I0018754

GNU tar Reference Manual

A catalogue record for this book is available from the Hong Kong Public Libraries.

Published in Hong Kong by Samurai Media Limited.

Email: info@samuraimedia.org

ISBN 978-988-8381-47-0

Copyright 1992, 1994 to 1997, 1999 to 2001, 2003 to 2013 Free Software Foundation, Inc.
Permission is granted to copy, distribute and/or modify this document under the terms of the GNU Free Documentation License, Version 1.3 or any later version published by the Free Software Foundation; with the Invariant Sections being GNU General Public License, with the Front-Cover Texts being A GNU Manual, and with the Back-Cover Texts as in (a) below. A copy of the license is included in the section entitled GNU Free Documentation License. (a) The FSFs Back-Cover Text is: You have the freedom to copy and modify this GNU manual.

Minor modifications for publication Copyright 2015 Samurai Media Limited.

Background Cover Image by https://www.flickr.com/people/webtreatsetc/

1 Introduction

GNU `tar` creates and manipulates *archives* which are actually collections of many other files; the program provides users with an organized and systematic method for controlling a large amount of data. The name "tar" originally came from the phrase "Tape ARchive", but archives need not (and these days, typically do not) reside on tapes.

1.1 What this Book Contains

The first part of this chapter introduces you to various terms that will recur throughout the book. It also tells you who has worked on GNU `tar` and its documentation, and where you should send bug reports or comments.

The second chapter is a tutorial (see Chapter 2 [Tutorial], page 5) which provides a gentle introduction for people who are new to using `tar`. It is meant to be self-contained, not requiring any reading from subsequent chapters to make sense. It moves from topic to topic in a logical, progressive order, building on information already explained.

Although the tutorial is paced and structured to allow beginners to learn how to use `tar`, it is not intended solely for beginners. The tutorial explains how to use the three most frequently used operations ('`create`', '`list`', and '`extract`') as well as two frequently used options ('`file`' and '`verbose`'). The other chapters do not refer to the tutorial frequently; however, if a section discusses something which is a complex variant of a basic concept, there may be a cross-reference to that basic concept. (The entire book, including the tutorial, assumes that the reader understands some basic concepts of using a Unix-type operating system; see Chapter 2 [Tutorial], page 5.)

The third chapter presents the remaining five operations, and information about using `tar` options and option syntax.

The other chapters are meant to be used as a reference. Each chapter presents everything that needs to be said about a specific topic.

One of the chapters (see Chapter 7 [Date input formats], page 123) exists in its entirety in other GNU manuals, and is mostly self-contained. In addition, one section of this manual (see [Standard], page 193) contains a big quote which is taken directly from `tar` sources.

In general, we give both long and short (abbreviated) option names at least once in each section where the relevant option is covered, so that novice readers will become familiar with both styles. (A few options have no short versions, and the relevant sections will indicate this.)

1.2 Some Definitions

The `tar` program is used to create and manipulate `tar` archives. An *archive* is a single file which contains the contents of many files, while still identifying the names of the files, their owner(s), and so forth. (In addition, archives record access permissions, user and group, size in bytes, and data modification time. Some archives also record the file names in each archived directory, as well as other file and directory information.) You can use `tar` to *create* a new archive in a specified directory.

The files inside an archive are called *members*. Within this manual, we use the term *file* to refer only to files accessible in the normal ways (by `ls`, `cat`, and so forth), and the term *member* to refer only to the members of an archive. Similarly, a *file name* is the name of a file, as it resides in the file system, and a *member name* is the name of an archive member within the archive.

The term *extraction* refers to the process of copying an archive member (or multiple members) into a file in the file system. Extracting all the members of an archive is often called *extracting the archive*. The term *unpack* can also be used to refer to the extraction of many or all the members of an archive. Extracting an archive does not destroy the archive's structure, just as creating an archive does not destroy the copies of the files that exist outside of the archive. You may also *list* the members in a given archive (this is often thought of as "printing" them to the standard output, or the command line), or *append* members to a pre-existing archive. All of these operations can be performed using `tar`.

1.3 What `tar` Does

The `tar` program provides the ability to create `tar` archives, as well as various other kinds of manipulation. For example, you can use `tar` on previously created archives to extract files, to store additional files, or to update or list files which were already stored.

Initially, `tar` archives were used to store files conveniently on magnetic tape. The name `tar` comes from this use; it stands for `tape` `ar`chiver. Despite the utility's name, `tar` can direct its output to available devices, files, or other programs (using pipes). `tar` may even access remote devices or files (as archives).

You can use `tar` archives in many ways. We want to stress a few of them: storage, backup, and transportation.

Storage   Often, `tar` archives are used to store related files for convenient file transfer over a network. For example, the GNU Project distributes its software bundled into `tar` archives, so that all the files relating to a particular program (or set of related programs) can be transferred as a single unit.

A magnetic tape can store several files in sequence. However, the tape has no names for these files; it only knows their relative position on the tape. One way to store several files on one tape and retain their names is by creating a `tar` archive. Even when the basic transfer mechanism can keep track of names, as

FTP can, the nuisance of handling multiple files, directories, and multiple links makes `tar` archives useful.

Archive files are also used for long-term storage. You can think of this as transportation from the present into the future. (It is a science-fiction idiom that you can move through time as well as in space; the idea here is that `tar` can be used to move archives in all dimensions, even time!)

Backup   Because the archive created by `tar` is capable of preserving file information and directory structure, `tar` is commonly used for performing full and incremental backups of disks. A backup puts a collection of files (possibly pertaining to many users and projects) together on a disk or a tape. This guards against accidental destruction of the information in those files. GNU `tar` has special features that allow it to be used to make incremental and full dumps of all the files in a file system.

Transportation
            You can create an archive on one system, transfer it to another system, and extract the contents there. This allows you to transport a group of files from one system to another.

1.4 How `tar` Archives are Named

Conventionally, `tar` archives are given names ending with '.tar'. This is not necessary for `tar` to operate properly, but this manual follows that convention in order to accustom readers to it and to make examples more clear.

Often, people refer to `tar` archives as "`tar` files," and archive members as "files" or "entries". For people familiar with the operation of `tar`, this causes no difficulty. However, in this manual, we consistently refer to "archives" and "archive members" to make learning to use `tar` easier for novice users.

1.5 GNU `tar` Authors

GNU `tar` was originally written by John Gilmore, and modified by many people. The GNU enhancements were written by Jay Fenlason, then Joy Kendall, and the whole package has been further maintained by Thomas Bushnell, n/BSG, François Pinard, Paul Eggert, and finally Sergey Poznyakoff with the help of numerous and kind users.

We wish to stress that `tar` is a collective work, and owes much to all those people who reported problems, offered solutions and other insights, or shared their thoughts and suggestions. An impressive, yet partial list of those contributors can be found in the '`THANKS`' file from the GNU `tar` distribution.

Jay Fenlason put together a draft of a GNU `tar` manual, borrowing notes from the original man page from John Gilmore. This was withdrawn in version 1.11. Thomas Bushnell, n/BSG and Amy Gorin worked on a tutorial and manual for GNU `tar`. François Pinard put version 1.11.8 of the manual together by taking information from all these sources and merging them. Melissa Weisshaus finally edited and redesigned the book to create version 1.12. The book for versions from 1.14 up to 1.28 were edited by the current maintainer, Sergey Poznyakoff.

For version 1.12, Daniel Hagerty contributed a great deal of technical consulting. In particular, he is the primary author of Chapter 5 [Backups], page 83.

In July, 2003 GNU `tar` was put on CVS at savannah.gnu.org (see `http://savannah.gnu.org/projects/tar`), and active development and maintenance work has started again. Currently GNU `tar` is being maintained by Paul Eggert, Sergey Poznyakoff and Jeff Bailey.

Support for POSIX archives was added by Sergey Poznyakoff.

1.6 Reporting bugs or suggestions

If you find problems or have suggestions about this program or manual, please report them to '`bug-tar@gnu.org`'.

When reporting a bug, please be sure to include as much detail as possible, in order to reproduce it.

2 Tutorial Introduction to `tar`

This chapter guides you through some basic examples of three `tar` operations: '`--create`', '`--list`', and '`--extract`'. If you already know how to use some other version of `tar`, then you may not need to read this chapter. This chapter omits most complicated details about how `tar` works.

2.1 Assumptions this Tutorial Makes

This chapter is paced to allow beginners to learn about `tar` slowly. At the same time, we will try to cover all the basic aspects of these three operations. In order to accomplish both of these tasks, we have made certain assumptions about your knowledge before reading this manual, and the hardware you will be using:

- Before you start to work through this tutorial, you should understand what the terms "archive" and "archive member" mean (see Section 1.2 [Definitions], page 1). In addition, you should understand something about how Unix-type operating systems work, and you should know how to use some basic utilities. For example, you should know how to create, list, copy, rename, edit, and delete files and directories; how to change between directories; and how to figure out where you are in the file system. You should have some basic understanding of directory structure and how files are named according to which directory they are in. You should understand concepts such as standard output and standard input, what various definitions of the term '`argument`' mean, and the differences between relative and absolute file names.

- This manual assumes that you are working from your own home directory (unless we state otherwise). In this tutorial, you will create a directory to practice `tar` commands in. When we show file names, we will assume that those names are relative to your home directory. For example, my home directory is '`/home/fsf/melissa`'. All of my examples are in a subdirectory of the directory named by that file name; the subdirectory is called '`practice`'.

- In general, we show examples of archives which exist on (or can be written to, or worked with from) a directory on a hard disk. In most cases, you could write those archives to, or work with them on any other device, such as a tape drive. However, some of the later examples in the tutorial and next chapter will not work on tape drives. Additionally, working with tapes is much more complicated than working with hard disks. For these reasons, the tutorial does not cover working with tape drives. See Chapter 9 [Media], page 155, for complete information on using `tar` archives with tape drives.

2.2 Stylistic Conventions

In the examples, '`$`' represents a typical shell prompt. It precedes lines you should type; to make this more clear, those lines are shown in `this font`, as opposed to lines which represent the computer's response; those lines are shown in `this font`, or sometimes '`like this`'.

2.3 Basic `tar` Operations and Options

`tar` can take a wide variety of arguments which specify and define the actions it will have on the particular set of files or the archive. The main types of arguments to `tar` fall into one of two classes: operations, and options.

Some arguments fall into a class called *operations*; exactly one of these is both allowed and required for any instance of using `tar`; you may *not* specify more than one. People sometimes speak of *operating modes*. You are in a particular operating mode when you have specified the operation which specifies it; there are eight operations in total, and thus there are eight operating modes.

The other arguments fall into the class known as *options*. You are not required to specify any options, and you are allowed to specify more than one at a time (depending on the way you are using `tar` at that time). Some options are used so frequently, and are so useful for helping you type commands more carefully that they are effectively "required". We will discuss them in this chapter.

You can write most of the `tar` operations and options in any of three forms: long (mnemonic) form, short form, and old style. Some of the operations and options have no short or "old" forms; however, the operations and options which we will cover in this tutorial have corresponding abbreviations. We will indicate those abbreviations appropriately to get you used to seeing them. Note, that the "old style" option forms exist in GNU `tar` for compatibility with Unix `tar`. In this book we present a full discussion of this way of writing options and operations (see Section 3.3.3 [Old Options], page 26), and we discuss the other two styles of writing options (See Section 3.3.1 [Long Options], page 24, and see Section 3.3.2 [Short Options], page 25).

In the examples and in the text of this tutorial, we usually use the long forms of operations and options; but the "short" forms produce the same result and can make typing long `tar` commands easier. For example, instead of typing

```
tar --create --verbose --file=afiles.tar apple angst aspic
```

you can type

```
tar -c -v -f afiles.tar apple angst aspic
```

or even

```
tar -cvf afiles.tar apple angst aspic
```

For more information on option syntax, see Section 4.2 [Advanced tar], page 62. In discussions in the text, when we name an option by its long form, we also give the corresponding short option in parentheses.

The term, "option", can be confusing at times, since "operations" are often lumped in with the actual, *optional* "options" in certain general class statements. For example, we just talked about "short and long forms of options and operations". However, experienced `tar` users often refer to these by shorthand terms such as, "short and long options". This term assumes that the "operations" are included, also. Context will help you determine which definition of "options" to use.

Similarly, the term "command" can be confusing, as it is often used in two different ways. People sometimes refer to `tar` "commands". A `tar` *command* is the entire command line of user input which tells `tar` what to do — including the operation, options, and any arguments (file names, pipes, other commands, etc.). However, you will also sometimes hear the term "the `tar` command". When the word "command" is used specifically like this, a person is usually referring to the `tar` *operation*, not the whole line. Again, use context to figure out which of the meanings the speaker intends.

2.4 The Three Most Frequently Used Operations

Here are the three most frequently used operations (both short and long forms), as well as a brief description of their meanings. The rest of this chapter will cover how to use these operations in detail. We will present the rest of the operations in the next chapter.

'`--create`'
'`-c`'   Create a new `tar` archive.

'`--list`'
'`-t`'   List the contents of an archive.

'`--extract`'
'`-x`'   Extract one or more members from an archive.

2.5 Two Frequently Used Options

To understand how to run `tar` in the three operating modes listed previously, you also need to understand how to use two of the options to `tar`: '`--file`' (which takes an archive file as an argument) and '`--verbose`'. (You are usually not *required* to specify either of these options when you run `tar`, but they can be very useful in making things more clear and helping you avoid errors.)

The '`--file`' Option

'--file=*archive-name*'
'-f *archive-name*'
> Specify the name of an archive file.

You can specify an argument for the '--file=*archive-name*' ('-f *archive-name*') option whenever you use `tar`; this option determines the name of the archive file that `tar` will work on.

If you don't specify this argument, then `tar` will examine the environment variable `TAPE`. If it is set, its value will be used as the archive name. Otherwise, `tar` will use the default archive, determined at compile time. Usually it is standard output or some physical tape drive attached to your machine (you can verify what the default is by running `tar --show-defaults`, see Section 3.6 [defaults], page 50). If there is no tape drive attached, or the default is not meaningful, then `tar` will print an error message. The error message might look roughly like one of the following:

```
tar: can't open /dev/rmt8 : No such device or address
tar: can't open /dev/rsmt0 : I/O error
```

To avoid confusion, we recommend that you always specify an archive file name by using '--file=*archive-name*' ('-f *archive-name*') when writing your `tar` commands. For more information on using the '--file=*archive-name*' ('-f *archive-name*') option, see Section 6.1 [file], page 97.

The '--verbose' Option

'--verbose'
'-v'   Show the files being worked on as `tar` is running.

'--verbose' ('-v') shows details about the results of running `tar`. This can be especially useful when the results might not be obvious. For example, if you want to see the progress of `tar` as it writes files into the archive, you can use the '--verbose' option. In the beginning, you may find it useful to use '--verbose' at all times; when you are more accustomed to `tar`, you will likely want to use it at certain times but not at others. We will use '--verbose' at times to help make something clear, and we will give many examples both using and not using '--verbose' to show the differences.

Each instance of '--verbose' on the command line increases the verbosity level by one, so if you need more details on the output, specify it twice.

When reading archives ('--list', '--extract', '--diff'), `tar` by default prints only the names of the members being extracted. Using '--verbose' will show a full, `ls` style member listing.

In contrast, when writing archives ('--create', '--append', '--update'), `tar` does not print file names by default. So, a single '--verbose' option shows the file names being added to the archive, while two '--verbose' options enable the full listing.

For example, to create an archive in verbose mode:

```
$ tar -cvf afiles.tar apple angst aspic
apple
```

```
angst
aspic
```

Creating the same archive with the verbosity level 2 could give:

```
$ tar -cvvf afiles.tar apple angst aspic
-rw-r--r-- gray/staff    62373 2006-06-09 12:06 apple
-rw-r--r-- gray/staff    11481 2006-06-09 12:06 angst
-rw-r--r-- gray/staff    23152 2006-06-09 12:06 aspic
```

This works equally well using short or long forms of options. Using long forms, you would simply write out the mnemonic form of the option twice, like this:

```
$ tar --create --verbose --verbose ...
```

Note that you must double the hyphens properly each time.

Later in the tutorial, we will give examples using '`--verbose --verbose`'.

The full output consists of six fields:

- File type and permissions in symbolic form. These are displayed in the same format as the first column of `ls -l` output (see section "Verbose listing" in *GNU file utilities*).

- Owner name and group separated by a slash character. If these data are not available (for example, when listing a '`v7`' format archive), numeric ID values are printed instead.

- Size of the file, in bytes.

- File modification date in ISO 8601 format.

- File modification time.

- File name. If the name contains any special characters (white space, newlines, etc.) these are displayed in an unambiguous form using so called *quoting style*. For the detailed discussion of available styles and on how to use them, see Section 6.6 [quoting styles], page 109.

Depending on the file type, the name can be followed by some additional information, described in the following table:

'`-> link-name`'
> The file or archive member is a *symbolic link* and *link-name* is the name of file it links to.

'`link to link-name`'
> The file or archive member is a *hard link* and *link-name* is the name of file it links to.

'`--Long Link--`'
> The archive member is an old GNU format long link. You will normally not encounter this.

'`--Long Name--`'
> The archive member is an old GNU format long name. You will normally not encounter this.

'--Volume Header--'

> The archive member is a GNU *volume header* (see Section 9.6.2 [Tape Files], page 173).

'--Continued at byte *n*--'

> Encountered only at the beginning of a multi-volume archive (see Section 9.6 [Using Multiple Tapes], page 168). This archive member is a continuation from the previous volume. The number *n* gives the offset where the original file was split.

'unknown file type *c*'

> An archive member of unknown type. *c* is the type character from the archive header. If you encounter such a message, it means that either your archive contains proprietary member types GNU `tar` is not able to handle, or the archive is corrupted.

For example, here is an archive listing containing most of the special suffixes explained above:

```
V--------- 0/0             1536 2006-06-09 13:07 MyVolume--Volume Header-
-
-rw-r--r-- gray/staff    456783 2006-06-09 12:06 aspic--Continued at byte 32456-
-
-rw-r--r-- gray/staff     62373 2006-06-09 12:06 apple
lrwxrwxrwx gray/staff         0 2006-06-09 13:01 angst -> apple
-rw-r--r-- gray/staff     35793 2006-06-09 12:06 blues
hrw-r--r-- gray/staff         0 2006-06-09 12:06 music link to blues
```

Getting Help: Using the '--help' Option

'--help'

> The '--help' option to `tar` prints out a very brief list of all operations and option available for the current version of `tar` available on your system.

2.6 How to Create Archives

(This message will disappear, once this node revised.)

One of the basic operations of `tar` is '--create' ('-c'), which you use to create a `tar` archive. We will explain '--create' first because, in order to learn about the other operations, you will find it useful to have an archive available to practice on.

To make this easier, in this section you will first create a directory containing three files. Then, we will show you how to create an *archive* (inside the new directory). Both the directory, and the archive are specifically for you to practice on. The rest of this chapter and the next chapter will show many examples using this directory and the files you will create: some of those files may be other directories and other archives.

The three files you will archive in this example are called '`blues`', '`folk`', and '`jazz`'. The archive is called '`collection.tar`'.

This section will proceed slowly, detailing how to use '`--create`' in `verbose` mode, and showing examples using both short and long forms. In the rest of the tutorial, and in the examples in the next chapter, we will proceed at a slightly quicker pace. This section moves more slowly to allow beginning users to understand how `tar` works.

2.6.1 Preparing a Practice Directory for Examples

To follow along with this and future examples, create a new directory called '`practice`' containing files called '`blues`', '`folk`' and '`jazz`'. The files can contain any information you like: ideally, they should contain information which relates to their names, and be of different lengths. Our examples assume that '`practice`' is a subdirectory of your home directory.

Now `cd` to the directory named '`practice`'; '`practice`' is now your *working directory*. (*Please note*: Although the full file name of this directory is '*/homedir*/`practice`', in our examples we will refer to this directory as '`practice`'; the *homedir* is presumed.)

In general, you should check that the files to be archived exist where you think they do (in the working directory) by running `ls`. Because you just created the directory and the files and have changed to that directory, you probably don't need to do that this time.

It is very important to make sure there isn't already a file in the working directory with the archive name you intend to use (in this case, '`collection.tar`'), or that you don't care about its contents. Whenever you use '`create`', `tar` will erase the current contents of the file named by '`--file=`*archive-name*' ('`-f` *archive-name*') if it exists. `tar` will not tell you if you are about to overwrite an archive unless you specify an option which does this (see Section 4.5 [backup], page 80, for the information on how to do so). To add files to an existing archive, you need to use a different option, such as '`--append`' ('`-r`'); see Section 4.2.2 [append], page 63 for information on how to do this.

2.6.2 Creating the Archive

To place the files '`blues`', '`folk`', and '`jazz`' into an archive named '`collection.tar`', use the following command:

```
$ tar --create --file=collection.tar blues folk jazz
```

The order of the arguments is not very important, *when using long option forms.* You could also say:

```
$ tar blues --create folk --file=collection.tar jazz
```

However, you can see that this order is harder to understand; this is why we will list the arguments in the order that makes the commands easiest to understand (and we encourage you to do the same when you use `tar`, to avoid errors).

Note that the sequence '`--file=collection.tar`' is considered to be *one* argument. If you substituted any other string of characters for `collection.tar`, then that string would become the name of the archive file you create.

The order of the options becomes more important when you begin to use short forms. With short forms, if you type commands in the wrong order (even if you type them correctly in all other ways), you may end up with results you don't expect. For this reason, it is a good idea to get into the habit of typing options in the order that makes inherent sense. See Section 2.6.4 [short create], page 13, for more information on this.

In this example, you type the command as shown above: '`--create`' is the operation which creates the new archive ('`collection.tar`'), and '`--file`' is the option which lets you give it the name you chose. The files, '`blues`', '`folk`', and '`jazz`', are now members of the archive, '`collection.tar`' (they are *file name arguments* to the '`--create`' operation. See Chapter 6 [Choosing], page 97, for the detailed discussion on these.) Now that they are in the archive, they are called *archive members*, not files. (see Section 1.2 [Definitions], page 1).

When you create an archive, you *must* specify which files you want placed in the archive. If you do not specify any archive members, GNU `tar` will complain.

If you now list the contents of the working directory (`ls`), you will find the archive file listed as well as the files you saw previously:

```
blues    folk    jazz    collection.tar
```

Creating the archive '`collection.tar`' did not destroy the copies of the files in the directory.

Keep in mind that if you don't indicate an operation, `tar` will not run and will prompt you for one. If you don't name any files, `tar` will complain. You must have write access to the working directory, or else you will not be able to create an archive in that directory.

Caution: Do not attempt to use '`--create`' ('`-c`') to add files to an existing archive; it will delete the archive and write a new one. Use '`--append`' ('`-r`') instead. See Section 4.2.2 [append], page 63.

2.6.3 Running '`--create`' with '`--verbose`'

If you include the '`--verbose`' ('`-v`') option on the command line, `tar` will list the files it is acting on as it is working. In verbose mode, the **create** example above would appear as:

```
$ tar --create --verbose --file=collection.tar blues folk jazz
blues
folk
jazz
```

This example is just like the example we showed which did not use '`--verbose`', except that `tar` generated the remaining lines (note the different font styles).

In the rest of the examples in this chapter, we will frequently use `verbose` mode so we can show actions or `tar` responses that you would otherwise not see, and which are important for you to understand.

2.6.4 Short Forms with '`create`'

As we said before, the '`--create`' ('`-c`') operation is one of the most basic uses of `tar`, and you will use it countless times. Eventually, you will probably want to use abbreviated (or "short") forms of options. A full discussion of the three different forms that options can take appears in Section 3.3 [Styles], page 24; for now, here is what the previous example (including the '`--verbose`' ('`-v`') option) looks like using short option forms:

```
$ tar -cvf collection.tar blues folk jazz
blues
folk
jazz
```

As you can see, the system responds the same no matter whether you use long or short option forms.

One difference between using short and long option forms is that, although the exact placement of arguments following options is no more specific when using short forms, it is easier to become confused and make a mistake when using short forms. For example, suppose you attempted the above example in the following way:

```
$ tar -cfv collection.tar blues folk jazz
```

In this case, `tar` will make an archive file called '`v`', containing the files '`blues`', '`folk`', and '`jazz`', because the '`v`' is the closest "file name" to the '`-f`' option, and is thus taken to be the chosen archive file name. `tar` will try to add a file called '`collection.tar`' to the '`v`' archive file; if the file '`collection.tar`' did not already exist, `tar` will report an error indicating that this file does not exist. If the file '`collection.tar`' does already exist (e.g., from a previous command you may have run), then `tar` will add this file to the archive. Because the '`-v`' option did not get registered, `tar` will not run under '`verbose`' mode, and will not report its progress.

The end result is that you may be quite confused about what happened, and possibly overwrite a file. To illustrate this further, we will show you how an example we showed previously would look using short forms.

This example,

```
$ tar blues --create folk --file=collection.tar jazz
```

is confusing as it is. When shown using short forms, however, it becomes much more so:

```
$ tar blues -c folk -f collection.tar jazz
```

It would be very easy to put the wrong string of characters immediately following the '-f', but doing that could sacrifice valuable data.

For this reason, we recommend that you pay very careful attention to the order of options and placement of file and archive names, especially when using short option forms. Not having the option name written out mnemonically can affect how well you remember which option does what, and therefore where different names have to be placed.

2.6.5 Archiving Directories

You can archive a directory by specifying its directory name as a file name argument to `tar`. The files in the directory will be archived relative to the working directory, and the directory will be re-created along with its contents when the archive is extracted.

To archive a directory, first move to its superior directory. If you have followed the previous instructions in this tutorial, you should type:

```
$ cd ..
$
```

This will put you into the directory which contains 'practice', i.e., your home directory. Once in the superior directory, you can specify the subdirectory, 'practice', as a file name argument. To store 'practice' in the new archive file 'music.tar', type:

```
$ tar --create --verbose --file=music.tar practice
```

`tar` should output:

```
practice/
practice/blues
practice/folk
practice/jazz
practice/collection.tar
```

Note that the archive thus created is not in the subdirectory 'practice', but rather in the current working directory—the directory from which `tar` was invoked. Before trying to archive a directory from its superior directory, you should make sure you have write access to the superior directory itself, not only the directory you are trying archive with `tar`. For example, you will probably not be able to store your home directory in an archive by invoking `tar` from the root directory; See Section 6.10.2 [absolute], page 120. (Note also that 'collection.tar', the original archive file, has itself been archived. `tar` will accept any file as a file to be archived, regardless of its content. When 'music.tar' is extracted, the archive file 'collection.tar' will be re-written into the file system).

If you give `tar` a command such as

```
$ tar --create --file=foo.tar .
```

`tar` will report 'tar: ./foo.tar is the archive; not dumped'. This happens because `tar` creates the archive 'foo.tar' in the current directory before putting any files into it. Then, when `tar` attempts to add all the files in the directory '.' to the archive, it notices that the file './foo.tar' is the same as the archive 'foo.tar', and skips it. (It makes no sense to put an archive into itself.) GNU `tar` will continue in this case, and create the archive normally, except for the exclusion of that one file. (*Please note:* Other implementations of `tar` may not be so clever; they will enter an infinite loop when this happens, so you should not depend on this behavior unless you are certain you are running GNU `tar`. In general, it is wise to always place the archive outside of the directory being dumped.)

2.7 How to List Archives

Frequently, you will find yourself wanting to determine exactly what a particular archive contains. You can use the '--list' ('-t') operation to get the member names as they currently appear in the archive, as well as various attributes of the files at the time they were archived. For example, you can examine the archive 'collection.tar' that you created in the last section with the command,

```
$ tar --list --file=collection.tar
```

The output of `tar` would then be:

```
blues
folk
jazz
```

The archive 'bfiles.tar' would list as follows:

```
./birds
baboon
./box
```

Be sure to use a '--file=*archive-name*' ('-f *archive-name*') option just as with '--create' ('-c') to specify the name of the archive.

If you use the '--verbose' ('-v') option with '--list', then `tar` will print out a listing reminiscent of 'ls -l', showing owner, file size, and so forth. This output is described in detail in [verbose member listing], page 9.

If you had used '--verbose' ('-v') mode, the example above would look like:

```
$ tar --list --verbose --file=collection.tar folk
-rw-r--r-- myself/user       62 1990-05-23 10:55 folk
```

It is important to notice that the output of `tar --list --verbose` does not necessarily match that produced by `tar --create --verbose` while creating the archive. It is because GNU `tar`, unless told explicitly not to do so, removes some directory prefixes from file names before storing them in the archive (See Section 6.10.2 [absolute], page 120, for more information). In other words, in verbose mode GNU `tar` shows *file names* when creating an archive and *member names* when listing it. Consider this example:

```
$ tar --create --verbose --file archive /etc/mail
tar: Removing leading '/' from member names
/etc/mail/
/etc/mail/sendmail.cf
/etc/mail/aliases
$ tar --test --file archive
etc/mail/
etc/mail/sendmail.cf
etc/mail/aliases
```

This default behavior can sometimes be inconvenient. You can force GNU `tar` show member names when creating archive by supplying '--show-stored-names' option.

'--show-stored-names'

Print member (as opposed to *file*) names when creating the archive.

You can specify one or more individual member names as arguments when using 'list'. In this case, `tar` will only list the names of members you identify. For example, `tar --list --file=afiles.tar apple` would only print 'apple'.

Because `tar` preserves file names, these must be specified as they appear in the archive (i.e., relative to the directory from which the archive was created). Therefore, it is essential when specifying member names to `tar` that you give the exact member names. For example, `tar --list --file=bfiles.tar birds` would produce an error message something like 'tar: birds: Not found in archive', because there is no member named 'birds', only one named './birds'. While the names 'birds' and './birds' name the same file, *member* names by default are compared verbatim.

However, `tar --list --file=bfiles.tar baboon` would respond with 'baboon', because this exact member name is in the archive file 'bfiles.tar'. If you are not sure of the exact file name, use *globbing patterns*, for example:

```
$ tar --list --file=bfiles.tar --wildcards '*b*'
```

will list all members whose name contains 'b'. See Section 6.5 [wildcards], page 106, for a detailed discussion of globbing patterns and related `tar` command line options.

Listing the Contents of a Stored Directory

To get information about the contents of an archived directory, use the directory name as a file name argument in conjunction with '--list' ('-t'). To find out file attributes, include the '--verbose' ('-v') option.

For example, to find out about files in the directory 'practice', in the archive file 'music.tar', type:

```
$ tar --list --verbose --file=music.tar practice
```

`tar` responds:

```
drwxrwxrwx myself/user         0 1990-05-31 21:49 practice/
-rw-r--r-- myself/user        42 1990-05-21 13:29 practice/blues
-rw-r--r-- myself/user        62 1990-05-23 10:55 practice/folk
-rw-r--r-- myself/user        40 1990-05-21 13:30 practice/jazz
-rw-r--r-- myself/user     10240 1990-05-31 21:49 practice/collection.tar
```

When you use a directory name as a file name argument, `tar` acts on all the files (including sub-directories) in that directory.

2.8 How to Extract Members from an Archive

Creating an archive is only half the job—there is no point in storing files in an archive if you can't retrieve them. The act of retrieving members from an archive so they can be used and manipulated as unarchived files again is called *extraction*. To extract files from an archive, use the '`--extract`' ('`--get`' or '`-x`') operation. As with '`--create`', specify the name of the archive with '`--file`' ('`-f`') option. Extracting an archive does not modify the archive in any way; you can extract it multiple times if you want or need to.

Using '`--extract`', you can extract an entire archive, or specific files. The files can be directories containing other files, or not. As with '`--create`' ('`-c`') and '`--list`' ('`-t`'), you may use the short or the long form of the operation without affecting the performance.

2.8.1 Extracting an Entire Archive

To extract an entire archive, specify the archive file name only, with no individual file names as arguments. For example,

```
$ tar -xvf collection.tar
```

produces this:

```
-rw-r--r-- me/user        28 1996-10-18 16:31 jazz
-rw-r--r-- me/user        21 1996-09-23 16:44 blues
-rw-r--r-- me/user        20 1996-09-23 16:44 folk
```

2.8.2 Extracting Specific Files

To extract specific archive members, give their exact member names as arguments, as printed by '`--list`' ('`-t`'). If you had mistakenly deleted one of the files you had placed in the archive '`collection.tar`' earlier (say, '`blues`'), you can extract it from the archive without changing the archive's structure. Its contents will be identical to the original file '`blues`' that you deleted.

First, make sure you are in the '`practice`' directory, and list the files in the directory. Now, delete the file, '`blues`', and list the files in the directory again.

You can now extract the member '`blues`' from the archive file '`collection.tar`' like this:

```
$ tar --extract --file=collection.tar blues
```

If you list the files in the directory again, you will see that the file 'blues' has been restored, with its original permissions, data modification times, and owner.[1] (These parameters will be identical to those which the file had when you originally placed it in the archive; any changes you may have made before deleting the file from the file system, however, will *not* have been made to the archive member.) The archive file, 'collection.tar', is the same as it was before you extracted 'blues'. You can confirm this by running tar with '--list' ('-t').

Remember that as with other operations, specifying the exact member name is important. *tar --extract --file=bfiles.tar birds* will fail, because there is no member named 'birds'. To extract the member named './birds', you must specify *tar --extract --file=bfiles.tar ./birds*. If you don't remember the exact member names, use '--list' ('-t') option (see Section 2.7 [list], page 15). You can also extract those members that match a specific *globbing pattern*. For example, to extract from 'bfiles.tar' all files that begin with 'b', no matter their directory prefix, you could type:

```
$ tar -x -f bfiles.tar --wildcards --no-anchored 'b*'
```

Here, '--wildcards' instructs tar to treat command line arguments as globbing patterns and '--no-anchored' informs it that the patterns apply to member names after any '/' delimiter. The use of globbing patterns is discussed in detail in See Section 6.5 [wildcards], page 106.

You can extract a file to standard output by combining the above options with the '--to-stdout' ('-O') option (see [Writing to Standard Output], page 77).

If you give the '--verbose' option, then '--extract' will print the names of the archive members as it extracts them.

2.8.3 Extracting Files that are Directories

Extracting directories which are members of an archive is similar to extracting other files. The main difference to be aware of is that if the extracted directory has the same name as any directory already in the working directory, then files in the extracted directory will be placed into the directory of the same name. Likewise, if there are files in the pre-existing directory with the same names as the members which you extract, the files from the extracted archive will replace the files already in the working directory (and possible subdirectories). This will happen regardless of whether or not the files in the working directory were more recent than those extracted (there exist, however, special options that alter this behavior see Section 4.4.2 [Writing], page 72).

---

[1] This is only accidentally true, but not in general. Whereas modification times are always restored, in most cases, one has to be root for restoring the owner, and use a special option for restoring permissions. Here, it just happens that the restoring user is also the owner of the archived members, and that the current umask is compatible with original permissions.

However, if a file was stored with a directory name as part of its file name, and that directory does not exist under the working directory when the file is extracted, `tar` will create the directory.

We can demonstrate how to use '`--extract`' to extract a directory file with an example. Change to the '`practice`' directory if you weren't there, and remove the files '`folk`' and '`jazz`'. Then, go back to the parent directory and extract the archive '`music.tar`'. You may either extract the entire archive, or you may extract only the files you just deleted. To extract the entire archive, don't give any file names as arguments after the archive name '`music.tar`'. To extract only the files you deleted, use the following command:

```
$ tar -xvf music.tar practice/folk practice/jazz
practice/folk
practice/jazz
```

If you were to specify two '`--verbose`' ('`-v`') options, `tar` would have displayed more detail about the extracted files, as shown in the example below:

```
$ tar -xvvf music.tar practice/folk practice/jazz
-rw-r--r-- me/user         28 1996-10-18 16:31 practice/jazz
-rw-r--r-- me/user         20 1996-09-23 16:44 practice/folk
```

Because you created the directory with '`practice`' as part of the file names of each of the files by archiving the '`practice`' directory as '`practice`', you must give '`practice`' as part of the file names when you extract those files from the archive.

2.8.4 Extracting Archives from Untrusted Sources

Extracting files from archives can overwrite files that already exist. If you receive an archive from an untrusted source, you should make a new directory and extract into that directory, so that you don't have to worry about the extraction overwriting one of your existing files. For example, if '`untrusted.tar`' came from somewhere else on the Internet, and you don't necessarily trust its contents, you can extract it as follows:

```
$ mkdir newdir
$ cd newdir
$ tar -xvf ../untrusted.tar
```

It is also a good practice to examine contents of the archive before extracting it, using '`--list`' ('`-t`') option, possibly combined with '`--verbose`' ('`-v`').

2.8.5 Commands That Will Fail

Here are some sample commands you might try which will not work, and why they won't work.

If you try to use this command,

```
$ tar -xvf music.tar folk jazz
```

you will get the following response:

```
tar: folk: Not found in archive
```

```
tar: jazz: Not found in archive
```

This is because these files were not originally *in* the parent directory '..',
where the archive is located; they were in the '**practice**' directory, and their
file names reflect this:

```
$ tar -tvf music.tar
practice/blues
practice/folk
practice/jazz
```

Likewise, if you try to use this command,

```
$ tar -tvf music.tar folk jazz
```

you would get a similar response. Members with those names are not in the
archive. You must use the correct member names, or wildcards, in order to
extract the files from the archive.

If you have forgotten the correct names of the files in the archive, use
`tar --list --verbose` to list them correctly.

2.9 Going Further Ahead in this Manual

(This message will disappear, once this node revised.)

3 Invoking GNU `tar`

This chapter is about how one invokes the GNU `tar` command, from the command synopsis (see Section 3.1 [Synopsis], page 21). There are numerous options, and many styles for writing them. One mandatory option specifies the operation `tar` should perform (see Section 3.4.1 [Operation Summary], page 28), other options are meant to detail how this operation should be performed (see Section 3.4.2 [Option Summary], page 29). Non-option arguments are not always interpreted the same way, depending on what the operation is.

You will find in this chapter everything about option styles and rules for writing them (see Section 3.3 [Styles], page 24). On the other hand, operations and options are fully described elsewhere, in other chapters. Here, you will find only synthetic descriptions for operations and options, together with pointers to other parts of the `tar` manual.

Some options are so special they are fully described right in this chapter. They have the effect of inhibiting the normal operation of `tar` or else, they globally alter the amount of feedback the user receives about what is going on. These are the '`--help`' and '`--version`' (see Section 3.5 [help], page 49), '`--verbose`' (see Section 3.7 [verbose], page 51) and '`--interactive`' options (see Section 3.10 [interactive], page 59).

3.1 General Synopsis of `tar`

The GNU `tar` program is invoked as either one of:

```
tar option... [name]...
tar letter... [argument]... [option]... [name]...
```

The second form is for when old options are being used.

You can use `tar` to store files in an archive, to extract them from an archive, and to do other types of archive manipulation. The primary argument to `tar`, which is called the *operation*, specifies which action to take. The other arguments to `tar` are either *options*, which change the way `tar` performs an operation, or file names or archive members, which specify the files or members `tar` is to act on.

You can actually type in arguments in any order, even if in this manual the options always precede the other arguments, to make examples easier to understand. Further, the option stating the main operation mode (the `tar` main command) is usually given first.

Each *name* in the synopsis above is interpreted as an archive member name when the main command is one of '`--compare`' ('`--diff`', '`-d`'), '`--delete`', '`--extract`' ('`--get`', '`-x`'), '`--list`' ('`-t`') or '`--update`' ('`-u`'). When naming archive members, you must give the exact name of the member in the archive, as it is printed by '`--list`'. For '`--append`' ('`-r`') and '`--create`' ('`-c`'), these *name* arguments specify the names of either files or directory hierarchies to place in the archive. These files or hierarchies should already exist in the file system, prior to the execution of the `tar` command.

`tar` interprets relative file names as being relative to the working directory. `tar` will make all file names relative (by removing leading slashes when archiving or restoring files), unless you specify otherwise (using the '`--absolute-names`' option). See Section 6.10.2 [absolute], page 120, for more information about '`--absolute-names`'.

If you give the name of a directory as either a file name or a member name, then `tar` acts recursively on all the files and directories beneath that directory. For example, the name '`/`' identifies all the files in the file system to `tar`.

The distinction between file names and archive member names is especially important when shell globbing is used, and sometimes a source of confusion for newcomers. See Section 6.5 [wildcards], page 106, for more information about globbing. The problem is that shells may only glob using existing files in the file system. Only `tar` itself may glob on archive members, so when needed, you must ensure that wildcard characters reach `tar` without being interpreted by the shell first. Using a backslash before '`*`' or '`?`', or putting the whole argument between quotes, is usually sufficient for this.

Even if *names* are often specified on the command line, they can also be read from a text file in the file system, using the '`--files-from=file-of-names`' ('`-T file-of-names`') option.

If you don't use any file name arguments, '`--append`' ('`-r`'), '`--delete`' and '`--concatenate`' ('`--catenate`', '`-A`') will do nothing, while '`--create`' ('`-c`') will usually yield a diagnostic and inhibit `tar` execution. The other operations of `tar` ('`--list`', '`--extract`', '`--compare`', and '`--update`') will act on the entire contents of the archive.

Besides successful exits, GNU `tar` may fail for many reasons. Some reasons correspond to bad usage, that is, when the `tar` command line is improperly written. Errors may be encountered later, while processing the archive or the files. Some errors are recoverable, in which case the failure is delayed until `tar` has completed all its work. Some errors are such that it would be not meaningful, or at least risky, to continue processing: `tar` then aborts processing immediately. All abnormal exits, whether immediate or delayed, should always be clearly diagnosed on `stderr`, after a line stating the nature of the error.

Possible exit codes of GNU `tar` are summarized in the following table:

0   '`Successful termination`'.

1   '`Some files differ`'. If tar was invoked with '`--compare`' ('`--diff`', '`-d`') command line option, this means that some files in the archive differ from their disk counterparts (see Section 4.2.6 [compare], page 69). If tar was given '`--create`', '`--append`' or '`--update`' option, this exit code means that some

files were changed while being archived and so the resulting archive does not contain the exact copy of the file set.

2   'Fatal error'. This means that some fatal, unrecoverable error occurred.

If `tar` has invoked a subprocess and that subprocess exited with a nonzero exit code, `tar` exits with that code as well. This can happen, for example, if `tar` was given some compression option (see Section 8.1.1 [gzip], page 132) and the external compressor program failed. Another example is `rmt` failure during backup to the remote device (see Section 9.2 [Remote Tape Server], page 157).

3.2 Using `tar` Options

GNU `tar` has a total of eight operating modes which allow you to perform a variety of tasks. You are required to choose one operating mode each time you employ the `tar` program by specifying one, and only one operation as an argument to the `tar` command (the corresponding options may be found at Section 2.4 [frequent operations], page 7 and Section 4.2.1 [Operations], page 62). Depending on circumstances, you may also wish to customize how the chosen operating mode behaves. For example, you may wish to change the way the output looks, or the format of the files that you wish to archive may require you to do something special in order to make the archive look right.

You can customize and control `tar`'s performance by running `tar` with one or more options (such as '`--verbose`' ('`-v`'), which we used in the tutorial). As we said in the tutorial, *options* are arguments to `tar` which are (as their name suggests) optional. Depending on the operating mode, you may specify one or more options. Different options will have different effects, but in general they all change details of the operation, such as archive format, archive name, or level of user interaction. Some options make sense with all operating modes, while others are meaningful only with particular modes. You will likely use some options frequently, while you will only use others infrequently, or not at all. (A full list of options is available in see Section 3.4 [All Options], page 28.)

The `TAR_OPTIONS` environment variable specifies default options to be placed in front of any explicit options. For example, if `TAR_OPTIONS` is '`-v --unlink-first`', `tar` behaves as if the two options '`-v`' and '`--unlink-first`' had been specified before any explicit options. Option specifications are separated by whitespace. A backslash escapes the next character, so it can be used to specify an option containing whitespace or a backslash.

Note that `tar` options are case sensitive. For example, the options '`-T`' and '`-t`' are different; the first requires an argument for stating the name of a file providing a list of *names*, while the second does not require an argument and is another way to write '`--list`' ('`-t`').

In addition to the eight operations, there are many options to `tar`, and three different styles for writing both: long (mnemonic) form, short form, and old style. These styles are discussed below. Both the options and the operations can be written in any of these three styles.

3.3 The Three Option Styles

There are three styles for writing operations and options to the command line invoking `tar`. The different styles were developed at different times during the history of `tar`. These styles will be presented below, from the most recent to the oldest.

Some options must take an argument[1]. Where you *place* the arguments generally depends on which style of options you choose. We will detail specific information relevant to each option style in the sections on the different option styles, below. The differences are subtle, yet can often be very important; incorrect option placement can cause you to overwrite a number of important files. We urge you to note these differences, and only use the option style(s) which makes the most sense to you until you feel comfortable with the others.

Some options *may* take an argument. Such options may have at most long and short forms, they do not have old style equivalent. The rules for specifying an argument for such options are stricter than those for specifying mandatory arguments. Please, pay special attention to them.

3.3.1 Long Option Style

Each option has at least one *long* (or *mnemonic*) name starting with two dashes in a row, e.g., '`--list`'. The long names are more clear than their corresponding short or old names. It sometimes happens that a single long option has many different names which are synonymous, such as '`--compare`' and '`--diff`'. In addition, long option names can be given unique abbreviations. For example, '`--cre`' can be used in place of '`--create`' because there is no other long option which begins with '`cre`'. (One way to find this out is by trying it and seeing what happens; if a particular abbreviation could represent more than one option, `tar` will tell you that that abbreviation is ambiguous and you'll know that that abbreviation won't work. You may also choose to run '`tar --help`' to see a list of options. Be aware that if you run `tar` with a unique abbreviation for the long name of an option you didn't want to use, you are stuck; `tar` will perform the command as ordered.)

Long options are meant to be obvious and easy to remember, and their meanings are generally easier to discern than those of their corresponding short options (see below). For example:

---

[1] For example, '`--file`' ('`-f`') takes the name of an archive file as an argument. If you do not supply an archive file name, `tar` will use a default, but this can be confusing; thus, we recommend that you always supply a specific archive file name.

```
$ tar --create --verbose --blocking-factor=20 --file=/dev/rmt0
```

gives a fairly good set of hints about what the command does, even for those not fully acquainted with `tar`.

Long options which require arguments take those arguments immediately following the option name. There are two ways of specifying a mandatory argument. It can be separated from the option name either by an equal sign, or by any amount of white space characters. For example, the '`--file`' option (which tells the name of the `tar` archive) is given a file such as '`archive.tar`' as argument by using any of the following notations: '`--file=archive.tar`' or '`--file archive.tar`'.

In contrast, optional arguments must always be introduced using an equal sign. For example, the '`--backup`' option takes an optional argument specifying backup type. It must be used as '`--backup=backup-type`'.

3.3.2 Short Option Style

Most options also have a *short option* name. Short options start with a single dash, and are followed by a single character, e.g., '`-t`' (which is equivalent to '`--list`'). The forms are absolutely identical in function; they are interchangeable.

The short option names are faster to type than long option names.

Short options which require arguments take their arguments immediately following the option, usually separated by white space. It is also possible to stick the argument right after the short option name, using no intervening space. For example, you might write '`-f archive.tar`' or '`-farchive.tar`' instead of using '`--file=archive.tar`'. Both '`--file=archive-name`' and '`-f archive-name`' denote the option which indicates a specific archive, here named '`archive.tar`'.

Short options which take optional arguments take their arguments immediately following the option letter, *without any intervening white space characters.*

Short options' letters may be clumped together, but you are not required to do this (as compared to old options; see below). When short options are clumped as a set, use one (single) dash for them all, e.g., '`tar -cvf`'. Only the last option in such a set is allowed to have an argument[2].

When the options are separated, the argument for each option which requires an argument directly follows that option, as is usual for Unix programs. For example:

```
$ tar -c -v -b 20 -f /dev/rmt0
```

If you reorder short options' locations, be sure to move any arguments that belong to them. If you do not move the arguments properly, you may end up overwriting files.

---

[2] Clustering many options, the last of which has an argument, is a rather opaque way to write options. Some wonder if GNU `getopt` should not even be made helpful enough for considering such usages as invalid.

3.3.3 Old Option Style

As far as we know, all `tar` programs, GNU and non-GNU, support *old options*: that is, if the first argument does not start with '-', it is assumed to specify option letters. GNU `tar` supports old options not only for historical reasons, but also because many people are used to them. If the first argument does not start with a dash, you are announcing the old option style instead of the short option style; old options are decoded differently.

Like short options, old options are single letters. However, old options must be written together as a single clumped set, without spaces separating them or dashes preceding them. This set of letters must be the first to appear on the command line, after the `tar` program name and some white space; old options cannot appear anywhere else. The letter of an old option is exactly the same letter as the corresponding short option. For example, the old option 't' is the same as the short option '-t', and consequently, the same as the long option '--list'. So for example, the command '`tar cv`' specifies the option '-v' in addition to the operation '-c'.

When options that need arguments are given together with the command, all the associated arguments follow, in the same order as the options. Thus, the example given previously could also be written in the old style as follows:

    $ tar cvbf 20 /dev/rmt0

Here, '20' is the argument of '-b' and '/dev/rmt0' is the argument of '-f'.

The old style syntax can make it difficult to match option letters with their corresponding arguments, and is often confusing. In the command '`tar cvbf 20 /dev/rmt0`', for example, '20' is the argument for '-b', '/dev/rmt0' is the argument for '-f', and '-v' does not have a corresponding argument. Even using short options like in '`tar -c -v -b 20 -f /dev/rmt0`' is clearer, putting all arguments next to the option they pertain to.

If you want to reorder the letters in the old option argument, be sure to reorder any corresponding argument appropriately.

This old way of writing `tar` options can surprise even experienced users. For example, the two commands:

    tar cfz archive.tar.gz file
    tar -cfz archive.tar.gz file

are quite different. The first example uses '`archive.tar.gz`' as the value for option 'f' and recognizes the option 'z'. The second example, however, uses 'z' as the value for option 'f' — probably not what was intended.

This second example could be corrected in many ways, among which the following are equivalent:

    tar -czf archive.tar.gz file
    tar -cf archive.tar.gz -z file
    tar cf archive.tar.gz -z file

3.3.4 Mixing Option Styles

All three styles may be intermixed in a single `tar` command, so long as the rules for each style are fully respected[3]. Old style options and either of the modern styles of options may be mixed within a single `tar` command. However, old style options must be introduced as the first arguments only, following the rule for old options (old options must appear directly after the `tar` command and some white space). Modern options may be given only after all arguments to the old options have been collected. If this rule is not respected, a modern option might be falsely interpreted as the value of the argument to one of the old style options.

For example, all the following commands are wholly equivalent, and illustrate the many combinations and orderings of option styles.

```
tar --create --file=archive.tar
tar --create -f archive.tar
tar --create -farchive.tar
tar --file=archive.tar --create
tar --file=archive.tar -c
tar -c --file=archive.tar
tar -c -f archive.tar
tar -c -farchive.tar
tar -cf archive.tar
tar -cfarchive.tar
tar -f archive.tar --create
tar -f archive.tar -c
tar -farchive.tar --create
tar -farchive.tar -c
tar c --file=archive.tar
tar c -f archive.tar
tar c -farchive.tar
tar cf archive.tar
tar f archive.tar --create
tar f archive.tar -c
tar fc archive.tar
```

On the other hand, the following commands are *not* equivalent to the previous set:

```
tar -f -c archive.tar
tar -fc archive.tar
tar -fcarchive.tar
tar -farchive.tarc
tar cfarchive.tar
```

These last examples mean something completely different from what the user intended (judging based on the example in the previous set which uses long options, whose intent is therefore very clear). The first four specify that the `tar` archive would be a file named '`-c`', '`c`', '`carchive.tar`' or '`archive.tarc`', respectively. The first two examples also specify a single

---

[3] Before GNU `tar` version 1.11.6, a bug prevented intermixing old style options with long options in some cases.

non-option, *name* argument having the value '`archive.tar`'. The last example contains only old style option letters (repeating option '`c`' twice), not all of which are meaningful (eg., '`.`', '`h`', or '`i`'), with no argument value.

3.4 All `tar` Options

The coming manual sections contain an alphabetical listing of all `tar` operations and options, with brief descriptions and cross-references to more in-depth explanations in the body of the manual. They also contain an alphabetically arranged table of the short option forms with their corresponding long option. You can use this table as a reference for deciphering `tar` commands in scripts.

3.4.1 Operations

'`--append`'
'`-r`'

> Appends files to the end of the archive. See Section 4.2.2 [append], page 63.

'`--catenate`'
'`-A`'

> Same as '`--concatenate`'. See Section 4.2.4 [concatenate], page 67.

'`--compare`'
'`-d`'

> Compares archive members with their counterparts in the file system, and reports differences in file size, mode, owner, modification date and contents. See Section 4.2.6 [compare], page 69.

'`--concatenate`'
'`-A`'

> Appends other `tar` archives to the end of the archive. See Section 4.2.4 [concatenate], page 67.

'`--create`'
'`-c`'

> Creates a new `tar` archive. See Section 2.6 [create], page 10.

'`--delete`'

> Deletes members from the archive. Don't try this on an archive on a tape! See Section 4.2.5 [delete], page 68.

'`--diff`'
'`-d`'

> Same '`--compare`'. See Section 4.2.6 [compare], page 69.

'`--extract`'
'`-x`'

>   Extracts members from the archive into the file system. See
>   Section 2.8 [extract], page 17.

'`--get`'
'`-x`'

>   Same as '`--extract`'. See Section 2.8 [extract], page 17.

'`--list`'
'`-t`'

>   Lists the members in an archive. See Section 2.7 [list], page 15.

'`--update`'
'`-u`'

>   Adds files to the end of the archive, but only if they are newer
>   than their counterparts already in the archive, or if they do not
>   already exist in the archive. See Section 4.2.3 [update], page 66.

3.4.2 `tar` Options

'`--absolute-names`'
'`-P`'

>   Normally when creating an archive, `tar` strips an initial '`/`' from
>   member names, and when extracting from an archive `tar` treats
>   names specially if they have initial '`/`' or internal '`..`'. This
>   option disables that behavior. See Section 6.10.2 [absolute],
>   page 120.

'`--after-date`'

>   (See '`--newer`', see Section 6.8 [after], page 116)

'`--anchored`'

>   A pattern must match an initial subsequence of the name's com-
>   ponents. See [controlling pattern-matching], page 107.

'`--atime-preserve`'
'`--atime-preserve=replace`'
'`--atime-preserve=system`'

>   Attempt to preserve the access time of files when reading them.
>   This option currently is effective only on files that you own,
>   unless you have superuser privileges.
>
>   '`--atime-preserve=replace`' remembers the access time of a
>   file before reading it, and then restores the access time after-
>   wards. This may cause problems if other programs are reading
>   the file at the same time, as the times of their accesses will be
>   lost. On most platforms restoring the access time also requires
>   `tar` to restore the data modification time too, so this option may

also cause problems if other programs are writing the file at the same time (`tar` attempts to detect this situation, but cannot do so reliably due to race conditions). Worse, on most platforms restoring the access time also updates the status change time, which means that this option is incompatible with incremental backups.

'`--atime-preserve=system`' avoids changing time stamps on files, without interfering with time stamp updates caused by other programs, so it works better with incremental backups. However, it requires a special `O_NOATIME` option from the underlying operating and file system implementation, and it also requires that searching directories does not update their access times. As of this writing (November 2005) this works only with Linux, and only with Linux kernels 2.6.8 and later. Worse, there is currently no reliable way to know whether this feature actually works. Sometimes `tar` knows that it does not work, and if you use '`--atime-preserve=system`' then `tar` complains and exits right away. But other times `tar` might think that the option works when it actually does not.

Currently '`--atime-preserve`' with no operand defaults to '`--atime-preserve=replace`', but this may change in the future as support for '`--atime-preserve=system`' improves.

If your operating or file system does not support '`--atime-preserve=system`', you might be able to preserve access times reliably by using the `mount` command. For example, you can mount the file system read-only, or access the file system via a read-only loopback mount, or use the '`noatime`' mount option available on some systems. However, mounting typically requires superuser privileges and can be a pain to manage.

'`--auto-compress`'
'`-a`'

> During a '`--create`' operation, enables automatic compressed format recognition based on the archive suffix. The effect of this option is cancelled by '`--no-auto-compress`'. See Section 8.1.1 [gzip], page 132.

'`--backup=backup-type`'
> Rather than deleting files from the file system, `tar` will back them up using simple or numbered backups, depending upon *backup-type*. See Section 4.5 [backup], page 80.

'`--block-number`'
'`-R`'

With this option present, `tar` prints error messages for read errors with the block number in the archive file. See [block-number], page 53.

'`--blocking-factor=blocking`'
'`-b blocking`'

Sets the blocking factor `tar` uses to *blocking* x 512 bytes per record. See Section 9.4.2 [Blocking Factor], page 161.

'`--bzip2`'
'`-j`'

This option tells `tar` to read or write archives through `bzip2`. See Section 8.1.1 [gzip], page 132.

'`--check-device`'

Check device numbers when creating a list of modified files for incremental archiving. This is the default. See [device numbers], page 85, for a detailed description.

'`--checkpoint[=number]`'

This option directs `tar` to print periodic checkpoint messages as it reads through the archive. It is intended for when you want a visual indication that `tar` is still running, but don't want to see '`--verbose`' output. You can also instruct `tar` to execute a list of actions on each checkpoint, see '`--checkpoint-action`' below. For a detailed description, see Section 3.8 [checkpoints], page 53.

'`--checkpoint-action=action`'

Instruct `tar` to execute an action upon hitting a breakpoint. Here we give only a brief outline. See Section 3.8 [checkpoints], page 53, for a complete description.

The *action* argument can be one of the following:

bell   Produce an audible bell on the console.

dot
.   Print a single dot on the standard listing stream.

echo   Display a textual message on the standard error, with the status and number of the checkpoint. This is the default.

echo=*string*
            Display *string* on the standard error. Before output, the string is subject to meta-character expansion.

exec=*command*
            Execute the given *command*.

sleep=*time*
            Wait for *time* seconds.

ttyout=*string*

> Output *string* on the current console ('/dev/tty').

Several '--checkpoint-action' options can be specified. The supplied actions will be executed in order of their appearance in the command line.

Using '--checkpoint-action' without '--checkpoint' assumes default checkpoint frequency of one checkpoint per 10 records.

'--check-links'
'-l'

> If this option was given, tar will check the number of links dumped for each processed file. If this number does not match the total number of hard links for the file, a warning message will be output[4].
>
> See Section 8.3.3 [hard links], page 141.

'--compress'
'--uncompress'
'-Z'

> tar will use the compress program when reading or writing the archive. This allows you to directly act on archives while saving space. See Section 8.1.1 [gzip], page 132.

'--confirmation'

> (See '--interactive'.) See Section 3.10 [interactive], page 59.

'--delay-directory-restore'

> Delay setting modification times and permissions of extracted directories until the end of extraction. See [Directory Modification Times and Permissions], page 75.

'--dereference'
'-h'

> When reading or writing a file to be archived, tar accesses the file that a symbolic link points to, rather than the symlink itself. See Section 8.3.2 [dereference], page 141.

'--directory=*dir*'
'-C *dir*'

> When this option is specified, tar will change its current directory to *dir* before performing any operations. When this option is used during archive creation, it is order sensitive. See Section 6.10.1 [directory], page 119.

'--exclude=*pattern*'

> When performing operations, tar will skip files that match *pattern*. See Section 6.4 [exclude], page 101.

---

[4] Earlier versions of GNU tar understood '-l' as a synonym for '--one-file-system'. The current semantics, which complies to UNIX98, was introduced with version 1.15.91. See Appendix A [Changes], page 185, for more information.

'`--exclude-backups`'

> Exclude backup and lock files. See Section 6.4 [exclude-backups], page 101.

'`--exclude-from=file`'
'`-X file`'

> Similar to '`--exclude`', except `tar` will use the list of patterns in the file *file*. See Section 6.4 [exclude], page 101.

'`--exclude-caches`'

> Exclude from dump any directory containing a valid cache directory tag file, but still dump the directory node and the tag file itself.
>
> See Section 6.4 [exclude-caches], page 101.

'`--exclude-caches-under`'

> Exclude from dump any directory containing a valid cache directory tag file, but still dump the directory node itself.
>
> See Section 6.4 [exclude], page 101.

'`--exclude-caches-all`'

> Exclude from dump any directory containing a valid cache directory tag file. See Section 6.4 [exclude], page 101.

'`--exclude-ignore=file`'

> Before dumping a directory, `tar` checks if it contains *file*. If so, exclusion patterns are read from this file. The patterns affect only the directory itself. See Section 6.4 [exclude], page 101.

'`--exclude-ignore-recursive=file`'

> Before dumping a directory, `tar` checks if it contains *file*. If so, exclusion patterns are read from this file. The patterns affect the directory and all itssubdirectories. See Section 6.4 [exclude], page 101.

'`--exclude-tag=file`'

> Exclude from dump any directory containing file named *file*, but dump the directory node and *file* itself. See Section 6.4 [exclude-tag], page 101.

'`--exclude-tag-under=file`'

> Exclude from dump the contents of any directory containing file named *file*, but dump the directory node itself. See Section 6.4 [exclude-tag-under], page 101.

'`--exclude-tag-all=file`'

> Exclude from dump any directory containing file named *file*. See Section 6.4 [exclude-tag-all], page 101.

'`--exclude-vcs`'

> Exclude from dump directories and files, that are internal for some widely used version control systems.

See [exclude-vcs], page 103.

'--exclude-vcs-ignores'

Exclude files that match patterns read from VCS-specific ignore files. Supported files are: '.cvsignore', '.gitignore', '.bzrignore', and '.hgignore'. The semantics of each file is the same as for the corresponding VCS, e.g. patterns read from '.gitignore' affect the directory and all its subdirectories. See [exclude-vcs-ignores], page 102.

'--file=archive'
'-f archive'

tar will use the file *archive* as the tar archive it performs operations on, rather than tar's compilation dependent default. See [file tutorial], page 7.

'--files-from=file'
'-T file'

tar will use the contents of *file* as a list of archive members or files to operate on, in addition to those specified on the command-line. See Section 6.3 [files], page 99.

'--force-local'

Forces tar to interpret the file name given to '--file' as a local file, even if it looks like a remote tape drive name. See [local and remote archives], page 98.

'--format=format'
'-H format'

Selects output archive format. *Format* may be one of the following:

'v7'   Creates an archive that is compatible with Unix V7 tar.

'oldgnu'   Creates an archive that is compatible with GNU tar version 1.12 or earlier.

'gnu'   Creates archive in GNU tar 1.13 format. Basically it is the same as 'oldgnu' with the only difference in the way it handles long numeric fields.

'ustar'   Creates a POSIX.1-1988 compatible archive.

'posix'   Creates a POSIX.1-2001 archive.

See Chapter 8 [Formats], page 131, for a detailed discussion of these formats.

'--full-time'

This option instructs tar to print file times to their full resolution. Usually this means 1-second resolution, but that depends on the underlying file system. The '`--full-time`' option takes effect only when detailed output (verbosity level 2 or higher) has been requested using the '`--verbose`' option, e.g., when listing or extracting archives:

```
$ tar -t -v --full-time -f archive.tar
```

or, when creating an archive:

```
$ tar -c -vv --full-time -f archive.tar .
```

Notice, thar when creating the archive you need to specify '`--verbose`' twice to get a detailed output (see [verbose tutorial], page 8).

'`--group=group`'

Files added to the `tar` archive will have a group ID of *group*, rather than the group from the source file. *group* can specify a symbolic name, or a numeric ID, or both as *name:id*. See Section 4.3.1 [override], page 69.

Also see the comments for the '`--owner=user`' option.

'`--gzip`'
'`--gunzip`'
'`--ungzip`'
'`-z`'

This option tells `tar` to read or write archives through `gzip`, allowing `tar` to directly operate on several kinds of compressed archives transparently. See Section 8.1.1 [gzip], page 132.

'`--hard-dereference`'

When creating an archive, dereference hard links and store the files they refer to, instead of creating usual hard link members.

See Section 8.3.3 [hard links], page 141.

'`--help`'
'`-?`'

`tar` will print out a short message summarizing the operations and options to `tar` and exit. See Section 3.5 [help], page 49.

'`--ignore-case`'

Ignore case when matching member or file names with patterns. See [controlling pattern-matching], page 107.

'`--ignore-command-error`'

Ignore exit codes of subprocesses. See [Writing to an External Program], page 77.

'`--ignore-failed-read`'

Do not exit unsuccessfully merely because an unreadable file was encountered. See Section 4.3.2 [Ignore Failed Read], page 71.

'--ignore-zeros'
'-i'

> With this option, tar will ignore zeroed blocks in the archive, which normally signals EOF. See Section 4.4.1 [Reading], page 71.

'--incremental'
'-G'

> Informs tar that it is working with an old GNU-format incremental backup archive. It is intended primarily for backwards compatibility only. See Section 5.2 [Incremental Dumps], page 84, for a detailed discussion of incremental archives.

'--index-file=file'
> Send verbose output to file instead of to standard output.

'--info-script=command'
'--new-volume-script=command'
'-F command'

> When tar is performing multi-tape backups, command is run at the end of each tape. If it exits with nonzero status, tar fails immediately. See [info-script], page 170, for a detailed discussion of this feature.

'--interactive'
'--confirmation'
'-w'

> Specifies that tar should ask the user for confirmation before performing potentially destructive options, such as overwriting files. See Section 3.10 [interactive], page 59.

'--keep-directory-symlink'
> This option changes the behavior of tar when it encounters a symlink with the same name as the directory that it is about to extract. By default, in this case tar would first remove the symlink and then proceed extracting the directory.

> The '--keep-directory-symlink' option disables this behavior and instructs tar to follow symlinks to directories when extracting from the archive.

> It is mainly intended to provide compatibility with the Slackware installation scripts.

'--keep-newer-files'
> Do not replace existing files that are newer than their archive copies when extracting files from an archive.

'--keep-old-files'
'-k'

Do not overwrite existing files when extracting files from an archive. Return error if such files exist. See also [–skip-old-files], page 44.

See [Keep Old Files], page 74.

'`--label=`*name*'
'`-V `*name*'

> When creating an archive, instructs `tar` to write *name* as a name record in the archive. When extracting or listing archives, `tar` will only operate on archives that have a label matching the pattern specified in *name*. See Section 9.6.2 [Tape Files], page 173.

'`--level=`*n*'

> Force incremental backup of level *n*. As of GNU `tar` version 1.28, the option '`--level=0`' truncates the snapshot file, thereby forcing the level 0 dump. Other values of *n* are effectively ignored. See [–level=0], page 85, for details and examples.

> The use of this option is valid only in conjunction with the '`--listed-incremental`' option. See Section 5.2 [Incremental Dumps], page 84, for a detailed description.

'`--listed-incremental=`*snapshot-file*'
'`-g `*snapshot-file*'

> During a '`--create`' operation, specifies that the archive that `tar` creates is a new GNU-format incremental backup, using *snapshot-file* to determine which files to backup. With other operations, informs `tar` that the archive is in incremental format. See Section 5.2 [Incremental Dumps], page 84.

'`--lzip`'

> This option tells `tar` to read or write archives through `lzip`. See Section 8.1.1 [gzip], page 132.

'`--lzma`'

> This option tells `tar` to read or write archives through `lzma`. See Section 8.1.1 [gzip], page 132.

'`--lzop`'

> This option tells `tar` to read or write archives through `lzop`. See Section 8.1.1 [gzip], page 132.

'`--mode=`*permissions*'

> When adding files to an archive, `tar` will use *permissions* for the archive members, rather than the permissions from the files. *permissions* can be specified either as an octal number or as symbolic permissions, like with `chmod`. See Section 4.3.1 [override], page 69.

'--mtime=*date*'

> When adding files to an archive, tar will use *date* as the modification time of members when creating archives, instead of their actual modification times. The value of *date* can be either a textual date representation (see Chapter 7 [Date input formats], page 123) or a name of the existing file, starting with '/' or '.'. In the latter case, the modification time of that file is used. See Section 4.3.1 [override], page 69.

'--multi-volume'
'-M'

> Informs tar that it should create or otherwise operate on a multi-volume tar archive. See Section 9.6 [Using Multiple Tapes], page 168.

'--new-volume-script'

> (see '--info-script')

'--newer=*date*'
'--after-date=*date*'
'-N'

> When creating an archive, tar will only add files that have changed since *date*. If *date* begins with '/' or '.', it is taken to be the name of a file whose data modification time specifies the date. See Section 6.8 [after], page 116.

'--newer-mtime=*date*'

> Like '--newer', but add only files whose contents have changed (as opposed to just '--newer', which will also back up files for which any status information has changed). See Section 6.8 [after], page 116.

'--no-anchored'

> An exclude pattern can match any subsequence of the name's components. See [controlling pattern-matching], page 107.

'--no-auto-compress'

> Disables automatic compressed format recognition based on the archive suffix. See [–auto-compress], page 30. See Section 8.1.1 [gzip], page 132.

'--no-check-device'

> Do not check device numbers when creating a list of modified files for incremental archiving. See [device numbers], page 85, for a detailed description.

'--no-delay-directory-restore'

> Modification times and permissions of extracted directories are set when all files from this directory have been extracted. This

is the default. See [Directory Modification Times and Permissions], page 75.

'`--no-ignore-case`'

Use case-sensitive matching. See [controlling pattern-matching], page 107.

'`--no-ignore-command-error`'

Print warnings about subprocesses that terminated with a nonzero exit code. See [Writing to an External Program], page 77.

'`--no-null`'

If the '`--null`' option was given previously, this option cancels its effect, so that any following '`--files-from`' options will expect their file lists to be newline-terminated.

'`--no-overwrite-dir`'

Preserve metadata of existing directories when extracting files from an archive. See [Overwrite Old Files], page 73.

'`--no-quote-chars=string`'

Remove characters listed in *string* from the list of quoted characters set by the previous '`--quote-chars`' option (see Section 6.6 [quoting styles], page 109).

'`--no-recursion`'

With this option, `tar` will not recurse into directories. See Section 6.9 [recurse], page 118.

'`--no-same-owner`'
'`-o`'

When extracting an archive, do not attempt to preserve the owner specified in the `tar` archive. This the default behavior for ordinary users.

'`--no-same-permissions`'

When extracting an archive, subtract the user's umask from files from the permissions specified in the archive. This is the default behavior for ordinary users.

'`--no-seek`'

The archive media does not support seeks to arbitrary locations. Usually `tar` determines automatically whether the archive can be seeked or not. Use this option to disable this mechanism.

'`--no-unquote`'

Treat all input file or member names literally, do not interpret escape sequences. See [input name quoting], page 98.

'`--no-wildcards`'

Do not use wildcards. See [controlling pattern-matching], page 107.

'--no-wildcards-match-slash'

>Wildcards do not match '/'. See [controlling pattern-matching], page 107.

'--null'

>When tar is using the '--files-from' option, this option instructs tar to expect file names terminated with NUL, so tar can correctly work with file names that contain newlines. See Section 6.3.1 [nul], page 101.

'--numeric-owner'

>This option will notify tar that it should use numeric user and group IDs when creating a tar file, rather than names. See Section 8.2 [Attributes], page 138.

'-o'

>The function of this option depends on the action tar is performing. When extracting files, '-o' is a synonym for '--no-same-owner', i.e., it prevents tar from restoring ownership of files being extracted.

>When creating an archive, it is a synonym for '--old-archive'. This behavior is for compatibility with previous versions of GNU tar, and will be removed in future releases.

>See Appendix A [Changes], page 185, for more information.

'--occurrence[=number]'

>This option can be used in conjunction with one of the subcommands '--delete', '--diff', '--extract' or '--list' when a list of files is given either on the command line or via '-T' option.

>This option instructs tar to process only the numberth occurrence of each named file. Number defaults to 1, so

```
tar -x -f archive.tar --occurrence filename
```

>will extract the first occurrence of the member 'filename' from 'archive.tar' and will terminate without scanning to the end of the archive.

'--old-archive'

>Synonym for '--format=v7'.

'--one-file-system'

>Used when creating an archive. Prevents tar from recursing into directories that are on different file systems from the current directory.

'--one-top-level[=dir]'

>Tells tar to create a new directory beneath the extraction directory (or the one passed to '-C') and use it to guard against tarbombs. In the absence of dir argument, the name of the new

directory will be equal to the base name of the archive (file name minus the archive suffix, if recognized). Any member names that do not begin with that directory name (after transformations from '`--transform`' and '`--strip-components`') will be prefixed with it. Recognized file name suffixes are '`.tar`', and any compression suffixes recognizable by See [–auto-compress], page 30.

'`--overwrite`'

> Overwrite existing files and directory metadata when extracting files from an archive. See [Overwrite Old Files], page 73.

'`--overwrite-dir`'

> Overwrite the metadata of existing directories when extracting files from an archive. See [Overwrite Old Files], page 73.

'`--owner=user`'

> Specifies that `tar` should use *user* as the owner of members when creating archives, instead of the user associated with the source file. *user* can specify a symbolic name, or a numeric ID, or both as *name:id*. See Section 4.3.1 [override], page 69.
>
> This option does not affect extraction from archives.

'`--pax-option=keyword-list`'

> This option enables creation of the archive in POSIX.1-2001 format (see Section 8.3.7 [posix], page 143) and modifies the way `tar` handles the extended header keywords. *Keyword-list* is a comma-separated list of keyword options. See Section 8.3.7.1 [PAX keywords], page 143, for a detailed discussion.

'`--portability`'
'`--old-archive`'

> Synonym for '`--format=v7`'.

'`--posix`'   Same as '`--format=posix`'.

'`--preserve`'

> Synonymous with specifying both '`--preserve-permissions`' and '`--same-order`'. See [Setting Access Permissions], page 75.

'`--preserve-order`'

> (See '`--same-order`'; see Section 4.4.1 [Reading], page 71.)

'`--preserve-permissions`'
'`--same-permissions`'
'`-p`'

> When `tar` is extracting an archive, it normally subtracts the users' umask from the permissions specified in the archive and uses that number as the permissions to create the destination file. Specifying this option instructs `tar` that it should use the

permissions directly from the archive. See [Setting Access Permissions], page 75.

'--quote-chars=*string*'

Always quote characters from *string*, even if the selected quoting style would not quote them (see Section 6.6 [quoting styles], page 109).

'--quoting-style=*style*'

Set quoting style to use when printing member and file names (see Section 6.6 [quoting styles], page 109). Valid *style* values are: `literal`, `shell`, `shell-always`, `c`, `escape`, `locale`, and `clocale`. Default quoting style is `escape`, unless overridden while configuring the package.

'--read-full-records'
'-B'

Specifies that `tar` should reblock its input, for reading from pipes on systems with buggy implementations. See Section 4.4.1 [Reading], page 71.

'--record-size=*size*[*suf*]'

Instructs `tar` to use *size* bytes per record when accessing the archive. The argument can be suffixed with a *size suffix*, e.g. '--record-size=10K' for 10 Kilobytes. See Table 9.1, for a list of valid suffixes. See Section 9.4.2 [Blocking Factor], page 161, for a detailed description of this option.

'--recursion'

With this option, `tar` recurses into directories (default). See Section 6.9 [recurse], page 118.

'--recursive-unlink'

Remove existing directory hierarchies before extracting directories of the same name from the archive. See [Recursive Unlink], page 75.

'--remove-files'

Directs `tar` to remove the source file from the file system after appending it to an archive. See [remove files], page 79.

'--restrict'

Disable use of some potentially harmful `tar` options. Currently this option disables shell invocation from multi-volume menu (see Section 9.6 [Using Multiple Tapes], page 168).

'--rmt-command=*cmd*'

Notifies `tar` that it should use *cmd* instead of the default '/usr/libexec/rmt' (see Section 9.2 [Remote Tape Server], page 157).

'--rsh-command=*cmd*'

> Notifies `tar` that is should use *cmd* to communicate with remote devices. See Section 9.1 [Device], page 155.

'--same-order'
'--preserve-order'
'-s'

> This option is an optimization for `tar` when running on machines with small amounts of memory. It informs `tar` that the list of file arguments has already been sorted to match the order of files in the archive. See Section 4.4.1 [Reading], page 71.

'--same-owner'

> When extracting an archive, `tar` will attempt to preserve the owner specified in the `tar` archive with this option present. This is the default behavior for the superuser; this option has an effect only for ordinary users. See Section 8.2 [Attributes], page 138.

'--same-permissions'

> (See '--preserve-permissions'; see [Setting Access Permissions], page 75.)

'--seek'
'-n'

> Assume that the archive media supports seeks to arbitrary locations. Usually `tar` determines automatically whether the archive can be seeked or not. This option is intended for use in cases when such recognition fails. It takes effect only if the archive is open for reading (e.g. with '--list' or '--extract' options).

'--show-defaults'

> Displays the default options used by `tar` and exits successfully. This option is intended for use in shell scripts. Here is an example of what you can see using this option:

```
$ tar --show-defaults
--format=gnu -f- -b20 --quoting-style=escape
--rmt-command=/usr/libexec/rmt --rsh-command=/usr/bin/rsh
```

> Notice, that this option outputs only one line. The example output above has been split to fit page boundaries. See Section 3.6 [defaults], page 50.

'--show-omitted-dirs'

> Instructs `tar` to mention the directories it is skipping when operating on a `tar` archive. See [show-omitted-dirs], page 53.

'--show-snapshot-field-ranges'

> Displays the range of values allowed by this version of `tar` for each field in the snapshot file, then exits successfully. See [Snapshot Files], page 205.

'--show-transformed-names'
'--show-stored-names'

> Display file or member names after applying any transformations (see Section 6.7 [transform], page 113). In particular, when used in conjunction with one of the archive creation operations it instructs tar to list the member names stored in the archive, as opposed to the actual file names. See [listing member and file names], page 15.

'--skip-old-files'

> Do not overwrite existing files when extracting files from an archive. See [Keep Old Files], page 74.
>
> This option differs from '--keep-old-files' in that it does not treat such files as an error, instead it just silently avoids overwriting them.
>
> The '--warning=existing-file' option can be used together with this option to produce warning messages about existing old files (see Section 3.9 [warnings], page 56).

'--sort=order'

> Specify the directory sorting order when reading directories. *Order* may be one of the following:
>
> 'none'   No directory sorting is performed. This is the default.
>
> 'name'   Sort the directory entries on name. The operating system may deliver directory entries in a more or less random order, and sorting them makes archive creation reproducible.
>
> 'inode'   Sort the directory entries on inode number. Sorting directories on inode number may reduce the amount of disk seek operations when creating an archive for some file systems.

'--sparse'
'-S'

> Invokes a GNU extension when adding files to an archive that handles sparse files efficiently. See Section 8.1.2 [sparse], page 137.

'--sparse-version=version'

> Specifies the *format version* to use when archiving sparse files. Implies '--sparse'. See Section 8.1.2 [sparse], page 137. For the description of the supported sparse formats, See [Sparse Formats], page 202.

'--starting-file=name'
'-K name'

This option affects extraction only; `tar` will skip extracting files in the archive until it finds one that matches *name*. See Section 4.4.3 [Scarce], page 79.

'`--strip-components=`*number*'

Strip given *number* of leading components from file names before extraction. For example, if archive '`archive.tar`' contained '`/some/file/name`', then running

```
tar --extract --file archive.tar --strip-components=2
```

would extract this file to file '`name`'.

'`--suffix=`*suffix*'

Alters the suffix `tar` uses when backing up files from the default '`~`'. See Section 4.5 [backup], page 80.

'`--tape-length=`*num* [*suf*]'
'`-L` *num* [*suf*]'

Specifies the length of tapes that `tar` is writing as being *num* x 1024 bytes long. If optional *suf* is given, it specifies a multiplicative factor to be used instead of 1024. For example, '`-L2M`' means 2 megabytes. See Table 9.1, for a list of allowed suffixes. See Section 9.6 [Using Multiple Tapes], page 168, for a detailed discussion of this option.

'`--test-label`'

Reads the volume label. If an argument is specified, test whether it matches the volume label. See [–test-label option], page 174.

'`--to-command=`*command*'

During extraction `tar` will pipe extracted files to the standard input of *command*. See [Writing to an External Program], page 77.

'`--to-stdout`'
'`-O`'

During extraction, `tar` will extract files to stdout rather than to the file system. See [Writing to Standard Output], page 77.

'`--totals`[=*signo*]'

Displays the total number of bytes transferred when processing an archive. If an argument is given, these data are displayed on request, when signal *signo* is delivered to `tar`. See [totals], page 52.

'`--touch`'
'`-m`'

Sets the data modification time of extracted files to the extraction time, rather than the data modification time stored in the archive. See [Data Modification Times], page 75.

'`--transform=`*sed-expr*'
'`--xform=`*sed-expr*'

> Transform file or member names using `sed` replacement expression *sed-expr*. For example,
>
> $ tar cf archive.tar --transform 's,^\./,usr/,' .
>
> will add to '`archive`' files from the current working directory, replacing initial '`./`' prefix with '`usr/`'. For the detailed discussion, See Section 6.7 [transform], page 113.
>
> To see transformed member names in verbose listings, use '`--show-transformed-names`' option (see [show-transformed-names], page 114).

'`--uncompress`'

> (See '`--compress`', see Section 8.1.1 [gzip], page 132)

'`--ungzip`'

> (See '`--gzip`', see Section 8.1.1 [gzip], page 132)

'`--unlink-first`'
'`-U`'

> Directs `tar` to remove the corresponding file from the file system before extracting it from the archive. See [Unlink First], page 74.

'`--unquote`'

> Enable unquoting input file or member names (default). See [input name quoting], page 98.

'`--use-compress-program=`*prog*'
'`-I=`*prog*'

> Instructs `tar` to access the archive through *prog*, which is presumed to be a compression program of some sort. See Section 8.1.1 [gzip], page 132.

'`--utc`'

> Display file modification dates in UTC. This option implies '`--verbose`'.

'`--verbose`'
'`-v`'

> Specifies that `tar` should be more verbose about the operations it is performing. This option can be specified multiple times for some operations to increase the amount of information displayed. See Section 3.7 [verbose], page 51.

'`--verify`'
'`-W`'

> Verifies that the archive was correctly written when creating an archive. See Section 9.8 [verify], page 176.

'`--version`'

> Print information about the program's name, version, origin and legal status, all on standard output, and then exit successfully. See Section 3.5 [help], page 49.

'`--volno-file=file`'

> Used in conjunction with '`--multi-volume`'. `tar` will keep track of which volume of a multi-volume archive it is working in *file*. See [volno-file], page 170.

'`--warning=keyword`'

> Enable or disable warning messages identified by *keyword*. The messages are suppressed if *keyword* is prefixed with '`no-`'. See Section 3.9 [warnings], page 56.

'`--wildcards`'

> Use wildcards when matching member names with patterns. See [controlling pattern-matching], page 107.

'`--wildcards-match-slash`'

> Wildcards match '`/`'. See [controlling pattern-matching], page 107.

'`--xz`'
'`-J`'   Use `xz` for compressing or decompressing the archives. See Section 8.1.1 [gzip], page 132.

3.4.3 Short Options Cross Reference

Here is an alphabetized list of all of the short option forms, matching them with the equivalent long option.

Short Option	Reference
-A	[–concatenate], page 28.
-B	[–read-full-records], page 42.
-C	[–directory], page 32.
-F	[–info-script], page 36.
-G	[–incremental], page 36.
-J	[–xz], page 47.
-K	[–starting-file], page 44.
-L	[–tape-length], page 45.

-M   [–multi-volume], page 38.

-N   [–newer], page 38.

-O   [–to-stdout], page 45.

-P   [–absolute-names], page 29.

-R   [–block-number], page 30.

-S   [–sparse], page 44.

-T   [–files-from], page 34.

-U   [–unlink-first], page 46.

-V   [–label], page 37.

-W   [–verify], page 46.

-X   [–exclude-from], page 33.

-Z   [–compress], page 32.

-b   [–blocking-factor], page 31.

-c   [–create], page 28.

-d   [–compare], page 28.

-f   [–file], page 34.

-g   [–listed-incremental], page 37.

-h   [–dereference], page 32.

-i   [–ignore-zeros], page 35.

-j   [–bzip2], page 31.

-k   [–keep-old-files], page 36.

-l   [–check-links], page 32.

-m   [–touch], page 45.

-o   When creating, [–no-same-owner], page 39, when extract-
                            ing — [–portability], page 41.
                            The latter usage is deprecated. It is retained for com-
                            patibility with the earlier versions of GNU `tar`. In future
                            releases '`-o`' will be equivalent to '`--no-same-owner`' only.

-p   [–preserve-permissions], page 41.

-r   [–append], page 28.

-s   [–same-order], page 43.

-t   [–list], page 29.

-u   [–update], page 29.

-v   [–verbose], page 46.

-w   [–interactive], page 36.

-x   [–extract], page 28.

-z   [–gzip], page 35.

3.5 GNU `tar` documentation

Being careful, the first thing is really checking that you are using GNU `tar`,
indeed. The '`--version`' option causes `tar` to print information about its
name, version, origin and legal status, all on standard output, and then exit
successfully. For example, '`tar --version`' might print:

```
tar (GNU tar) 1.28
Copyright (C) 2013-2014 Free Software Foundation, Inc.
License GPLv3+: GNU GPL version 3 or later <http://gnu.org/licenses/gpl.html>.
This is free software: you are free to change and redistribute it.
There is NO WARRANTY, to the extent permitted by law.

Written by John Gilmore and Jay Fenlason.
```

The first occurrence of '`tar`' in the result above is the program name in the
package (for example, `rmt` is another program), while the second occurrence
of '`tar`' is the name of the package itself, containing possibly many programs.
The package is currently named '`tar`', after the name of the main program
it contains[5].

Another thing you might want to do is checking the spelling or meaning
of some particular `tar` option, without resorting to this manual, for once you

---

[5] There are plans to merge the `cpio` and `tar` packages into a single one which would be
called `paxutils`. So, who knows if, one of this days, the '`--version`' would not output
'`tar (GNU paxutils) 3.2`'.

have carefully read it. GNU `tar` has a short help feature, triggerable through the '`--help`' option. By using this option, `tar` will print a usage message listing all available options on standard output, then exit successfully, without doing anything else and ignoring all other options. Even if this is only a brief summary, it may be several screens long. So, if you are not using some kind of scrollable window, you might prefer to use something like:

```
$ tar --help | less
```

presuming, here, that you like using `less` for a pager. Other popular pagers are `more` and `pg`. If you know about some *keyword* which interests you and do not want to read all the '`--help`' output, another common idiom is doing:

```
tar --help | grep keyword
```

for getting only the pertinent lines. Notice, however, that some `tar` options have long description lines and the above command will list only the first of them.

The exact look of the option summary displayed by *tar --help* is configurable. See Appendix B [Configuring Help Summary], page 187, for a detailed description.

If you only wish to check the spelling of an option, running *tar --usage* may be a better choice. This will display a terse list of `tar` options without accompanying explanations.

The short help output is quite succinct, and you might have to get back to the full documentation for precise points. If you are reading this paragraph, you already have the `tar` manual in some form. This manual is available in a variety of forms from `http://www.gnu.org/software/tar/manual`. It may be printed out of the GNU `tar` distribution, provided you have TeX already installed somewhere, and a laser printer around. Just configure the distribution, execute the command '`make dvi`', then print '`doc/tar.dvi`' the usual way (contact your local guru to know how). If GNU `tar` has been conveniently installed at your place, this manual is also available in interactive, hypertextual form as an Info file. Just call '`info tar`' or, if you do not have the `info` program handy, use the Info reader provided within GNU Emacs, calling '`tar`' from the main Info menu.

There is currently no `man` page for GNU `tar`. If you observe such a `man` page on the system you are running, either it does not belong to GNU `tar`, or it has not been produced by GNU. Some package maintainers convert *tar --help* output to a man page, using `help2man`. In any case, please bear in mind that the authoritative source of information about GNU `tar` is this Texinfo documentation.

3.6 Obtaining GNU `tar` default values

GNU `tar` has some predefined defaults that are used when you do not explicitly specify another values. To obtain a list of such defaults, use '`--show-defaults`' option. This will output the values in the form of `tar` command line options:

```
$ tar --show-defaults
--format=gnu -f- -b20 --quoting-style=escape
--rmt-command=/etc/rmt --rsh-command=/usr/bin/rsh
```

Notice, that this option outputs only one line. The example output above has been split to fit page boundaries.

The above output shows that this version of GNU `tar` defaults to using 'gnu' archive format (see Chapter 8 [Formats], page 131), it uses standard output as the archive, if no '`--file`' option has been given (see [file tutorial], page 7), the default blocking factor is 20 (see Section 9.4.2 [Blocking Factor], page 161). It also shows the default locations where `tar` will look for `rmt` and `rsh` binaries.

3.7 Checking `tar` progress

Typically, `tar` performs most operations without reporting any information to the user except error messages. When using `tar` with many options, particularly ones with complicated or difficult-to-predict behavior, it is possible to make serious mistakes. `tar` provides several options that make observing `tar` easier. These options cause `tar` to print information as it progresses in its job, and you might want to use them just for being more careful about what is going on, or merely for entertaining yourself. If you have encountered a problem when operating on an archive, however, you may need more information than just an error message in order to solve the problem. The following options can be helpful diagnostic tools.

Normally, the '`--list`' ('`-t`') command to list an archive prints just the file names (one per line) and the other commands are silent. When used with most operations, the '`--verbose`' ('`-v`') option causes `tar` to print the name of each file or archive member as it is processed. This and the other options which make `tar` print status information can be useful in monitoring `tar`.

With '`--create`' or '`--extract`', '`--verbose`' used once just prints the names of the files or members as they are processed. Using it twice causes `tar` to print a longer listing (See [verbose member listing], page 9, for the description) for each member. Since '`--list`' already prints the names of the members, '`--verbose`' used once with '`--list`' causes `tar` to print an '`ls -l`' type listing of the files in the archive. The following examples both extract members with long list output:

```
$ tar --extract --file=archive.tar --verbose --verbose
$ tar xvvf archive.tar
```

Verbose output appears on the standard output except when an archive is being written to the standard output, as with '`tar --create --file=- --verbose`' ('`tar cvf -`', or even '`tar cv`'—if the installer let standard output be the default archive). In that case `tar` writes verbose output to the standard error stream.

If '--index-file=*file*' is specified, `tar` sends verbose output to *file* rather than to standard output or standard error.

The '--totals' option causes `tar` to print on the standard error the total amount of bytes transferred when processing an archive. When creating or appending to an archive, this option prints the number of bytes written to the archive and the average speed at which they have been written, e.g.:

```
$ tar -c -f archive.tar --totals /home
Total bytes written: 7924664320 (7.4GiB, 85MiB/s)
```

When reading an archive, this option displays the number of bytes read:

```
$ tar -x -f archive.tar --totals
Total bytes read: 7924664320 (7.4GiB, 95MiB/s)
```

Finally, when deleting from an archive, the '--totals' option displays both numbers plus number of bytes removed from the archive:

```
$ tar --delete -f foo.tar --totals --wildcards '*~'
Total bytes read: 9543680 (9.2MiB, 201MiB/s)
Total bytes written: 3829760 (3.7MiB, 81MiB/s)
Total bytes deleted: 1474048
```

You can also obtain this information on request. When '--totals' is used with an argument, this argument is interpreted as a symbolic name of a signal, upon delivery of which the statistics is to be printed:

'--totals=*signo*'

Print statistics upon delivery of signal *signo*. Valid arguments are: SIGHUP, SIGQUIT, SIGINT, SIGUSR1 and SIGUSR2. Shortened names without 'SIG' prefix are also accepted.

Both forms of '--totals' option can be used simultaneously. Thus, `tar -x --totals --totals=USR1` instructs `tar` to extract all members from its default archive and print statistics after finishing the extraction, as well as when receiving signal SIGUSR1.

The '--checkpoint' option prints an occasional message as `tar` reads or writes the archive. It is designed for those who don't need the more detailed (and voluminous) output of '--block-number' ('-R'), but do want visual confirmation that `tar` is actually making forward progress. By default it prints a message each 10 records read or written. This can be changed by giving it a numeric argument after an equal sign:

```
$ tar -c --checkpoint=1000 /var
tar: Write checkpoint 1000
tar: Write checkpoint 2000
tar: Write checkpoint 3000
```

This example shows the default checkpoint message used by `tar`. If you place a dot immediately after the equal sign, it will print a '.' at each checkpoint[6]. For example:

```
$ tar -c --checkpoint=.1000 /var
```

---

[6] This is actually a shortcut for '--checkpoint=*n* --checkpoint-action=dot'. See Section 3.8 [checkpoints], page 53.

. . .

The '`--checkpoint`' option provides a flexible mechanism for executing arbitrary actions upon hitting checkpoints, see the next section (see Section 3.8 [checkpoints], page 53), for more information on it.

The '`--show-omitted-dirs`' option, when reading an archive—with '`--list`' or '`--extract`', for example—causes a message to be printed for each directory in the archive which is skipped. This happens regardless of the reason for skipping: the directory might not have been named on the command line (implicitly or explicitly), it might be excluded by the use of the '`--exclude=pattern`' option, or some other reason.

If '`--block-number`' ('`-R`') is used, `tar` prints, along with every message it would normally produce, the block number within the archive where the message was triggered. Also, supplementary messages are triggered when reading blocks full of NULs, or when hitting end of file on the archive. As of now, if the archive is properly terminated with a NUL block, the reading of the file may stop before end of file is met, so the position of end of file will not usually show when '`--block-number`' ('`-R`') is used. Note that GNU `tar` drains the archive before exiting when reading the archive from a pipe.

This option is especially useful when reading damaged archives, since it helps pinpoint the damaged sections. It can also be used with '`--list`' ('`-t`') when listing a file-system backup tape, allowing you to choose among several backup tapes when retrieving a file later, in favor of the tape where the file appears earliest (closest to the front of the tape). See Section 4.5 [backup], page 80.

3.8 Checkpoints

A *checkpoint* is a moment of time before writing nth record to the archive (a *write checkpoint*), or before reading nth record from the archive (a *read checkpoint*). Checkpoints allow to periodically execute arbitrary actions.

The checkpoint facility is enabled using the following option:

'`--checkpoint[=n]`'

> Schedule checkpoints before writing or reading each nth record. The default value for n is 10.

A list of arbitrary *actions* can be executed at each checkpoint. These actions include: pausing, displaying textual messages, and executing arbitrary external programs. Actions are defined using the '`--checkpoint-action`' option.

'`--checkpoint-action=action`'

> Execute an *action* at each checkpoint.

The simplest value of *action* is '`echo`'. It instructs `tar` to display the default message on the standard error stream upon arriving at each checkpoint. The default message is (in POSIX locale) '`Write checkpoint n`', for write checkpoints, and 'Read checkpoint *n* ', for read checkpoints. Here, *n* represents ordinal number of the checkpoint.

In another locales, translated versions of this message are used.

This is the default action, so running:

```
$ tar -c --checkpoint=1000 --checkpoint-action=echo /var
```

is equivalent to:

```
$ tar -c --checkpoint=1000 /var
```

The 'echo' action also allows to supply a customized message. You do so by placing an equals sign and the message right after it, e.g.:

```
--checkpoint-action="echo=Hit %s checkpoint #%u"
```

The '%s' and '%u' in the above example are *format specifiers*. The '%s' specifier is replaced with the *type* of the checkpoint: 'write' or 'read' (or a corresponding translated version in locales other than POSIX). The '%u' specifier is replaced with the ordinal number of the checkpoint. Thus, the above example could produce the following output when used with the '--create' option:

```
tar: Hit write checkpoint #10
tar: Hit write checkpoint #20
tar: Hit write checkpoint #30
```

The complete list of available format specifiers follows. Some of them can take optional arguments. These arguments, if given, are supplied in curly braces between the percent sign and the specifier letter.

'%s'   Print type of the checkpoint ('write' or 'read').

'%u'   Print number of the checkpoint.

'%{r,w,d}T'

Print number of bytes transferred so far and approximate transfer speed. Optional arguments supply prefixes to be used before number of bytes read, written and deleted, correspondingly. If absent, they default to 'R'. 'W', 'D'. Any or all of them can be omitted, so, that e.g. '%{}T' means to print corresponding statistics without any prefixes. Any surplus arguments, if present, are silently ignored.

```
$ tar --delete -f f.tar --checkpoint-action=echo="#%u:
tar: #1: R: 0 (0B, 0B/s),W: 0 (0B, 0B/s),D: 0
tar: #2: R: 10240 (10KiB, 19MiB/s),W: 0 (0B, 0B/s),D: 1
```

See also the 'totals' action, described below.

'%{fmt}t'   Output current local time using *fmt* as format for strftime (see section "strftime" in *strftime(3) man page*). The '{fmt}' part is optional. If not present, the default format is '%c', i.e. the preferred date and time representation for the current locale.

'%{n}*'   Pad output with spaces to the *n*th column. If the '{n}' part is omitted, the current screen width is assumed.

'%c'   This is a shortcut for '%{%Y-%m-%d %H:%M:%S}t: %ds,
              %{read,wrote}T%*\r', intended mainly for use with 'ttyout'
              action (see below).

Aside from format expansion, the message string is subject to *unquoting*, during which the backslash *escape sequences* are replaced with their corresponding ASCII characters (see [escape sequences], page 109). E.g. the following action will produce an audible bell and the message described above at each checkpoint:

```
--checkpoint-action='echo=\aHit %s checkpoint #%u'
```

There is also a special action which produces an audible signal: 'bell'. It is not equivalent to 'echo='\a'', because 'bell' sends the bell directly to the console ('/dev/tty'), whereas 'echo='\a'' sends it to the standard error.

The 'ttyout=*string*' action outputs *string* to '/dev/tty', so it can be used even if the standard output is redirected elsewhere. The *string* is subject to the same modifications as with 'echo' action. In contrast to the latter, 'ttyout' does not prepend `tar` executable name to the string, nor does it output a newline after it. For example, the following action will print the checkpoint message at the same screen line, overwriting any previous message:

```
--checkpoint-action="ttyout=Hit %s checkpoint #%u%*\r"
```

Notice the use of '%*' specifier to clear out any eventual remains of the prior output line. As as more complex example, consider this:

```
--checkpoint-action=ttyout='%{%Y-%m-%d %H:%M:%S}t (%d sec): #%u, %T%*\r'
```

This prints the current local time, number of seconds expired since tar was started, the checkpoint ordinal number, transferred bytes and average computed I/O speed.

Another available checkpoint action is 'dot' (or '.'). It instructs `tar` to print a single dot on the standard listing stream, e.g.:

```
$ tar -c --checkpoint=1000 --checkpoint-action=dot /var
...
```

For compatibility with previous GNU `tar` versions, this action can be abbreviated by placing a dot in front of the checkpoint frequency, as shown in the previous section.

The 'totals' action prints the total number of bytes transferred so far. The format of the data is the same as for the '--totals' option (see [totals], page 52). See also '%T' format specifier of the 'echo' or 'ttyout' action.

Yet another action, 'sleep', pauses `tar` for a specified amount of seconds. The following example will stop for 30 seconds at each checkpoint:

```
$ tar -c --checkpoint=1000 --checkpoint-action=sleep=30
```

Finally, the **exec** action executes a given external command. For example:

```
$ tar -c --checkpoint=1000 --checkpoint-action=exec=/sbin/cpoint
```

The supplied command can be any valid command invocation, with or without additional command line arguments. If it does contain arguments, don't forget to quote it to prevent it from being split by the shell. See Section 3.11 [external], page 59, for more detail.

The command gets a copy of **tar**'s environment plus the following variables:

TAR_VERSION
> GNU **tar** version number.

TAR_ARCHIVE
> The name of the archive **tar** is processing.

TAR_BLOCKING_FACTOR
> Current blocking factor (see Section 9.4 [Blocking], page 159).

TAR_CHECKPOINT
> Number of the checkpoint.

TAR_SUBCOMMAND
> A short option describing the operation **tar** is executing. See Section 4.2.1 [Operations], page 62, for a complete list of subcommand options.

TAR_FORMAT
> Format of the archive being processed. See Chapter 8 [Formats], page 131, for a complete list of archive format names.

These environment variables can also be passed as arguments to the command, provided that they are properly escaped, for example:

```
tar -c -f arc.tar \
    --checkpoint-action='exec=/sbin/cpoint $TAR_FILENAME'
```

Notice single quotes to prevent variable names from being expanded by the shell when invoking **tar**.

Any number of actions can be defined, by supplying several '--checkpoint-action' options in the command line. For example, the command below displays two messages, pauses execution for 30 seconds and executes the '/sbin/cpoint' script:

```
$ tar -c -f arc.tar \
      --checkpoint-action='\aecho=Hit %s checkpoint #%u' \
      --checkpoint-action='echo=Sleeping for 30 seconds' \
      --checkpoint-action='sleep=30' \
      --checkpoint-action='exec=/sbin/cpoint'
```

This example also illustrates the fact that '--checkpoint-action' can be used without '--checkpoint'. In this case, the default checkpoint frequency (at each 10th record) is assumed.

3.9 Controlling Warning Messages

Sometimes, while performing the requested task, GNU **tar** notices some conditions that are not exactly errors, but which the user should be aware of.

When this happens, `tar` issues a *warning message* describing the condition. Warning messages are output to the standard error and they do not affect the exit code of `tar` command.

GNU `tar` allows the user to suppress some or all of its warning messages:

'`--warning=keyword`'

> Control display of the warning messages identified by *keyword*. If *keyword* starts with the prefix '`no-`', such messages are suppressed. Otherwise, they are enabled.
>
> Multiple '`--warning`' messages accumulate.
>
> The tables below list allowed values for *keyword* along with the warning messages they control.

Keywords controlling `tar` operation

all   Enable all warning messages. This is the default.

none   Disable all warning messages.

filename-with-nuls
                '`%s: file name read contains nul character`'

alone-zero-block
                '`A lone zero block at %s`'

Keywords applicable for `tar --create`

cachedir   '`%s: contains a cache directory tag %s; %s`'

file-shrank   '`%s: File shrank by %s bytes; padding with zeros`'

xdev   '`%s: file is on a different filesystem; not dumped`'

file-ignored
                '`%s: Unknown file type; file ignored`'
                '`%s: socket ignored`'
                '`%s: door ignored`'

file-unchanged
                '`%s: file is unchanged; not dumped`'

ignore-archive
                '`%s: file is the archive; not dumped`'

file-removed
                '`%s: File removed before we read it`'

file-changed
                '`%s: file changed as we read it`'

Keywords applicable for `tar --extract`

timestamp '%s: implausibly old time stamp %s'
'%s: time stamp %s is %s s in the future'

contiguous-cast
'Extracting contiguous files as regular files'

symlink-cast
'Attempting extraction of symbolic links as hard links'

unknown-cast
'%s: Unknown file type '%c', extracted as normal file'

ignore-newer
'Current %s is newer or same age'

unknown-keyword
'Ignoring unknown extended header keyword '%s''

decompress-program
Controls verbose description of failures occurring when trying to run alternative decompressor programs (see [alternative decompression programs], page 133). This warning is disabled by default (unless '--verbose' is used). A common example of what you can get when using this warning is:

```
$ tar --warning=decompress-program -x -f archive.Z
tar (child): cannot run compress: No such file or directory
tar (child): trying gzip
```

This means that `tar` first tried to decompress 'archive.Z' using `compress`, and, when that failed, switched to `gzip`.

record-size
'Record size = %lu blocks'

Keywords controlling incremental extraction:

rename-directory
'%s: Directory has been renamed from %s'
'%s: Directory has been renamed'

new-directory
'%s: Directory is new'

xdev   '%s: directory is on a different device: not purging'

bad-dumpdir
'Malformed dumpdir: 'X' never used'

3.10 Asking for Confirmation During Operations

Typically, `tar` carries out a command without stopping for further instructions. In some situations however, you may want to exclude some files and archive members from the operation (for instance if disk or storage space is tight). You can do this by excluding certain files automatically (see Chapter 6 [Choosing], page 97), or by performing an operation interactively, using the '`--interactive`' ('`-w`') option. `tar` also accepts '`--confirmation`' for this option.

When the '`--interactive`' ('`-w`') option is specified, before reading, writing, or deleting files, `tar` first prints a message for each such file, telling what operation it intends to take, then asks for confirmation on the terminal. The actions which require confirmation include adding a file to the archive, extracting a file from the archive, deleting a file from the archive, and deleting a file from disk. To confirm the action, you must type a line of input beginning with '`y`'. If your input line begins with anything other than '`y`', `tar` skips that file.

If `tar` is reading the archive from the standard input, `tar` opens the file '`/dev/tty`' to support the interactive communications.

Verbose output is normally sent to standard output, separate from other error messages. However, if the archive is produced directly on standard output, then verbose output is mixed with errors on `stderr`. Producing the archive on standard output may be used as a way to avoid using disk space, when the archive is soon to be consumed by another process reading it, say. Some people felt the need of producing an archive on stdout, still willing to segregate between verbose output and error output. A possible approach would be using a named pipe to receive the archive, and having the consumer process to read from that named pipe. This has the advantage of letting standard output free to receive verbose output, all separate from errors.

3.11 Running External Commands

Certain GNU `tar` operations imply running external commands that you supply on the command line. One of such operations is checkpointing, described above (see [checkpoint exec], page 55). Another example of this feature is the '`-I`' option, which allows you to supply the program to use for compressing or decompressing the archive (see [use-compress-program], page 135).

Whenever such operation is requested, `tar` first splits the supplied command into words much like the shell does. It then treats the first word as the name of the program or the shell script to execute and the rest of words as its command line arguments. The program, unless given as an absolute file name, is searched in the shell's `PATH`.

Any additional information is normally supplied to external commands in environment variables, specific to each particular operation. For example,

the '`--checkpoint-action=exec`' option, defines the `TAR_ARCHIVE` variable
to the name of the archive being worked upon. You can, should the need
be, use these variables in the command line of the external command. For
example:

```
$ tar -x -f archive.tar \
     --checkpoint=exec='printf "%04d in %32s\r" $TAR_CHECKPOINT $TAR_ARCHIVE'
```

This command prints for each checkpoint its number and the name of the
archive, using the same output line on the screen.

Notice the use of single quotes to prevent variable names from being
expanded by the shell when invoking `tar`.

4 GNU `tar` Operations

4.1 Basic GNU `tar` Operations

The basic `tar` operations, '`--create`' ('`-c`'), '`--list`' ('`-t`') and '`--extract`' ('`--get`', '`-x`'), are currently presented and described in the tutorial chapter of this manual. This section provides some complementary notes for these operations.

'`--create`'
'`-c`'

Creating an empty archive would have some kind of elegance. One can initialize an empty archive and later use '`--append`' ('`-r`') for adding all members. Some applications would not welcome making an exception in the way of adding the first archive member. On the other hand, many people reported that it is dangerously too easy for `tar` to destroy a magnetic tape with an empty archive[1]. The two most common errors are:

1. Mistakingly using `create` instead of `extract`, when the intent was to extract the full contents of an archive. This error is likely: keys `c` and `x` are right next to each other on the QWERTY keyboard. Instead of being unpacked, the archive then gets wholly destroyed. When users speak about *exploding* an archive, they usually mean something else :-).

2. Forgetting the argument to `file`, when the intent was to create an archive with a single file in it. This error is likely because a tired user can easily add the `f` key to the cluster of option letters, by the mere force of habit, without realizing the full consequence of doing so. The usual consequence is that the single file, which was meant to be saved, is rather destroyed.

So, recognizing the likelihood and the catastrophic nature of these errors, GNU `tar` now takes some distance from elegance, and cowardly refuses to create an archive when '`--create`' option is given, there are no arguments besides options, and '`--files-from`' ('`-T`') option is *not* used. To get around the cautiousness of GNU `tar` and nevertheless create an archive with nothing in it, one may still use, as the value for the '`--files-from`' option, a file with no names in it, as shown in the following commands:

---

[1] This is well described in *Unix-haters Handbook*, by Simson Garfinkel, Daniel Weise & Steven Strassmann, IDG Books, ISBN 1-56884-203-1.

```
tar --create --file=empty-archive.tar --files-from=/dev/null
tar -cf empty-archive.tar -T /dev/null
```

'`--extract`'
'`--get`'
'`-x`'

>A socket is stored, within a GNU `tar` archive, as a pipe.

''`--list`' ('`-t`')'

>GNU `tar` now shows dates as '`1996-08-30`', while it used to show them as '`Aug 30 1996`'. Preferably, people should get used to ISO 8601 dates. Local American dates should be made available again with full date localization support, once ready. In the meantime, programs not being localizable for dates should prefer international dates, that's really the way to go.

>Look up `http://www.cl.cam.ac.uk/~mgk25/iso-time.html` if you are curious, it contains a detailed explanation of the ISO 8601 standard.

4.2 Advanced GNU `tar` Operations

Now that you have learned the basics of using GNU `tar`, you may want to learn about further ways in which `tar` can help you.

This chapter presents five, more advanced operations which you probably won't use on a daily basis, but which serve more specialized functions. We also explain the different styles of options and why you might want to use one or another, or a combination of them in your `tar` commands. Additionally, this chapter includes options which allow you to define the output from `tar` more carefully, and provide help and error correction in special circumstances.

4.2.1 The Five Advanced `tar` Operations

In the last chapter, you learned about the first three operations to `tar`. This chapter presents the remaining five operations to `tar`: '`--append`', '`--update`', '`--concatenate`', '`--delete`', and '`--compare`'.

You are not likely to use these operations as frequently as those covered in the last chapter; however, since they perform specialized functions, they are quite useful when you do need to use them. We will give examples using the same directory and files that you created in the last chapter. As you may recall, the directory is called '`practice`', the files are '`jazz`', '`blues`', '`folk`', and the two archive files you created are '`collection.tar`' and '`music.tar`'.

We will also use the archive files '`afiles.tar`' and '`bfiles.tar`'. The archive '`afiles.tar`' contains the members '`apple`', '`angst`', and '`aspic`'; '`bfiles.tar`' contains the members '`./birds`', '`baboon`', and '`./box`'.

Unless we state otherwise, all practicing you do and examples you follow in this chapter will take place in the '`practice`' directory that you created in the previous chapter; see Section 2.6.1 [prepare for examples], page 11. (Below in this section, we will remind you of the state of the examples where the last chapter left them.)

The five operations that we will cover in this chapter are:

'`--append`'
'`-r`'   Add new entries to an archive that already exists.

'`--update`'
'`-u`'   Add more recent copies of archive members to the end of an archive, if they exist.

'`--concatenate`'
'`--catenate`'
'`-A`'   Add one or more pre-existing archives to the end of another archive.

'`--delete`'
              Delete items from an archive (does not work on tapes).

'`--compare`'
'`--diff`'
'`-d`'   Compare archive members to their counterparts in the file system.

4.2.2 How to Add Files to Existing Archives: '`--append`'

If you want to add files to an existing archive, you don't need to create a new archive; you can use '`--append`' ('`-r`'). The archive must already exist in order to use '`--append`'. (A related operation is the '`--update`' operation; you can use this to add newer versions of archive members to an existing archive. To learn how to do this with '`--update`', see Section 4.2.3 [update], page 66.)

If you use '`--append`' to add a file that has the same name as an archive member to an archive containing that archive member, then the old member is not deleted. What does happen, however, is somewhat complex. `tar` *allows* you to have infinite number of files with the same name. Some operations treat these same-named members no differently than any other set of archive members: for example, if you view an archive with '`--list`' ('`-t`'), you will see all of those members listed, with their data modification times, owners, etc.

Other operations don't deal with these members as perfectly as you might prefer; if you were to use '`--extract`' to extract the archive, only the most recently added copy of a member with the same name as other members would end up in the working directory. This is because '`--extract`' extracts an archive in the order the members appeared in the archive; the most recently archived members will be extracted last. Additionally, an extracted member will *replace* a file of the same name which existed in the directory already, and `tar` will not prompt you about this[2]. Thus, only the most recently archived member will end up being extracted, as it will replace the one extracted before it, and so on.

There exists a special option that allows you to get around this behavior and extract (or list) only a particular copy of the file. This is '`--occurrence`' option. If you run `tar` with this option, it will extract only the first copy of the file. You may also give this option an argument specifying the number of copy to be extracted. Thus, for example if the archive '`archive.tar`' contained three copies of file '`myfile`', then the command

```
tar --extract --file archive.tar --occurrence=2 myfile
```

would extract only the second copy. See Section 3.4.2 [Option Summary], page 29, for the description of '`--occurrence`' option.

If you want to replace an archive member, use '`--delete`' to delete the member you want to remove from the archive, and then use '`--append`' to add the member you want to be in the archive. Note that you can not change the order of the archive; the most recently added member will still appear last. In this sense, you cannot truly "replace" one member with another. (Replacing one member with another will not work on certain types of media, such as tapes; see Section 4.2.5 [delete], page 68 and Chapter 9 [Media], page 155, for more information.)

4.2.2.1 Appending Files to an Archive

The simplest way to add a file to an already existing archive is the '`--append`' ('`-r`') operation, which writes specified files into the archive whether or not they are already among the archived files.

When you use '`--append`', you *must* specify file name arguments, as there is no default. If you specify a file that already exists in the archive, another copy of the file will be added to the end of the archive. As with other operations, the member names of the newly added files will be exactly the same as their names given on the command line. The '`--verbose`' ('`-v`') option will print out the names of the files as they are written into the archive.

'`--append`' cannot be performed on some tape drives, unfortunately, due to deficiencies in the formats those tape drives use. The archive must be a valid `tar` archive, or else the results of using this operation will be unpredictable. See Chapter 9 [Media], page 155.

To demonstrate using '`--append`' to add a file to an archive, create a file called '`rock`' in the '`practice`' directory. Make sure you are in the '`practice`' directory. Then, run the following `tar` command to add '`rock`' to '`collection.tar`':

```
$ tar --append --file=collection.tar rock
```

---

[2] Unless you give it '`--keep-old-files`' (or '`--skip-old-files`') option, or the disk copy is newer than the one in the archive and you invoke `tar` with '`--keep-newer-files`' option.

If you now use the '--list' ('-t') operation, you will see that 'rock' has been added to the archive:

```
$ tar --list --file=collection.tar
-rw-r--r-- me/user          28 1996-10-18 16:31 jazz
-rw-r--r-- me/user          21 1996-09-23 16:44 blues
-rw-r--r-- me/user          20 1996-09-23 16:44 folk
-rw-r--r-- me/user          20 1996-09-23 16:44 rock
```

4.2.2.2 Multiple Members with the Same Name

You can use '--append' ('-r') to add copies of files which have been updated since the archive was created. (However, we do not recommend doing this since there is another `tar` option called '--update'; See Section 4.2.3 [update], page 66, for more information. We describe this use of '--append' here for the sake of completeness.) When you extract the archive, the older version will be effectively lost. This works because files are extracted from an archive in the order in which they were archived. Thus, when the archive is extracted, a file archived later in time will replace a file of the same name which was archived earlier, even though the older version of the file will remain in the archive unless you delete all versions of the file.

Supposing you change the file 'blues' and then append the changed version to 'collection.tar'. As you saw above, the original 'blues' is in the archive 'collection.tar'. If you change the file and append the new version of the file to the archive, there will be two copies in the archive. When you extract the archive, the older version of the file will be extracted first, and then replaced by the newer version when it is extracted.

You can append the new, changed copy of the file 'blues' to the archive in this way:

```
$ tar --append --verbose --file=collection.tar blues
blues
```

Because you specified the '--verbose' option, `tar` has printed the name of the file being appended as it was acted on. Now list the contents of the archive:

```
$ tar --list --verbose --file=collection.tar
-rw-r--r-- me/user          28 1996-10-18 16:31 jazz
-rw-r--r-- me/user          21 1996-09-23 16:44 blues
-rw-r--r-- me/user          20 1996-09-23 16:44 folk
-rw-r--r-- me/user          20 1996-09-23 16:44 rock
-rw-r--r-- me/user          58 1996-10-24 18:30 blues
```

The newest version of 'blues' is now at the end of the archive (note the different creation dates and file sizes). If you extract the archive, the older version of the file 'blues' will be replaced by the newer version. You can confirm this by extracting the archive and running 'ls' on the directory.

If you wish to extract the first occurrence of the file 'blues' from the archive, use '--occurrence' option, as shown in the following example:

```
$ tar --extract -vv --occurrence --file=collection.tar blues
-rw-r--r-- me/user          21 1996-09-23 16:44 blues
```

See Section 4.4.2 [Writing], page 72, for more information on '--extract' and see Section 3.4.2 [Option Summary], page 29, for a description of '--occurrence' option.

4.2.3 Updating an Archive

In the previous section, you learned how to use '--append' to add a file to an existing archive. A related operation is '--update' ('-u'). The '--update' operation updates a `tar` archive by comparing the date of the specified archive members against the date of the file with the same name. If the file has been modified more recently than the archive member, then the newer version of the file is added to the archive (as with '--append').

Unfortunately, you cannot use '--update' with magnetic tape drives. The operation will fail.

Both '--update' and '--append' work by adding to the end of the archive. When you extract a file from the archive, only the version stored last will wind up in the file system, unless you use the '--backup' option. See Section 4.2.2.2 [multiple], page 65, for a detailed discussion.

4.2.3.1 How to Update an Archive Using '--update'

You must use file name arguments with the '--update' ('-u') operation. If you don't specify any files, `tar` won't act on any files and won't tell you that it didn't do anything (which may end up confusing you).

To see the '--update' option at work, create a new file, '`classical`', in your practice directory, and some extra text to the file '`blues`', using any text editor. Then invoke `tar` with the '`update`' operation and the '--verbose' ('-v') option specified, using the names of all the files in the '`practice`' directory as file name arguments:

```
$ tar --update -v -f collection.tar blues folk rock classical
blues
classical
$
```

Because we have specified verbose mode, `tar` prints out the names of the files it is working on, which in this case are the names of the files that needed to be updated. If you run '`tar --list`' and look at the archive, you will see '`blues`' and '`classical`' at its end. There will be a total of two versions of the member '`blues`'; the one at the end will be newer and larger, since you added text before updating it.

The reason `tar` does not overwrite the older file when updating it is because writing to the middle of a section of tape is a difficult process. Tapes are not designed to go backward. See Chapter 9 [Media], page 155, for more information about tapes.

'--update' ('-u') is not suitable for performing backups for two reasons: it does not change directory content entries, and it lengthens the archive every time it is used. The GNU `tar` options intended specifically for backups are more efficient. If you need to run backups, please consult Chapter 5 [Backups], page 83.

4.2.4 Combining Archives with '--concatenate'

Sometimes it may be convenient to add a second archive onto the end of an archive rather than adding individual files to the archive. To add one or more archives to the end of another archive, you should use the '--concatenate' ('--catenate', '-A') operation.

To use '--concatenate', give the first archive with '--file' option and name the rest of archives to be concatenated on the command line. The members, and their member names, will be copied verbatim from those archives to the first one[3]. The new, concatenated archive will be called by the same name as the one given with the '--file' option. As usual, if you omit '--file', `tar` will use the value of the environment variable TAPE, or, if this has not been set, the default archive name.

To demonstrate how '--concatenate' works, create two small archives called 'bluesrock.tar' and 'folkjazz.tar', using the relevant files from 'practice':

```
$ tar -cvf bluesrock.tar blues rock
blues
rock
$ tar -cvf folkjazz.tar folk jazz
folk
jazz
```

If you like, You can run 'tar --list' to make sure the archives contain what they are supposed to:

```
$ tar -tvf bluesrock.tar
-rw-r--r-- melissa/user     105 1997-01-21 19:42 blues
-rw-r--r-- melissa/user      33 1997-01-20 15:34 rock
$ tar -tvf jazzfolk.tar
-rw-r--r-- melissa/user      20 1996-09-23 16:44 folk
-rw-r--r-- melissa/user      65 1997-01-30 14:15 jazz
```

We can concatenate these two archives with `tar`:

```
$ cd ..
$ tar --concatenate --file=bluesrock.tar jazzfolk.tar
```

If you now list the contents of the 'bluesrock.tar', you will see that now it also contains the archive members of 'jazzfolk.tar':

```
$ tar --list --file=bluesrock.tar
blues
rock
folk
jazz
```

When you use '--concatenate', the source and target archives must already exist and must have been created using compatible format parameters.

---

[3] This can cause multiple members to have the same name. For information on how this affects reading the archive, see Section 4.2.2.2 [multiple], page 65.

Notice, that `tar` does not check whether the archives it concatenates have compatible formats, it does not even check if the files are really tar archives.

Like '`--append`' ('`-r`'), this operation cannot be performed on some tape drives, due to deficiencies in the formats those tape drives use.

It may seem more intuitive to you to want or try to use `cat` to concatenate two archives instead of using the '`--concatenate`' operation; after all, `cat` is the utility for combining files.

However, `tar` archives incorporate an end-of-file marker which must be removed if the concatenated archives are to be read properly as one archive. '`--concatenate`' removes the end-of-archive marker from the target archive before each new archive is appended. If you use `cat` to combine the archives, the result will not be a valid `tar` format archive. If you need to retrieve files from an archive that was added to using the `cat` utility, use the '`--ignore-zeros`' ('`-i`') option. See [Ignore Zeros], page 72, for further information on dealing with archives improperly combined using the `cat` shell utility.

4.2.5 Removing Archive Members Using '`--delete`'

You can remove members from an archive by using the '`--delete`' option. Specify the name of the archive with '`--file`' ('`-f`') and then specify the names of the members to be deleted; if you list no member names, nothing will be deleted. The '`--verbose`' option will cause `tar` to print the names of the members as they are deleted. As with '`--extract`', you must give the exact member names when using '`tar --delete`'. '`--delete`' will remove all versions of the named file from the archive. The '`--delete`' operation can run very slowly.

Unlike other operations, '`--delete`' has no short form.

This operation will rewrite the archive. You can only use '`--delete`' on an archive if the archive device allows you to write to any point on the media, such as a disk; because of this, it does not work on magnetic tapes. Do not try to delete an archive member from a magnetic tape; the action will not succeed, and you will be likely to scramble the archive and damage your tape. There is no safe way (except by completely re-writing the archive) to delete files from most kinds of magnetic tape. See Chapter 9 [Media], page 155.

To delete all versions of the file '`blues`' from the archive '`collection.tar`' in the '`practice`' directory, make sure you are in that directory, and then,

```
$ tar --list --file=collection.tar
blues
folk
jazz
rock
$ tar --delete --file=collection.tar blues
$ tar --list --file=collection.tar
```

```
folk
jazz
rock
```

The '`--delete`' option has been reported to work properly when `tar` acts as a filter from `stdin` to `stdout`.

4.2.6 Comparing Archive Members with the File System

The '`--compare`' ('`-d`'), or '`--diff`' operation compares specified archive members against files with the same names, and then reports differences in file size, mode, owner, modification date and contents. You should *only* specify archive member names, not file names. If you do not name any members, then `tar` will compare the entire archive. If a file is represented in the archive but does not exist in the file system, `tar` reports a difference.

You have to specify the record size of the archive when modifying an archive with a non-default record size.

`tar` ignores files in the file system that do not have corresponding members in the archive.

The following example compares the archive members '`rock`', '`blues`' and '`funk`' in the archive '`bluesrock.tar`' with files of the same name in the file system. (Note that there is no file, '`funk`'; `tar` will report an error message.)

```
$ tar --compare --file=bluesrock.tar rock blues funk
rock
blues
tar: funk not found in archive
```

The spirit behind the '`--compare`' ('`--diff`', '`-d`') option is to check whether the archive represents the current state of files on disk, more than validating the integrity of the archive media. For this latter goal, see Section 9.8 [verify], page 176.

4.3 Options Used by '`--create`'

The previous chapter described the basics of how to use '`--create`' ('`-c`') to create an archive from a set of files. See Section 2.6 [create], page 10. This section described advanced options to be used with '`--create`'.

4.3.1 Overriding File Metadata

As described above, a `tar` archive keeps, for each member it contains, its *metadata*, such as modification time, mode and ownership of the file. GNU `tar` allows to replace these data with other values when adding files to the archive. The options described in this section affect creation of archives of any type. For POSIX archives, see also Section 8.3.7.1 [PAX keywords], page 143, for additional ways of controlling metadata, stored in the archive.

'--mode=*permissions*'
> When adding files to an archive, **tar** will use *permissions* for
> the archive members, rather than the permissions from the files.
> *permissions* can be specified either as an octal number or as
> symbolic permissions, like with **chmod** (See section "File permis-
> sions" in *GNU file utilities*. This reference also has useful infor-
> mation for those not being overly familiar with the UNIX per-
> mission system). Using latter syntax allows for more flexibility.
> For example, the value '**a+rw**' adds read and write permissions
> for everybody, while retaining executable bits on directories or
> on any other file already marked as executable:
>
> ```
> $ tar -c -f archive.tar --mode='a+rw' .
> ```

'--mtime=*date*'
> When adding files to an archive, **tar** will use *date* as the modifi-
> cation time of members when creating archives, instead of their
> actual modification times. The argument *date* can be either
> a textual date representation in almost arbitrary format (see
> Chapter 7 [Date input formats], page 123) or a name of an ex-
> isting file, starting with '/' or '.'. In the latter case, the modi-
> fication time of that file will be used.
>
> The following example will set the modification date to 00:00:00,
> January 1, 1970:
>
> ```
> $ tar -c -f archive.tar --mtime='1970-01-01' .
> ```
>
> When used with '**--verbose**' (see [verbose tutorial], page 8)
> GNU **tar** will try to convert the specified date back to its textual
> representation and compare it with the one given with '**--mtime**'
> options. If the two dates differ, **tar** will print a warning saying
> what date it will use. This is to help user ensure he is using the
> right date.
>
> For example:
>
> ```
> $ tar -c -f archive.tar -v --mtime=yesterday .
> tar: Option --mtime: Treating date 'yesterday' as 2006-06-20
> 13:06:29.152478
> ...
> ```

'--owner=*user*'
> Specifies that **tar** should use *user* as the owner of members when
> creating archives, instead of the user associated with the source
> file.
>
> If *user* contains a colon, it is taken to be of the form *name*:*id*
> where a nonempty *name* specifies the user name and a nonempty
> *id* specifies the decimal numeric user ID. If *user* does not contain
> a colon, it is taken to be a user number if it is one or more decimal
> digits; otherwise it is taken to be a user name.

If a name is given but no number, the number is inferred from the current host's user database if possible, and the file's user number is used otherwise. If a number is given but no name, the name is inferred from the number if possible, and an empty name is used otherwise. If both name and number are given, the user database is not consulted, and the name and number need not be valid on the current host.

There is no value indicating a missing number, and '0' usually means `root`. Some people like to force '0' as the value to offer in their distributions for the owner of files, because the `root` user is anonymous anyway, so that might as well be the owner of anonymous archives. For example:

```
$ tar -c -f archive.tar --owner=0 .
```

or:

```
$ tar -c -f archive.tar --owner=root .
```

'--group=*group*'

Files added to the `tar` archive will have a group ID of *group*, rather than the group from the source file. As with '--owner', the argument *group* can be an existing group symbolic name, or a decimal numeric group ID, or *name:id*.

4.3.2 Ignore Fail Read

'--ignore-failed-read'

Do not exit with nonzero on unreadable files or directories.

4.4 Options Used by '--extract'

The previous chapter showed how to use '--extract' to extract an archive into the file system. Various options cause `tar` to extract more information than just file contents, such as the owner, the permissions, the modification date, and so forth. This section presents options to be used with '--extract' when certain special considerations arise. You may review the information presented in Section 2.8 [extract], page 17 for more basic information about the '--extract' operation.

4.4.1 Options to Help Read Archives

Normally, `tar` will request data in full record increments from an archive storage device. If the device cannot return a full record, `tar` will report an error. However, some devices do not always return full records, or do not require the last record of an archive to be padded out to the next record boundary. To keep reading until you obtain a full record, or to accept an incomplete record if it contains an end-of-archive marker, specify the '--read-full-records' ('-B') option in conjunction with the '--extract' or '--list' operations. See Section 9.4 [Blocking], page 159.

The '--read-full-records' ('-B') option is turned on by default when tar reads an archive from standard input, or from a remote machine. This is because on BSD Unix systems, attempting to read a pipe returns however much happens to be in the pipe, even if it is less than was requested. If this option were not enabled, tar would fail as soon as it read an incomplete record from the pipe.

If you're not sure of the blocking factor of an archive, you can read the archive by specifying '--read-full-records' ('-B') and '--blocking-factor=512-size' ('-b 512-size'), using a blocking factor larger than what the archive uses. This lets you avoid having to determine the blocking factor of an archive. See Section 9.4.2 [Blocking Factor], page 161.

Reading Full Records

'--read-full-records'

'-B'   Use in conjunction with '--extract' ('--get', '-x') to read an archive which contains incomplete records, or one which has a blocking factor less than the one specified.

Ignoring Blocks of Zeros

Normally, tar stops reading when it encounters a block of zeros between file entries (which usually indicates the end of the archive). '--ignore-zeros' ('-i') allows tar to completely read an archive which contains a block of zeros before the end (i.e., a damaged archive, or one that was created by concatenating several archives together).

The '--ignore-zeros' ('-i') option is turned off by default because many versions of tar write garbage after the end-of-archive entry, since that part of the media is never supposed to be read. GNU tar does not write after the end of an archive, but seeks to maintain compatibility among archiving utilities.

'--ignore-zeros'

'-i'   To ignore blocks of zeros (i.e., end-of-archive entries) which may be encountered while reading an archive. Use in conjunction with '--extract' or '--list'.

4.4.2 Changing How tar Writes Files

(This message will disappear, once this node revised.)

Options Controlling the Overwriting of Existing Files

When extracting files, if tar discovers that the extracted file already exists, it normally replaces the file by removing it before extracting it, to prevent confusion in the presence of hard or symbolic links. (If the existing file is a symbolic link, it is removed, not followed.) However, if a directory cannot be removed because it is nonempty, `tar` normally overwrites its metadata (ownership, permission, etc.). The '`--overwrite-dir`' option enables this default behavior. To be more cautious and preserve the metadata of such a directory, use the '`--no-overwrite-dir`' option.

To be even more cautious and prevent existing files from being replaced, use the '`--keep-old-files`' ('`-k`') option. It causes `tar` to refuse to replace or update a file that already exists, i.e., a file with the same name as an archive member prevents extraction of that archive member. Instead, it reports an error. For example:

```
$ ls
blues
$ tar -x -k -f archive.tar
tar: blues: Cannot open: File exists
tar: Exiting with failure status due to previous errors
```

If you wish to preserve old files untouched, but don't want `tar` to treat them as errors, use the '`--skip-old-files`' option. This option causes `tar` to silently skip extracting over existing files.

To be more aggressive about altering existing files, use the '`--overwrite`' option. It causes `tar` to overwrite existing files and to follow existing symbolic links when extracting.

Some people argue that GNU `tar` should not hesitate to overwrite files with other files when extracting. When extracting a `tar` archive, they expect to see a faithful copy of the state of the file system when the archive was created. It is debatable that this would always be a proper behavior. For example, suppose one has an archive in which '`usr/local`' is a link to '`usr/local2`'. Since then, maybe the site removed the link and renamed the whole hierarchy from '`/usr/local2`' to '`/usr/local`'. Such things happen all the time. I guess it would not be welcome at all that GNU `tar` removes the whole hierarchy just to make room for the link to be reinstated (unless it *also* simultaneously restores the full '`/usr/local2`', of course!) GNU `tar` is indeed able to remove a whole hierarchy to reestablish a symbolic link, for example, but *only if* '`--recursive-unlink`' is specified to allow this behavior. In any case, single files are silently removed.

Finally, the '`--unlink-first`' ('`-U`') option can improve performance in some cases by causing `tar` to remove files unconditionally before extracting them.

Overwrite Old Files

'`--overwrite`'

> Overwrite existing files and directory metadata when extracting files from an archive.
>
> This causes `tar` to write extracted files into the file system without regard to the files already on the system; i.e., files with the same names as archive members are overwritten when the

archive is extracted. It also causes `tar` to extract the ownership, permissions, and time stamps onto any preexisting files or directories. If the name of a corresponding file name is a symbolic link, the file pointed to by the symbolic link will be overwritten instead of the symbolic link itself (if this is possible). Moreover, special devices, empty directories and even symbolic links are automatically removed if they are in the way of extraction.

Be careful when using the '`--overwrite`' option, particularly when combined with the '`--absolute-names`' ('`-P`') option, as this combination can change the contents, ownership or permissions of any file on your system. Also, many systems do not take kindly to overwriting files that are currently being executed.

'`--overwrite-dir`'
> Overwrite the metadata of directories when extracting files from an archive, but remove other files before extracting.

Keep Old Files

GNU `tar` provides two options to control its actions in a situation when it is about to extract a file which already exists on disk.

'`--keep-old-files`'
'`-k`'
> Do not replace existing files from archive. When such a file is encountered, `tar` issues an error message. Upon end of extraction, `tar` exits with code 2 (see [exit status], page 22).

'`--skip-old-files`'
> Do not replace existing files from archive, but do not treat that as error. Such files are silently skipped and do not affect `tar` exit status.
>
> Additional verbosity can be obtained using '`--warning=existing-file`' together with that option (see Section 3.9 [warnings], page 56).

Keep Newer Files

'`--keep-newer-files`'
> Do not replace existing files that are newer than their archive copies. This option is meaningless with '`--list`' ('`-t`').

Unlink First

'`--unlink-first`'
'`-U`'
> Remove files before extracting over them. This can make `tar` run a bit faster if you know in advance that the extracted files all need to be removed. Normally this option slows `tar` down slightly, so it is disabled by default.

Recursive Unlink

'`--recursive-unlink`'

>When this option is specified, try removing files and directory hierarchies before extracting over them. *This is a dangerous option!*

If you specify the '`--recursive-unlink`' option, `tar` removes *anything* that keeps you from extracting a file as far as current permissions will allow it. This could include removal of the contents of a full directory hierarchy.

Setting Data Modification Times

Normally, `tar` sets the data modification times of extracted files to the corresponding times recorded for the files in the archive, but limits the permissions of extracted files by the current `umask` setting.

To set the data modification times of extracted files to the time when the files were extracted, use the '`--touch`' ('`-m`') option in conjunction with '`--extract`' ('`--get`', '`-x`').

'`--touch`'
'`-m`'   Sets the data modification time of extracted archive members to the time they were extracted, not the time recorded for them in the archive. Use in conjunction with '`--extract`' ('`--get`', '`-x`').

Setting Access Permissions

To set the modes (access permissions) of extracted files to those recorded for those files in the archive, use '`--same-permissions`' in conjunction with the '`--extract`' ('`--get`', '`-x`') operation.

'`--preserve-permissions`'
'`--same-permissions`'
'`-p`'   Set modes of extracted archive members to those recorded in the archive, instead of current umask settings. Use in conjunction with '`--extract`' ('`--get`', '`-x`').

Directory Modification Times and Permissions

After successfully extracting a file member, GNU `tar` normally restores its permissions and modification times, as described in the previous sections. This cannot be done for directories, because after extracting a directory `tar` will almost certainly extract files into that directory and this will cause the directory modification time to be updated. Moreover, restoring that directory permissions may not permit file creation within it. Thus, restoring directory permissions and modification times must be delayed at least until all files have been extracted into that directory. GNU `tar` restores directories using the following approach.

The extracted directories are created with the mode specified in the archive, as modified by the umask of the user, which gives sufficient permissions to allow file creation. The meta-information about the directory is recorded in the temporary list of directories. When preparing to extract next archive member, GNU tar checks if the directory prefix of this file contains the remembered directory. If it does not, the program assumes that all files have been extracted into that directory, restores its modification time and permissions and removes its entry from the internal list. This approach allows to correctly restore directory meta-information in the majority of cases, while keeping memory requirements sufficiently small. It is based on the fact, that most tar archives use the predefined order of members: first the directory, then all the files and subdirectories in that directory.

However, this is not always true. The most important exception are incremental archives (see Section 5.2 [Incremental Dumps], page 84). The member order in an incremental archive is reversed: first all directory members are stored, followed by other (non-directory) members. So, when extracting from incremental archives, GNU tar alters the above procedure. It remembers all restored directories, and restores their meta-data only after the entire archive has been processed. Notice, that you do not need to specify any special options for that, as GNU tar automatically detects archives in incremental format.

There may be cases, when such processing is required for normal archives too. Consider the following example:

```
$ tar --no-recursion -cvf archive \
    foo foo/file1 bar bar/file foo/file2
foo/
foo/file1
bar/
bar/file
foo/file2
```

During the normal operation, after encountering 'bar' GNU tar will assume that all files from the directory 'foo' were already extracted and will therefore restore its timestamp and permission bits. However, after extracting 'foo/file2' the directory timestamp will be offset again.

To correctly restore directory meta-information in such cases, use the '--delay-directory-restore' command line option:

'--delay-directory-restore'

Delays restoring of the modification times and permissions of extracted directories until the end of extraction. This way, correct meta-information is restored even if the archive has unusual member ordering.

'--no-delay-directory-restore'

Cancel the effect of the previous '--delay-directory-restore'. Use this option if you have used '--delay-directory-restore' in `TAR_OPTIONS` variable (see [TAR_OPTIONS], page 23) and wish to temporarily disable it.

Writing to Standard Output

To write the extracted files to the standard output, instead of creating the files on the file system, use '`--to-stdout`' ('`-O`') in conjunction with '`--extract`' ('`--get`', '`-x`'). This option is useful if you are extracting files to send them through a pipe, and do not need to preserve them in the file system. If you extract multiple members, they appear on standard output concatenated, in the order they are found in the archive.

'`--to-stdout`'
'`-O`'   Writes files to the standard output. Use only in conjunction with '`--extract`' ('`--get`', '`-x`'). When this option is used, instead of creating the files specified, `tar` writes the contents of the files extracted to its standard output. This may be useful if you are only extracting the files in order to send them through a pipe. This option is meaningless with '`--list`' ('`-t`').

This can be useful, for example, if you have a tar archive containing a big file and don't want to store the file on disk before processing it. You can use a command like this:

```
tar -xOzf foo.tgz bigfile | process
```

or even like this if you want to process the concatenation of the files:

```
tar -xOzf foo.tgz bigfile1 bigfile2 | process
```

However, '`--to-command`' may be more convenient for use with multiple files. See the next section.

Writing to an External Program

You can instruct `tar` to send the contents of each extracted file to the standard input of an external program:

'`--to-command=command`'
                Extract files and pipe their contents to the standard input of *command*. When this option is used, instead of creating the files specified, `tar` invokes *command* and pipes the contents of the files to its standard output. The *command* may contain command line arguments (see Section 3.11 [external], page 59, for more detail).

                Notice, that *command* is executed once for each regular file extracted. Non-regular files (directories, etc.) are ignored when this option is used.

The command can obtain the information about the file it processes from the following environment variables:

`TAR_FILETYPE`
                Type of the file. It is a single letter with the following meaning:

f	Regular file
d	Directory
l	Symbolic link
h	Hard link
b	Block device
c	Character device

Currently only regular files are supported.

TAR_MODE   File mode, an octal number.

TAR_FILENAME
        The name of the file.

TAR_REALNAME
        Name of the file as stored in the archive.

TAR_UNAME
        Name of the file owner.

TAR_GNAME
        Name of the file owner group.

TAR_ATIME
        Time of last access. It is a decimal number, representing seconds since the Epoch. If the archive provides times with nanosecond precision, the nanoseconds are appended to the timestamp after a decimal point.

TAR_MTIME
        Time of last modification.

TAR_CTIME
        Time of last status change.

TAR_SIZE   Size of the file.

TAR_UID   UID of the file owner.

TAR_GID   GID of the file owner.

Additionally, the following variables contain information about tar mode and the archive being processed:

TAR_VERSION
        GNU tar version number.

TAR_ARCHIVE
        The name of the archive tar is processing.

TAR_BLOCKING_FACTOR
        Current blocking factor (see Section 9.4 [Blocking], page 159).

TAR_VOLUME
        Ordinal number of the volume tar is processing.

```
TAR_FORMAT
```
> Format of the archive being processed. See Chapter 8 [Formats], page 131, for a complete list of archive format names.

These variables are defined prior to executing the command, so you can pass them as arguments, if you prefer. For example, if the command *proc* takes the member name and size as its arguments, then you could do:

```
$ tar -x -f archive.tar \
        --to-command='proc $TAR_FILENAME $TAR_SIZE'
```

Notice single quotes to prevent variable names from being expanded by the shell when invoking `tar`.

If *command* exits with a non-0 status, `tar` will print an error message similar to the following:

```
tar: 2345: Child returned status 1
```

Here, '2345' is the PID of the finished process.

If this behavior is not wanted, use '`--ignore-command-error`':

'`--ignore-command-error`'
> Ignore exit codes of subprocesses. Notice that if the program exits on signal or otherwise terminates abnormally, the error message will be printed even if this option is used.

'`--no-ignore-command-error`'
> Cancel the effect of any previous '`--ignore-command-error`' option. This option is useful if you have set '`--ignore-command-error`' in `TAR_OPTIONS` (see [TAR_OPTIONS], page 23) and wish to temporarily cancel it.

Removing Files

'`--remove-files`'
> Remove files after adding them to the archive.

4.4.3 Coping with Scarce Resources

(This message will disappear, once this node revised.)

Starting File

'`--starting-file=name`'
'`-K name`'   Starts an operation in the middle of an archive. Use in conjunction with '`--extract`' ('`--get`', '`-x`') or '`--list`' ('`-t`').

If a previous attempt to extract files failed due to lack of disk space, you can use '`--starting-file=name`' ('`-K name`') to start extracting only after member *name* of the archive. This assumes, of course, that there is now free space, or that you are now extracting into a different file system. (You could also choose to suspend `tar`, remove unnecessary files from the file system, and then resume the same `tar` operation. In this case, '`--starting-file`' is not necessary.) See also Section 3.10 [interactive], page 59, and Section 6.4 [exclude], page 101.

Same Order

'`--same-order`'
'`--preserve-order`'
'`-s`'   To process large lists of file names on machines with small amounts of memory. Use in conjunction with '`--compare`' ('`--diff`', '`-d`'), '`--list`' ('`-t`') or '`--extract`' ('`--get`', '`-x`').

The '`--same-order`' ('`--preserve-order`', '`-s`') option tells `tar` that the list of file names to be listed or extracted is sorted in the same order as the files in the archive. This allows a large list of names to be used, even on a small machine that would not otherwise be able to hold all the names in memory at the same time. Such a sorted list can easily be created by running '`tar -t`' on the archive and editing its output.

This option is probably never needed on modern computer systems.

4.5 Backup options

GNU `tar` offers options for making backups of files before writing new versions. These options control the details of these backups. They may apply to the archive itself before it is created or rewritten, as well as individual extracted members. Other GNU programs (`cp`, `install`, `ln`, and `mv`, for example) offer similar options.

Backup options may prove unexpectedly useful when extracting archives containing many members having identical name, or when extracting archives on systems having file name limitations, making different members appear as having similar names through the side-effect of name truncation.

When any existing file is backed up before being overwritten by extraction, then clashing files are automatically be renamed to be unique, and the true name is kept for only the last file of a series of clashing files. By using verbose mode, users may track exactly what happens.

At the detail level, some decisions are still experimental, and may change in the future, we are waiting comments from our users. So, please do not learn to depend blindly on the details of the backup features. For example, currently, directories themselves are never renamed through using these options, so, extracting a file over a directory still has good chances to fail. Also, backup options apply to created archives, not only to extracted members. For created archives, backups will not be attempted when the archive is a block or character device, or when it refers to a remote file.

For the sake of simplicity and efficiency, backups are made by renaming old files prior to creation or extraction, and not by copying. The original name is restored if the file creation fails. If a failure occurs after a partial extraction of a file, both the backup and the partially extracted file are kept.

'`--backup[=method]`'

> Back up files that are about to be overwritten or removed. Without this option, the original versions are destroyed.
>
> Use *method* to determine the type of backups made. If *method* is not specified, use the value of the `VERSION_CONTROL` environment variable. And if `VERSION_CONTROL` is not set, use the '`existing`' method.
>
> This option corresponds to the Emacs variable '`version-control`'; the same values for *method* are accepted as in Emacs. This option also allows more descriptive names. The valid *method*s are:
>
> '`t`'
> '`numbered`'
>> Always make numbered backups.
>
> '`nil`'
> '`existing`'
>> Make numbered backups of files that already have them, simple backups of the others.
>
> '`never`'
> '`simple`'   Always make simple backups.

'`--suffix=suffix`'

> Append *suffix* to each backup file made with '`--backup`'. If this option is not specified, the value of the `SIMPLE_BACKUP_SUFFIX` environment variable is used. And if `SIMPLE_BACKUP_SUFFIX` is not set, the default is '`~`', just as in Emacs.

4.6 Notable `tar` Usages

(This message will disappear, once this node revised.)

You can easily use archive files to transport a group of files from one system to another: put all relevant files into an archive on one computer system, transfer the archive to another system, and extract the contents there. The basic transfer medium might be magnetic tape, Internet FTP, or even electronic mail (though you must encode the archive with `uuencode` in order to transport it properly by mail). Both machines do not have to use the same operating system, as long as they both support the `tar` program.

For example, here is how you might copy a directory's contents from one disk to another, while preserving the dates, modes, owners and link-structure of all the files therein. In this case, the transfer medium is a *pipe*:

```
$ (cd sourcedir; tar -cf - .) | (cd targetdir; tar -xf -)
```

You can avoid subshells by using '`-C`' option:

```
$ tar -C sourcedir -cf - . | tar -C targetdir -xf -
```
The command also works using long option forms:
```
$ (cd sourcedir; tar --create --file=- . ) \
       | (cd targetdir; tar --extract --file=-)
```
or
```
$ tar --directory sourcedir --create --file=- . \
       | tar --directory targetdir --extract --file=-
```
This is one of the easiest methods to transfer a `tar` archive.

4.7 Looking Ahead: The Rest of this Manual

You have now seen how to use all eight of the operations available to `tar`, and a number of the possible options. The next chapter explains how to choose and change file and archive names, how to use files to store names of other files which you can then call as arguments to `tar` (this can help you save time if you expect to archive the same list of files a number of times), and so forth.

If there are too many files to conveniently list on the command line, you can list the names in a file, and `tar` will read that file. See Section 6.3 [files], page 99.

There are various ways of causing `tar` to skip over some files, and not archive them. See Chapter 6 [Choosing], page 97.

5 Performing Backups and Restoring Files

GNU `tar` is distributed along with the scripts for performing backups and restores. Even if there is a good chance those scripts may be satisfying to you, they are not the only scripts or methods available for doing backups and restore. You may well create your own, or use more sophisticated packages dedicated to that purpose.

Some users are enthusiastic about **Amanda** (The Advanced Maryland Automatic Network Disk Archiver), a backup system developed by James da Silva '`jds@cs.umd.edu`' and available on many Unix systems. This is free software, and it is available from http://www.amanda.org.

This chapter documents both the provided shell scripts and `tar` options which are more specific to usage as a backup tool.

To *back up* a file system means to create archives that contain all the files in that file system. Those archives can then be used to restore any or all of those files (for instance if a disk crashes or a file is accidentally deleted). File system *backups* are also called *dumps*.

5.1 Using `tar` to Perform Full Dumps

(This message will disappear, once this node revised.)

Full dumps should only be made when no other people or programs are modifying files in the file system. If files are modified while `tar` is making the backup, they may not be stored properly in the archive, in which case you won't be able to restore them if you have to. (Files not being modified are written with no trouble, and do not corrupt the entire archive.)

You will want to use the '`--label=archive-label`' ('`-V archive-label`') option to give the archive a volume label, so you can tell what this archive is even if the label falls off the tape, or anything like that.

Unless the file system you are dumping is guaranteed to fit on one volume, you will need to use the '`--multi-volume`' ('`-M`') option. Make sure you have enough tapes on hand to complete the backup.

If you want to dump each file system separately you will need to use the '`--one-file-system`' option to prevent `tar` from crossing file system boundaries when storing (sub)directories.

The '`--incremental`' ('`-G`') (see Section 5.2 [Incremental Dumps], page 84) option is not needed, since this is a complete copy of everything in the file system, and a full restore from this backup would only be done onto a completely empty disk.

Unless you are in a hurry, and trust the `tar` program (and your tapes), it is a good idea to use the '`--verify`' ('`-W`') option, to make sure your files really made it onto the dump properly. This will also detect cases where the file was modified while (or just after) it was being archived. Not all media (notably cartridge tapes) are capable of being verified, unfortunately.

5.2 Using `tar` to Perform Incremental Dumps

Incremental backup is a special form of GNU `tar` archive that stores additional metadata so that exact state of the file system can be restored when extracting the archive.

GNU `tar` currently offers two options for handling incremental backups: '`--listed-incremental=snapshot-file`' ('`-g snapshot-file`') and '`--incremental`' ('`-G`').

The option '`--listed-incremental`' instructs tar to operate on an incremental archive with additional metadata stored in a standalone file, called a *snapshot file*. The purpose of this file is to help determine which files have been changed, added or deleted since the last backup, so that the next incremental backup will contain only modified files. The name of the snapshot file is given as an argument to the option:

'`--listed-incremental=file`'
'`-g file`'   Handle incremental backups with snapshot data in *file*.

To create an incremental backup, you would use '`--listed-incremental`' together with '`--create`' (see Section 2.6 [create], page 10). For example:

```
$ tar --create \
          --file=archive.1.tar \
          --listed-incremental=/var/log/usr.snar \
          /usr
```

This will create in '`archive.1.tar`' an incremental backup of the '`/usr`' file system, storing additional metadata in the file '`/var/log/usr.snar`'. If this file does not exist, it will be created. The created archive will then be a *level 0 backup*; please see the next section for more on backup levels.

Otherwise, if the file '`/var/log/usr.snar`' exists, it determines which files are modified. In this case only these files will be stored in the archive. Suppose, for example, that after running the above command, you delete file '`/usr/doc/old`' and create directory '`/usr/local/db`' with the following contents:

```
$ ls /usr/local/db
/usr/local/db/data
/usr/local/db/index
```

Some time later you create another incremental backup. You will then see:

```
$ tar --create \
          --file=archive.2.tar \
          --listed-incremental=/var/log/usr.snar \
          /usr
tar: usr/local/db: Directory is new
```

```
usr/local/db/
usr/local/db/data
usr/local/db/index
```

The created archive 'archive.2.tar' will contain only these three members. This archive is called a *level 1 backup*. Notice that '/var/log/usr.snar' will be updated with the new data, so if you plan to create more 'level 1' backups, it is necessary to create a working copy of the snapshot file before running tar. The above example will then be modified as follows:

```
$ cp /var/log/usr.snar /var/log/usr.snar-1
$ tar --create \
        --file=archive.2.tar \
        --listed-incremental=/var/log/usr.snar-1 \
        /usr
```

You can force 'level 0' backups either by removing the snapshot file before running tar, or by supplying the '--level=0' option, e.g.:

```
$ tar --create \
        --file=archive.2.tar \
        --listed-incremental=/var/log/usr.snar-0 \
        --level=0 \
        /usr
```

Incremental dumps depend crucially on time stamps, so the results are unreliable if you modify a file's time stamps during dumping (e.g., with the '--atime-preserve=replace' option), or if you set the clock backwards.

Metadata stored in snapshot files include device numbers, which, obviously are supposed to be non-volatile values. However, it turns out that NFS devices have undependable values when an automounter gets in the picture. This can lead to a great deal of spurious redumping in incremental dumps, so it is somewhat useless to compare two NFS devices numbers over time. The solution implemented currently is to consider all NFS devices as being equal when it comes to comparing directories; this is fairly gross, but there does not seem to be a better way to go.

Apart from using NFS, there are a number of cases where relying on device numbers can cause spurious redumping of unmodified files. For example, this occurs when archiving LVM snapshot volumes. To avoid this, use '--no-check-device' option:

'--no-check-device'
> Do not rely on device numbers when preparing a list of changed files for an incremental dump.

'--check-device'
> Use device numbers when preparing a list of changed files for an incremental dump. This is the default behavior. The purpose of this option is to undo the effect of the '--no-check-device' if it was given in TAR_OPTIONS environment variable (see [TAR_OPTIONS], page 23).

There is also another way to cope with changing device numbers. It is described in detail in Appendix C [Fixing Snapshot Files], page 191.

Note that incremental archives use **tar** extensions and may not be readable by non-GNU versions of the **tar** program.

To extract from the incremental dumps, use '--listed-incremental' together with '--extract' option (see Section 2.8.2 [extracting files], page 17). In this case, **tar** does not need to access snapshot file, since all the data necessary for extraction are stored in the archive itself. So, when extracting, you can give whatever argument to '--listed-incremental', the usual practice is to use '--listed-incremental=/dev/null'. Alternatively, you can use '--incremental', which needs no arguments. In general, '--incremental' ('-G') can be used as a shortcut for '--listed-incremental' when listing or extracting incremental backups (for more information regarding this option, see [incremental-op], page 87).

When extracting from the incremental backup GNU **tar** attempts to restore the exact state the file system had when the archive was created. In particular, it will *delete* those files in the file system that did not exist in their directories when the archive was created. If you have created several levels of incremental files, then in order to restore the exact contents the file system had when the last level was created, you will need to restore from all backups in turn. Continuing our example, to restore the state of '/usr' file system, one would do[1]:

```
$ tar --extract \
          --listed-incremental=/dev/null \
          --file archive.1.tar
$ tar --extract \
          --listed-incremental=/dev/null \
          --file archive.2.tar
```

To list the contents of an incremental archive, use '--list' (see Section 2.7 [list], page 15), as usual. To obtain more information about the archive, use '--listed-incremental' or '--incremental' combined with two '--verbose' options[2]:

```
tar --list --incremental --verbose --verbose archive.tar
```

This command will print, for each directory in the archive, the list of files in that directory at the time the archive was created. This information is

---

[1] Notice, that since both archives were created without '-P' option (see Section 6.10.2 [absolute], page 120), these commands should be run from the root file system.

[2] Two '--verbose' options were selected to avoid breaking usual verbose listing output ('--list --verbose') when using in scripts.

Versions of GNU **tar** up to 1.15.1 used to dump verbatim binary contents of the DUMPDIR header (with terminating nulls) when '--incremental' or '--listed-incremental' option was given, no matter what the verbosity level. This behavior, and, especially, the binary output it produced were considered inconvenient and were changed in version 1.16.

put out in a format which is both human-readable and unambiguous for a program: each file name is printed as

```
    x file
```

where x is a letter describing the status of the file: 'Y' if the file is present in the archive, 'N' if the file is not included in the archive, or a 'D' if the file is a directory (and is included in the archive). See [Dumpdir], page 207, for the detailed description of dumpdirs and status codes. Each such line is terminated by a newline character. The last line is followed by an additional newline to indicate the end of the data.

The option '--incremental' ('-G') gives the same behavior as '--listed-incremental' when used with '--list' and '--extract' options. When used with '--create' option, it creates an incremental archive without creating snapshot file. Thus, it is impossible to create several levels of incremental backups with '--incremental' option.

5.3 Levels of Backups

An archive containing all the files in the file system is called a *full backup* or *full dump*. You could insure your data by creating a full dump every day. This strategy, however, would waste a substantial amount of archive media and user time, as unchanged files are daily re-archived.

It is more efficient to do a full dump only occasionally. To back up files between full dumps, you can use *incremental dumps*. A *level one* dump archives all the files that have changed since the last full dump.

A typical dump strategy would be to perform a full dump once a week, and a level one dump once a day. This means some versions of files will in fact be archived more than once, but this dump strategy makes it possible to restore a file system to within one day of accuracy by only extracting two archives—the last weekly (full) dump and the last daily (level one) dump. The only information lost would be in files changed or created since the last daily backup. (Doing dumps more than once a day is usually not worth the trouble.)

GNU `tar` comes with scripts you can use to do full and level-one (actually, even level-two and so on) dumps. Using scripts (shell programs) to perform backups and restoration is a convenient and reliable alternative to typing out file name lists and `tar` commands by hand.

Before you use these scripts, you need to edit the file 'backup-specs', which specifies parameters used by the backup scripts and by the restore script. This file is usually located in '/etc/backup' directory. See Section 5.4 [Backup Parameters], page 88, for its detailed description. Once the backup parameters are set, you can perform backups or restoration by running the appropriate script.

The name of the backup script is `backup`. The name of the restore script is `restore`. The following sections describe their use in detail.

Please Note: The backup and restoration scripts are designed to be used together. While it is possible to restore files by hand from an archive which was created using a backup script, and to create an archive by hand which could then be extracted using the restore script, it is easier to use the scripts. See Section 5.2 [Incremental Dumps], page 84, before making such an attempt.

5.4 Setting Parameters for Backups and Restoration

The file 'backup-specs' specifies backup parameters for the backup and restoration scripts provided with tar. You must edit 'backup-specs' to fit your system configuration and schedule before using these scripts.

Syntactically, 'backup-specs' is a shell script, containing mainly variable assignments. However, any valid shell construct is allowed in this file. Particularly, you may wish to define functions within that script (e.g., see RESTORE_BEGIN below). For more information about shell script syntax, please refer to the definition of the Shell Command Language. See also section "Bash Features" in *Bash Reference Manual*.

The shell variables controlling behavior of backup and restore are described in the following subsections.

5.4.1 General-Purpose Variables

ADMINISTRATOR   [Backup variable]
    The user name of the backup administrator. Backup scripts sends a backup report to this address.

BACKUP_HOUR   [Backup variable]
    The hour at which the backups are done. This can be a number from 0 to 23, or the time specification in form *hours:minutes*, or the string 'now'. This variable is used by backup. Its value may be overridden using '--time' option (see Section 5.5 [Scripted Backups], page 92).

TAPE_FILE   [Backup variable]
    The device tar writes the archive to. If *TAPE_FILE* is a remote archive (see [remote-dev], page 98), backup script will suppose that your mt is able to access remote devices. If *RSH* (see [RSH], page 89) is set, '--rsh-command' option will be added to invocations of mt.

BLOCKING   [Backup variable]
    The blocking factor tar will use when writing the dump archive. See Section 9.4.2 [Blocking Factor], page 161.

BACKUP_DIRS   [Backup variable]
    A list of file systems to be dumped (for backup), or restored (for restore). You can include any directory name in the list — subdirectories on that

file system will be included, regardless of how they may look to other networked machines. Subdirectories on other file systems will be ignored.

The host name specifies which host to run `tar` on, and should normally be the host that actually contains the file system. However, the host machine must have GNU `tar` installed, and must be able to access the directory containing the backup scripts and their support files using the same file name that is used on the machine where the scripts are run (i.e., what `pwd` will print when in that directory on that machine). If the host that contains the file system does not have this capability, you can specify another host as long as it can access the file system through NFS.

If the list of file systems is very long you may wish to put it in a separate file. This file is usually named '`/etc/backup/dirs`', but this name may be overridden in '`backup-specs`' using DIRLIST variable.

DIRLIST   [Backup variable]
The name of the file that contains a list of file systems to backup or restore. By default it is '`/etc/backup/dirs`'.

BACKUP_FILES   [Backup variable]
A list of individual files to be dumped (for `backup`), or restored (for `restore`). These should be accessible from the machine on which the backup script is run.

If the list of individual files is very long you may wish to store it in a separate file. This file is usually named '`/etc/backup/files`', but this name may be overridden in '`backup-specs`' using FILELIST variable.

FILELIST   [Backup variable]
The name of the file that contains a list of individual files to backup or restore. By default it is '`/etc/backup/files`'.

MT   [Backup variable]
Full file name of `mt` binary.

RSH   [Backup variable]
Full file name of `rsh` binary or its equivalent. You may wish to set it to `ssh`, to improve security. In this case you will have to use public key authentication.

RSH_COMMAND   [Backup variable]
Full file name of `rsh` binary on remote machines. This will be passed via '`--rsh-command`' option to the remote invocation of GNU `tar`.

VOLNO_FILE   [Backup variable]
Name of temporary file to hold volume numbers. This needs to be accessible by all the machines which have file systems to be dumped.

XLIST   [Backup variable]
Name of *exclude file list*. An *exclude file list* is a file located on the remote machine and containing the list of files to be excluded from the backup.

Exclude file lists are searched in /etc/tar-backup directory. A common use for exclude file lists is to exclude files containing security-sensitive information (e.g., '/etc/shadow' from backups).

This variable affects only **backup**.

SLEEP_TIME   [Backup variable]

Time to sleep between dumps of any two successive file systems

This variable affects only **backup**.

DUMP_REMIND_SCRIPT   [Backup variable]

Script to be run when it's time to insert a new tape in for the next volume. Administrators may want to tailor this script for their site. If this variable isn't set, GNU **tar** will display its built-in prompt, and will expect confirmation from the console. For the description of the default prompt, see [change volume prompt], page 170.

SLEEP_MESSAGE   [Backup variable]

Message to display on the terminal while waiting for dump time. Usually this will just be some literal text.

TAR   [Backup variable]

Full file name of the GNU **tar** executable. If this is not set, backup scripts will search **tar** in the current shell path.

5.4.2 Magnetic Tape Control

Backup scripts access tape device using special *hook functions*. These functions take a single argument — the name of the tape device. Their names are kept in the following variables:

MT_BEGIN   [Backup variable]

The name of *begin* function. This function is called before accessing the drive. By default it retensions the tape:

```
MT_BEGIN=mt_begin

mt_begin() {
    mt -f "$1" retension
}
```

MT_REWIND   [Backup variable]

The name of *rewind* function. The default definition is as follows:

```
MT_REWIND=mt_rewind

mt_rewind() {
    mt -f "$1" rewind
}
```

MT_OFFLINE   [Backup variable]

The name of the function switching the tape off line. By default it is defined as follows:

```
MT_OFFLINE=mt_offline

mt_offline() {
    mt -f "$1" offl
}
```

MT_STATUS   [Backup variable]
The name of the function used to obtain the status of the archive device, including error count. Default definition:

```
MT_STATUS=mt_status

mt_status() {
    mt -f "$1" status
}
```

5.4.3 User Hooks

User hooks are shell functions executed before and after each `tar` invocation. Thus, there are *backup hooks*, which are executed before and after dumping each file system, and *restore hooks*, executed before and after restoring a file system. Each user hook is a shell function taking four arguments:

hook *level host fs fsname*   [User Hook Function]
Its arguments are:

level   Current backup or restore level.

host   Name or IP address of the host machine being dumped or restored.

fs   Full file name of the file system being dumped or restored.

fsname   File system name with directory separators replaced with colons. This is useful, e.g., for creating unique files.

Following variables keep the names of user hook functions:

DUMP_BEGIN   [Backup variable]
Dump begin function. It is executed before dumping the file system.

DUMP_END   [Backup variable]
Executed after dumping the file system.

RESTORE_BEGIN   [Backup variable]
Executed before restoring the file system.

RESTORE_END   [Backup variable]
Executed after restoring the file system.

5.4.4 An Example Text of 'Backup-specs'

The following is an example of 'backup-specs':

```
# site-specific parameters for file system backup.

ADMINISTRATOR=friedman
BACKUP_HOUR=1
TAPE_FILE=/dev/nrsmt0

# Use ssh instead of the less secure rsh
RSH=/usr/bin/ssh
RSH_COMMAND=/usr/bin/ssh

# Override MT_STATUS function:
my_status() {
        mts -t $TAPE_FILE
}
MT_STATUS=my_status

# Disable MT_OFFLINE function
MT_OFFLINE=:

BLOCKING=124
BACKUP_DIRS="
        albert:/fs/fsf
        apple-gunkies:/gd
        albert:/fs/gd2
        albert:/fs/gp
        geech:/usr/jla
        churchy:/usr/roland
        albert:/
        albert:/usr
        apple-gunkies:/
        apple-gunkies:/usr
        gnu:/hack
        gnu:/u
        apple-gunkies:/com/mailer/gnu
        apple-gunkies:/com/archive/gnu"

BACKUP_FILES="/com/mailer/aliases /com/mailer/league*[a-z]"
```

5.5 Using the Backup Scripts

The syntax for running a backup script is:

```
backup --level=level --time=time
```

The '--level' option requests the dump level. Thus, to produce a full
dump, specify --level=0 (this is the default, so '--level' may be omitted
if its value is 0)[3].

---

[3] For backward compatibility, the backup will also try to deduce the requested dump
level from the name of the script itself. If the name consists of a string 'level-' followed

The '`--time`' option determines when should the backup be run. *Time* may take three forms:

hh:mm

> The dump must be run at *hh* hours *mm* minutes.

hh

> The dump must be run at *hh* hours.

now

> The dump must be run immediately.

You should start a script with a tape or disk mounted. Once you start a script, it prompts you for new tapes or disks as it needs them. Media volumes don't have to correspond to archive files — a multi-volume archive can be started in the middle of a tape that already contains the end of another multi-volume archive. The `restore` script prompts for media by its archive volume, so to avoid an error message you should keep track of which tape (or disk) contains which volume of the archive (see Section 5.6 [Scripted Restoration], page 94).

The backup scripts write two files on the file system. The first is a record file in '`/etc/tar-backup/`', which is used by the scripts to store and retrieve information about which files were dumped. This file is not meant to be read by humans, and should not be deleted by them. See [Snapshot Files], page 205, for a more detailed explanation of this file.

The second file is a log file containing the names of the file systems and files dumped, what time the backup was made, and any error messages that were generated, as well as how much space was left in the media volume after the last volume of the archive was written. You should check this log file after every backup. The file name is '`log-mm-dd-yyyy-level-n`', where *mm-dd-yyyy* represents current date, and *n* represents current dump level number.

The script also prints the name of each system being dumped to the standard output.

Following is the full list of options accepted by `backup` script:

'`-l level`'
'`--level=level`'
> Do backup level *level* (default 0).

'`-f`'
'`--force`'   Force backup even if today's log file already exists.

---

by a single decimal digit, that digit is taken as the dump level number. Thus, you may create a link from `backup` to `level-1` and then run `level-1` whenever you need to create a level one dump.

'-v[*level*]'
'--verbose[=*level*]'

> Set verbosity level. The higher the level is, the more debugging information will be output during execution. Default *level* is 100, which means the highest debugging level.

'-t *start-time*'
'--time=*start-time*'

> Wait till *time*, then do backup.

'-h'
'--help'   Display short help message and exit.

'-V'
'--version'

> Display information about the program's name, version, origin and legal status, all on standard output, and then exit successfully.

5.6 Using the Restore Script

To restore files that were archived using a scripted backup, use the **restore** script. Its usage is quite straightforward. In the simplest form, invoke **restore --all**, it will then restore all the file systems and files specified in 'backup-specs' (see Section 5.4.1 [General-Purpose Variables], page 88).

You may select the file systems (and/or files) to restore by giving **restore** a list of *patterns* in its command line. For example, running

```
restore 'albert:*'
```

will restore all file systems on the machine 'albert'. A more complicated example:

```
restore 'albert:*' '*:/var'
```

This command will restore all file systems on the machine 'albert' as well as '/var' file system on all machines.

By default **restore** will start restoring files from the lowest available dump level (usually zero) and will continue through all available dump levels. There may be situations where such a thorough restore is not necessary. For example, you may wish to restore only files from the recent level one backup. To do so, use '--level' option, as shown in the example below:

```
restore --level=1
```

The full list of options accepted by **restore** follows:

'-a'
'--all'   Restore all file systems and files specified in 'backup-specs'.

'-l *level*'
'--level=*level*'

> Start restoring from the given backup level, instead of the default 0.

'`-v[level]`'
'`--verbose[=level]`'

> Set verbosity level. The higher the level is, the more debugging information will be output during execution. Default *level* is 100, which means the highest debugging level.

'`-h`'
'`--help`'   Display short help message and exit.

'`-V`'
'`--version`'

> Display information about the program's name, version, origin and legal status, all on standard output, and then exit successfully.

You should start the restore script with the media containing the first volume of the archive mounted. The script will prompt for other volumes as they are needed. If the archive is on tape, you don't need to rewind the tape to to its beginning—if the tape head is positioned past the beginning of the archive, the script will rewind the tape as needed. See Section 9.5.1 [Tape Positioning], page 167, for a discussion of tape positioning.

Warning: The script will delete files from the active file system if they were not in the file system when the archive was made.

See Section 5.2 [Incremental Dumps], page 84, for an explanation of how the script makes that determination.

6 Choosing Files and Names for `tar`

Certain options to `tar` enable you to specify a name for your archive. Other options let you decide which files to include or exclude from the archive, based on when or whether files were modified, whether the file names do or don't match specified patterns, or whether files are in specified directories.

This chapter discusses these options in detail.

6.1 Choosing and Naming Archive Files

By default, `tar` uses an archive file name that was compiled when it was built on the system; usually this name refers to some physical tape drive on the machine. However, the person who installed `tar` on the system may not have set the default to a meaningful value as far as most users are concerned. As a result, you will usually want to tell `tar` where to find (or create) the archive. The '`--file=archive-name`' ('`-f archive-name`') option allows you to either specify or name a file to use as the archive instead of the default archive file location.

'`--file=archive-name`'
'`-f archive-name`'

> Name the archive to create or operate on. Use in conjunction with any operation.

For example, in this `tar` command,

```
$ tar -cvf collection.tar blues folk jazz
```

'`collection.tar`' is the name of the archive. It must directly follow the '`-f`' option, since whatever directly follows '`-f`' *will* end up naming the archive. If you neglect to specify an archive name, you may end up overwriting a file in the working directory with the archive you create since `tar` will use this file's name for the archive name.

An archive can be saved as a file in the file system, sent through a pipe or over a network, or written to an I/O device such as a tape, floppy disk, or CD write drive.

If you do not name the archive, `tar` uses the value of the environment variable `TAPE` as the file name for the archive. If that is not available, `tar` uses a default, compiled-in archive name, usually that for tape unit zero (i.e., '`/dev/tu00`').

If you use '`-`' as an *archive-name*, `tar` reads the archive from standard input (when listing or extracting files), or writes it to standard output (when creating an archive). If you use '`-`' as an *archive-name* when modifying an archive, `tar` reads the original archive from its standard input and writes the entire new archive to its standard output.

The following example is a convenient way of copying directory hierarchy from '`sourcedir`' to '`targetdir`'.

```
$ (cd sourcedir; tar -cf - .) | (cd targetdir; tar -xpf -)
```

The '-C' option allows to avoid using subshells:

```
$ tar -C sourcedir -cf - . | tar -C targetdir -xpf -
```

In both examples above, the leftmost **tar** invocation archives the contents of 'sourcedir' to the standard output, while the rightmost one reads this archive from its standard input and extracts it. The '-p' option tells it to restore permissions of the extracted files.

To specify an archive file on a device attached to a remote machine, use the following:

```
--file=hostname:/dev/file-name
```

tar will set up the remote connection, if possible, and prompt you for a username and password. If you use '--file=@hostname:/dev/file-name', **tar** will attempt to set up the remote connection using your username as the username on the remote machine.

If the archive file name includes a colon (':'), then it is assumed to be a file on another machine. If the archive file is 'user@host:file', then *file* is used on the host *host*. The remote host is accessed using the **rsh** program, with a username of *user*. If the username is omitted (along with the '@' sign), then your user name will be used. (This is the normal **rsh** behavior.) It is necessary for the remote machine, in addition to permitting your **rsh** access, to have the 'rmt' program installed (this command is included in the GNU **tar** distribution and by default is installed under 'prefix/libexec/rmt', where *prefix* means your installation prefix). If you need to use a file whose name includes a colon, then the remote tape drive behavior can be inhibited by using the '--force-local' option.

When the archive is being created to '/dev/null', GNU **tar** tries to minimize input and output operations. The Amanda backup system, when used with GNU **tar**, has an initial sizing pass which uses this feature.

6.2 Selecting Archive Members

File Name arguments specify which files in the file system **tar** operates on, when creating or adding to an archive, or which archive members **tar** operates on, when reading or deleting from an archive. See Section 4.2.1 [Operations], page 62.

To specify file names, you can include them as the last arguments on the command line, as follows:

```
tar operation [option1 option2 ...] [file name-1 file name-2 ...]
```

If a file name begins with dash ('-'), precede it with '--add-file' option to prevent it from being treated as an option.

By default GNU **tar** attempts to *unquote* each file or member name, replacing *escape sequences* according to the following table:

Escape   **Replaced with**

`\a`	Audible bell (ASCII 7)
`\b`	Backspace (ASCII 8)
`\f`	Form feed (ASCII 12)
`\n`	New line (ASCII 10)
`\r`	Carriage return (ASCII 13)
`\t`	Horizontal tabulation (ASCII 9)
`\v`	Vertical tabulation (ASCII 11)
`\?`	ASCII 127
`\n`	ASCII n (n should be an octal number of up to 3 digits)

A backslash followed by any other symbol is retained.

This default behavior is controlled by the following command line option:

'`--unquote`'
> Enable unquoting input file or member names (default).

'`--no-unquote`'
> Disable unquoting input file or member names.

If you specify a directory name as a file name argument, all the files in that directory are operated on by `tar`.

If you do not specify files, `tar` behavior differs depending on the operation mode as described below:

When `tar` is invoked with '`--create`' ('`-c`'), `tar` will stop immediately, reporting the following:

```
$ tar cf a.tar
tar: Cowardly refusing to create an empty archive
Try 'tar --help' or 'tar --usage' for more information.
```

If you specify either '`--list`' ('`-t`') or '`--extract`' ('`--get`', '`-x`'), `tar` operates on all the archive members in the archive.

If run with '`--diff`' option, tar will compare the archive with the contents of the current working directory.

If you specify any other operation, `tar` does nothing.

By default, `tar` takes file names from the command line. However, there are other ways to specify file or member names, or to modify the manner in which `tar` selects the files or members upon which to operate. In general, these methods work both for specifying the names of files and archive members.

6.3 Reading Names from a File

Instead of giving the names of files or archive members on the command line, you can put the names into a file, and then use the '`--files-from=file-of-names`' ('`-T file-of-names`') option to `tar`. Give the name of the file which contains the list of files to include as the argument to '`--files-from`'. In the list, the file names should be separated by newlines. You will frequently use this option when you have generated the list of files to archive with the `find` utility.

'`--files-from=file-name`'
'`-T file-name`'
> Get names to extract or create from file *file-name*.

If you give a single dash as a file name for '`--files-from`', (i.e., you specify either `--files-from=-` or `-T -`), then the file names are read from standard input.

Unless you are running `tar` with '`--create`', you can not use both `--files-from=-` and `--file=-` (`-f -`) in the same command.

Any number of '`-T`' options can be given in the command line.

The following example shows how to use `find` to generate a list of files smaller than 400K in length and put that list into a file called '`small-files`'. You can then use the '`-T`' option to `tar` to specify the files from that file, '`small-files`', to create the archive '`little.tgz`'. (The '`-z`' option to `tar` compresses the archive with `gzip`; see Section 8.1.1 [gzip], page 132 for more information.)

```
$ find . -size -400 -print > small-files
$ tar -c -v -z -T small-files -f little.tgz
```

In the file list given by '`-T`' option, any file name beginning with '`-`' character is considered a `tar` option and is processed accordingly[1]. For example, the common use of this feature is to change to another directory by specifying '`-C`' option:

```
$ cat list
-C/etc
passwd
hosts
-C/lib
libc.a
$ tar -c -f foo.tar --files-from list
```

In this example, `tar` will first switch to '`/etc`' directory and add files '`passwd`' and '`hosts`' to the archive. Then it will change to '`/lib`' directory and will archive the file '`libc.a`'. Thus, the resulting archive '`foo.tar`' will contain:

```
$ tar tf foo.tar
passwd
hosts
libc.a
```

If you happen to have a file whose name starts with '`-`', precede it with '`--add-file`' option to prevent it from being recognized as an option. For example: `--add-file=--my-file`.

---

[1] Versions of GNU `tar` up to 1.15.1 recognized only '`-C`' option in file lists, and only if the option and its argument occupied two consecutive lines.

6.3.1 NUL-Terminated File Names

The '`--null`' option causes '`--files-from=file-of-names`' ('`-T file-of-names`') to read file names terminated by a NUL instead of a newline, so files whose names contain newlines can be archived using '`--files-from`'.

'`--null`' Only consider NUL-terminated file names, instead of files that terminate in a newline.

'`--no-null`'

Undo the effect of any previous '`--null`' option.

The '`--null`' option is just like the one in GNU `xargs` and `cpio`, and is useful with the '`-print0`' predicate of GNU `find`. In `tar`, '`--null`' also disables special handling for file names that begin with dash.

This example shows how to use `find` to generate a list of files larger than 800K in length and put that list into a file called '`long-files`'. The '`-print0`' option to `find` is just like '`-print`', except that it separates files with a NUL rather than with a newline. You can then run `tar` with both the '`--null`' and '`-T`' options to specify that `tar` gets the files from that file, '`long-files`', to create the archive '`big.tgz`'. The '`--null`' option to `tar` will cause `tar` to recognize the NUL separator between files.

```
$ find . -size +800 -print0 > long-files
$ tar -c -v --null --files-from=long-files --file=big.tar
```

The '`--no-null`' option can be used if you need to read both NUL-terminated and newline-terminated files on the same command line. For example, if '`flist`' is a newline-terminated file, then the following command can be used to combine it with the above command:

```
$ find . -size +800 -print0 |
    tar -c -f big.tar --null -T - --no-null -T flist
```

This example uses short options for typographic reasons, to avoid very long lines.

GNU `tar` is tries to automatically detect NUL-terminated file lists, so in many cases it is safe to use them even without the '`--null`' option. In this case `tar` will print a warning and continue reading such a file as if '`--null`' were actually given:

```
$ find . -size +800 -print0 | tar -c -f big.tar -T -
tar: -: file name read contains nul character
```

The null terminator, however, remains in effect only for this particular file, any following '`-T`' options will assume newline termination. Of course, the null autodetection applies to these eventual surplus '`-T`' options as well.

6.4 Excluding Some Files

To avoid operating on files whose names match a particular pattern, use the '`--exclude`' or '`--exclude-from`' options.

'`--exclude=pattern`'

Causes `tar` to ignore files that match the *pattern*.

The '--exclude=*pattern*' option prevents any file or member whose name matches the shell wildcard (*pattern*) from being operated on. For example, to create an archive with all the contents of the directory 'src' except for files whose names end in '.o', use the command 'tar -cf src.tar --exclude='*.o' src'.

You may give multiple '--exclude' options.

'--exclude-from=*file*'
'-X *file*'   Causes tar to ignore files that match the patterns listed in *file*.

Use the '--exclude-from' option to read a list of patterns, one per line, from *file*; tar will ignore files matching those patterns. Thus if tar is called as 'tar -c -X foo .' and the file 'foo' contains a single line '*.o', no files whose names end in '.o' will be added to the archive.

Notice, that lines from *file* are read verbatim. One of the frequent errors is leaving some extra whitespace after a file name, which is difficult to catch using text editors.

However, empty lines are OK.

When archiving directories that are under some version control system (VCS), it is often convenient to read exclusion patterns from this VCS' ignore files (e.g. '.cvsignore', '.gitignore', etc.) The following options provide such possibilty:

'--exclude-vcs-ignores'
               Before archiving a directory, see if it contains any of the following files: 'cvsignore', '.gitignore', '.bzrignore', or '.hgignore'. If so, read ignore patterns from these files.

               The patterns are treated much as the corresponding VCS would treat them, i.e.:

               '.cvsignore'
                         Contains shell-style globbing patterns that apply only to the directory where this file resides. No comments are allowed in the file. Empty lines are ignored.

               '.gitignore'
                         Contains shell-style globbing patterns. Applies to the directory where '.gitfile' is located and all its subdirectories.

                         Any line beginning with a '#' is a comment. Back-slash escapes the comment character.

'`.bzrignore`'

> Contains shell globbing-patterns and regular expressions (if prefixed with '`RE:`'[2]. Patterns affect the directory and all its subdirectories.
>
> Any line beginning with a '`#`' is a comment.

'`.hgignore`'

> Contains posix regular expressions[3]. The line '`syntax: glob`' switches to shell globbing patterns. The line '`syntax: regexp`' switches back. Comments begin with a '`#`'. Patterns affect the directory and all its subdirectories.

'`--exclude-ignore=file`'

> Before dumping a directory, `tar` checks if it contains *file*. If so, exclusion patterns are read from this file. The patterns affect only the directory itself.

'`--exclude-ignore-recursive=file`'

> Same as '`--exclude-ignore`', except that the patterns read affect both the directory where *file* resides and all its subdirectories.

'`--exclude-vcs`'

> Exclude files and directories used by following version control systems: '`CVS`', '`RCS`', '`SCCS`', '`SVN`', '`Arch`', '`Bazaar`', '`Mercurial`', and '`Darcs`'.
>
> As of version 1.28, the following files are excluded:
>
> - '`CVS/`', and everything under it
> - '`RCS/`', and everything under it
> - '`SCCS/`', and everything under it
> - '`.git/`', and everything under it
> - '`.gitignore`'
> - '`.cvsignore`'
> - '`.svn/`', and everything under it
> - '`.arch-ids/`', and everything under it
> - '`{arch}/`', and everything under it
> - '`=RELEASE-ID`'
> - '`=meta-update`'
> - '`=update`'

---

[2] According to the Bazaar docs, globbing-patterns are Korn-shell style and regular expressions are perl-style. As of GNU `tar` version 1.28, these are treated as shell-style globs and posix extended regexps. This will be fixed in future releases.

[3] Support for perl-style regexps will appear in future releases.

- '.bzr'
- '.bzrignore'
- '.bzrtags'
- '.hg'
- '.hgignore'
- '.hgrags'
- '_darcs'

'--exclude-backups'
>   Exclude backup and lock files. This option causes exclusion of
>   files that match the following shell globbing patterns:
>
>   .#*
>
>   *~
>
>   #*#

When creating an archive, the '--exclude-caches' option family causes tar to exclude all directories that contain a *cache directory tag*. A cache directory tag is a short file with the well-known name 'CACHEDIR.TAG' and having a standard header specified in http://www.brynosaurus.com/cachedir/spec.html. Various applications write cache directory tags into directories they use to hold regenerable, non-precious data, so that such data can be more easily excluded from backups.

There are three 'exclude-caches' options, each providing a different exclusion semantics:

'--exclude-caches'
>   Do not archive the contents of the directory, but archive the
>   directory itself and the 'CACHEDIR.TAG' file.

'--exclude-caches-under'
>   Do not archive the contents of the directory, nor the
>   'CACHEDIR.TAG' file, archive only the directory itself.

'--exclude-caches-all'
>   Omit directories containing 'CACHEDIR.TAG' file entirely.

Another option family, '--exclude-tag', provides a generalization of this concept. It takes a single argument, a file name to look for. Any directory that contains this file will be excluded from the dump. Similarly to 'exclude-caches', there are three options in this option family:

'--exclude-tag=*file*'
>   Do not dump the contents of the directory, but dump the directory itself and the *file*.

'`--exclude-tag-under=file`'
>Do not dump the contents of the directory, nor the *file*, archive only the directory itself.

'`--exclude-tag-all=file`'
>Omit directories containing *file* file entirely.

Multiple '`--exclude-tag*`' options can be given.

For example, given this directory:

```
$ find dir
dir
dir/blues
dir/jazz
dir/folk
dir/folk/tagfile
dir/folk/sanjuan
dir/folk/trote
```

The '`--exclude-tag`' will produce the following:

```
$ tar -cf archive.tar --exclude-tag=tagfile -v dir
dir/
dir/blues
dir/jazz
dir/folk/
tar: dir/folk/: contains a cache directory tag tagfile;
  contents not dumped
dir/folk/tagfile
```

Both the '`dir/folk`' directory and its tagfile are preserved in the archive, however the rest of files in this directory are not.

Now, using the '`--exclude-tag-under`' option will exclude '`tagfile`' from the dump, while still preserving the directory itself, as shown in this example:

```
$ tar -cf archive.tar --exclude-tag-under=tagfile -v dir
dir/
dir/blues
dir/jazz
dir/folk/
./tar: dir/folk/: contains a cache directory tag tagfile;
  contents not dumped
```

Finally, using '`--exclude-tag-all`' omits the '`dir/folk`' directory entirely:

```
$ tar -cf archive.tar --exclude-tag-all=tagfile -v dir
dir/
dir/blues
dir/jazz
./tar: dir/folk/: contains a cache directory tag tagfile;
  directory not dumped
```

Problems with Using the `exclude` Options

Some users find '`exclude`' options confusing. Here are some common pitfalls:

- The main operating mode of **tar** does not act on a file name explicitly listed on the command line, if one of its file name components is excluded. In the example above, if you create an archive and exclude files that end with '*.o', but explicitly name the file 'dir.o/foo' after all the options have been listed, 'dir.o/foo' will be excluded from the archive.

- You can sometimes confuse the meanings of '--exclude' and '--exclude-from'. Be careful: use '--exclude' when files to be excluded are given as a pattern on the command line. Use '--exclude-from' to introduce the name of a file which contains a list of patterns, one per line; each of these patterns can exclude zero, one, or many files.

- When you use '--exclude=*pattern*', be sure to quote the *pattern* parameter, so GNU **tar** sees wildcard characters like '*'. If you do not do this, the shell might expand the '*' itself using files at hand, so **tar** might receive a list of files instead of one pattern, or none at all, making the command somewhat illegal. This might not correspond to what you want.

  For example, write:

  ```
  $ tar -c -f archive.tar --exclude '*.o' directory
  ```

  rather than:

  ```
  # Wrong!
  $ tar -c -f archive.tar --exclude *.o directory
  ```

- You must use use shell syntax, or globbing, rather than **regexp** syntax, when using exclude options in **tar**. If you try to use **regexp** syntax to describe files to be excluded, your command might fail.

-

  In earlier versions of **tar**, what is now the '--exclude-from' option was called '--exclude' instead. Now, '--exclude' applies to patterns listed on the command line and '--exclude-from' applies to patterns listed in a file.

6.5 Wildcards Patterns and Matching

Globbing is the operation by which *wildcard* characters, '*' or '?' for example, are replaced and expanded into all existing files matching the given pattern. GNU **tar** can use wildcard patterns for matching (or globbing) archive members when extracting from or listing an archive. Wildcard patterns are also used for verifying volume labels of **tar** archives. This section has the purpose of explaining wildcard syntax for **tar**.

A *pattern* should be written according to shell syntax, using wildcard characters to effect globbing. Most characters in the pattern stand for themselves in the matched string, and case is significant: 'a' will match only 'a', and not 'A'. The character '?' in the pattern matches any single character in the matched string. The character '*' in the pattern matches zero, one, or more single characters in the matched string. The character '\' says to take the following character of the pattern *literally*; it is useful when one needs to match the '?', '*', '[' or '\' characters, themselves.

The character '[', up to the matching ']', introduces a character class. A *character class* is a list of acceptable characters for the next single character of the matched string. For example, '[abcde]' would match any of the first five letters of the alphabet. Note that within a character class, all of the "special characters" listed above other than '\' lose their special meaning; for example, '[-\\[*?]]' would match any of the characters, '-', '\', '[', '*', '?', or ']'. (Due to parsing constraints, the characters '-' and ']' must either come *first* or *last* in a character class.)

If the first character of the class after the opening '[' is '!' or '^', then the meaning of the class is reversed. Rather than listing character to match, it lists those characters which are *forbidden* as the next single character of the matched string.

Other characters of the class stand for themselves. The special construction '[a-e]', using an hyphen between two letters, is meant to represent all characters between *a* and *e*, inclusive.

Periods ('.') or forward slashes ('/') are not considered special for wildcard matches. However, if a pattern completely matches a directory prefix of a matched string, then it matches the full matched string: thus, excluding a directory also excludes all the files beneath it.

Controlling Pattern-Matching

For the purposes of this section, we call *exclusion members* all member names obtained while processing '--exclude' and '--exclude-from' options, and *inclusion members* those member names that were given in the command line or read from the file specified with '--files-from' option.

These two pairs of member lists are used in the following operations: '--diff', '--extract', '--list', '--update'.

There are no inclusion members in create mode ('--create' and '--append'), since in this mode the names obtained from the command line refer to *files*, not archive members.

By default, inclusion members are compared with archive members literally[4] and exclusion members are treated as globbing patterns. For example:

---

[4] Notice that earlier GNU `tar` versions used globbing for inclusion members, which contradicted to UNIX98 specification and was not documented. See Appendix A [Changes], page 185, for more information on this and other changes.

```
$ tar tf foo.tar
a.c
b.c
a.txt
[remarks]
# Member names are used verbatim:
$ tar -xf foo.tar -v '[remarks]'
[remarks]
# Exclude member names are globbed:
$ tar -xf foo.tar -v --exclude '*.c'
a.txt
[remarks]
```

This behavior can be altered by using the following options:

'--wildcards'
> Treat all member names as wildcards.

'--no-wildcards'
> Treat all member names as literal strings.

Thus, to extract files whose names end in '.c', you can use:

```
$ tar -xf foo.tar -v --wildcards '*.c'
a.c
b.c
```

Notice quoting of the pattern to prevent the shell from interpreting it.

The effect of '--wildcards' option is canceled by '--no-wildcards'. This can be used to pass part of the command line arguments verbatim and other part as globbing patterns. For example, the following invocation:

```
$ tar -xf foo.tar --wildcards '*.txt' --no-wildcards '[remarks]'
```

instructs `tar` to extract from 'foo.tar' all files whose names end in '.txt' and the file named '[remarks]'.

Normally, a pattern matches a name if an initial subsequence of the name's components matches the pattern, where '*', '?', and '[...]' are the usual shell wildcards, '\' escapes wildcards, and wildcards can match '/'.

Other than optionally stripping leading '/' from names (see Section 6.10.2 [absolute], page 120), patterns and names are used as-is. For example, trailing '/' is not trimmed from a user-specified name before deciding whether to exclude it.

However, this matching procedure can be altered by the options listed below. These options accumulate. For example:

```
--ignore-case --exclude='makefile' --no-ignore-case ---exclude='readme'
```

ignores case when excluding 'makefile', but not when excluding 'readme'.

'--anchored'
'--no-anchored'
> If anchored, a pattern must match an initial subsequence of the name's components. Otherwise, the pattern can match any sub-

sequence. Default is '`--no-anchored`' for exclusion members and '`--anchored`' inclusion members.

'`--ignore-case`'
'`--no-ignore-case`'

> When ignoring case, upper-case patterns match lower-case names and vice versa. When not ignoring case (the default), matching is case-sensitive.

'`--wildcards-match-slash`'
'`--no-wildcards-match-slash`'

> When wildcards match slash (the default for exclusion members), a wildcard like '`*`' in the pattern can match a '`/`' in the name. Otherwise, '`/`' is matched only by '`/`'.

The '`--recursion`' and '`--no-recursion`' options (see Section 6.9 [recurse], page 118) also affect how member patterns are interpreted. If recursion is in effect, a pattern matches a name if it matches any of the name's parent directories.

The following table summarizes pattern-matching default values:

Members	Default settings
Inclusion	'`--no-wildcards --anchored` `--no-wildcards-match-slash`'
Exclusion	'`--wildcards --no-anchored` `--wildcards-match-slash`'

6.6 Quoting Member Names

When displaying member names, `tar` takes care to avoid ambiguities caused by certain characters. This is called *name quoting*. The characters in question are:

- Non-printable control characters:

Character	ASCII	Character name
\a	7	Audible bell
\b	8	Backspace
\f	12	Form feed
\n	10	New line
\r	13	Carriage return
\t	9	Horizontal tabulation
\v	11	Vertical tabulation

- Space (ASCII 32)

- Single and double quotes (''' and '"')

- Backslash ('\')

The exact way `tar` uses to quote these characters depends on the *quoting style*. The default quoting style, called *escape* (see below), uses backslash notation to represent control characters, space and backslash. Using this quoting style, control characters are represented as listed in column 'Character' in the above table, a space is printed as '\ ' and a backslash as '\\'.

GNU `tar` offers seven distinct quoting styles, which can be selected using '--quoting-style' option:

'--quoting-style=*style*'

> Sets quoting style. Valid values for *style* argument are: literal, shell, shell-always, c, escape, locale, clocale.

These styles are described in detail below. To illustrate their effect, we will use an imaginary tar archive '`arch.tar`' containing the following members:

```
# 1. Contains horizontal tabulation character.
a       tab
# 2. Contains newline character
a
newline
# 3. Contains a space
a space
# 4. Contains double quotes
a"double"quote
# 5. Contains single quotes
a'single'quote
# 6. Contains a backslash character:
a\backslash
```

Here is how usual `ls` command would have listed them, if they had existed in the current working directory:

```
$ ls
a\ttab
a\nnewline
a\ space
a"double"quote
a'single'quote
a\\backslash
```

Quoting styles:

'`literal`'   No quoting, display each character as is:

```
$ tar tf arch.tar --quoting-style=literal
./
./a space
./a'single'quote
./a"double"quote
./a\backslash
./a       tab
./a
newline
```

'`shell`'   Display characters the same way Bourne shell does: control char-
                acters, except '\t' and '\n', are printed using backslash escapes,
                '\t' and '\n' are printed as is, and a single quote is printed as
                '\''. If a name contains any quoted characters, it is enclosed in
                single quotes. In particular, if a name contains single quotes, it
                is printed as several single-quoted strings:

```
$ tar tf arch.tar --quoting-style=shell
./
'./a space'
'./a'\''single'\''quote'
'./a"double"quote'
'./a\backslash'
'./a	tab'
'./a
newline'
```

'`shell-always`'
                Same as '`shell`', but the names are always enclosed in single
                quotes:

```
$ tar tf arch.tar --quoting-style=shell-always
'./'
'./a space'
'./a'\''single'\''quote'
'./a"double"quote'
'./a\backslash'
'./a	tab'
'./a
newline'
```

'`c`'   Use the notation of the C programming language. All names
                are enclosed in double quotes. Control characters are quoted
                using backslash notations, double quotes are represented as '\"',
                backslash characters are represented as '\\'. Single quotes and
                spaces are not quoted:

```
$ tar tf arch.tar --quoting-style=c
"./"
"./a space"
"./a'single'quote"
"./a\"double\"quote"
"./a\\backslash"
"./a\ttab"
"./a\nnewline"
```

'`escape`'   Control characters are printed using backslash notation, a space
                is printed as '\ ' and a backslash as '\\'. This is the default
                quoting style, unless it was changed when configured the pack-
                age.

```
$ tar tf arch.tar --quoting-style=escape
./
./a space
./a'single'quote
./a"double"quote
./a\\backslash
./a\ttab
./a\nnewline
```

'locale'   Control characters, single quote and backslash are printed using backslash notation. All names are quoted using left and right quotation marks, appropriate to the current locale. If it does not define quotation marks, use '' as left and as right quotation marks. Any occurrences of the right quotation mark in a name are escaped with '\', for example:

For example:

```
$ tar tf arch.tar --quoting-style=locale
'./'
'./a space'
'./a\'single\'quote'
'./a"double"quote'
'./a\\backslash'
'./a\ttab'
'./a\nnewline'
```

'clocale' Same as 'locale', but '"' is used for both left and right quotation marks, if not provided by the currently selected locale:

```
$ tar tf arch.tar --quoting-style=clocale
"./"
"./a space"
"./a'single'quote"
"./a\"double\"quote"
"./a\\backslash"
"./a\ttab"
"./a\nnewline"
```

You can specify which characters should be quoted in addition to those implied by the current quoting style:

'--quote-chars=string'
          Always quote characters from string, even if the selected quoting style would not quote them.

For example, using 'escape' quoting (compare with the usual escape listing above):

```
$ tar tf arch.tar --quoting-style=escape --quote-chars=' "'
./
./a\ space
./a'single'quote
./a\"double\"quote
./a\\backslash
./a\ttab
./a\nnewline
```

To disable quoting of such additional characters, use the following option:

'`--no-quote-chars=string`'

> Remove characters listed in *string* from the list of quoted characters set by the previous '`--quote-chars`' option.

This option is particularly useful if you have added '`--quote-chars`' to your `TAR_OPTIONS` (see [TAR_OPTIONS], page 23) and wish to disable it for the current invocation.

Note, that '`--no-quote-chars`' does *not* disable those characters that are quoted by default in the selected quoting style.

6.7 Modifying File and Member Names

`Tar` archives contain detailed information about files stored in them and full file names are part of that information. When storing a file to an archive, its file name is recorded in it, along with the actual file contents. When restoring from an archive, a file is created on disk with exactly the same name as that stored in the archive. In the majority of cases this is the desired behavior of a file archiver. However, there are some cases when it is not.

First of all, it is often unsafe to extract archive members with absolute file names or those that begin with a '`../`'. GNU `tar` takes special precautions when extracting such names and provides a special option for handling them, which is described in Section 6.10.2 [absolute], page 120.

Secondly, you may wish to extract file names without some leading directory components, or with otherwise modified names. In other cases it is desirable to store files under differing names in the archive.

GNU `tar` provides several options for these needs.

'`--strip-components=number`'

> Strip given *number* of leading components from file names before extraction.

For example, suppose you have archived whole '`/usr`' hierarchy to a tar archive named '`usr.tar`'. Among other files, this archive contains '`usr/include/stdlib.h`', which you wish to extract to the current working directory. To do so, you type:

```
$ tar -xf usr.tar --strip=2 usr/include/stdlib.h
```

The option '`--strip=2`' instructs `tar` to strip the two leading components ('`usr/`' and '`include/`') off the file name.

If you add the '--verbose' ('-v') option to the invocation above, you will note that the verbose listing still contains the full file name, with the two removed components still in place. This can be inconvenient, so `tar` provides a special option for altering this behavior:

'--show-transformed-names'

Display file or member names with all requested transformations applied.

For example:

```
$ tar -xf usr.tar -v --strip=2 usr/include/stdlib.h
usr/include/stdlib.h
$ tar -xf usr.tar -v --strip=2 --show-transformed usr/include/stdlib.h
stdlib.h
```

Notice that in both cases the file 'stdlib.h' is extracted to the current working directory, '--show-transformed-names' affects only the way its name is displayed.

This option is especially useful for verifying whether the invocation will have the desired effect. Thus, before running

```
$ tar -x --strip=n
```

it is often advisable to run

```
$ tar -t -v --show-transformed --strip=n
```

to make sure the command will produce the intended results.

In case you need to apply more complex modifications to the file name, GNU `tar` provides a general-purpose transformation option:

'--transform=*expression*'
'--xform=*expression*'

Modify file names using supplied *expression*.

The *expression* is a `sed`-like replace expression of the form:

```
s/regexp/replace/[flags]
```

where *regexp* is a *regular expression*, *replace* is a replacement for each file name part that matches *regexp*. Both *regexp* and *replace* are described in detail in section "The 's' Command" in *GNU sed*.

Any delimiter can be used in lieu of '/', the only requirement being that it be used consistently throughout the expression. For example, the following two expressions are equivalent:

```
s/one/two/
s,one,two,
```

Changing delimiters is often useful when the *regex* contains slashes. For example, it is more convenient to write `s,/,-,` than `s/\//-/`.

As in `sed`, you can give several replace expressions, separated by a semi-colon.

Supported *flags* are:

'g'   Apply the replacement to *all* matches to the *regexp*, not just the first.

'`i`'   Use case-insensitive matching.

'`x`'   *regexp* is an *extended regular expression* (see section "Extended regular expressions" in *GNU sed*).

'`number`'   Only replace the *number*th match of the *regexp*.

Note: the POSIX standard does not specify what should happen when you mix the '`g`' and *number* modifiers. GNU `tar` follows the GNU `sed` implementation in this regard, so the interaction is defined to be: ignore matches before the *number*th, and then match and replace all matches from the *number*th on.

In addition, several *transformation scope* flags are supported, that control to what files transformations apply. These are:

'`r`'   Apply transformation to regular archive members.

'`R`'   Do not apply transformation to regular archive members.

'`s`'   Apply transformation to symbolic link targets.

'`S`'   Do not apply transformation to symbolic link targets.

'`h`'   Apply transformation to hard link targets.

'`H`'   Do not apply transformation to hard link targets.

Default is '`rsh`', which means to apply tranformations to both archive members and targets of symbolic and hard links.

Default scope flags can also be changed using '`flags=`' statement in the transform expression. The flags set this way remain in force until next '`flags=`' statement or end of expression, whichever occurs first. For example:

```
--transform 'flags=S;s|^|/usr/local/|'
```

Here are several examples of '`--transform`' usage:

1. Extract '`usr/`' hierarchy into '`usr/local/`':

   ```
   $ tar --transform='s,usr/,usr/local/,' -x -f arch.tar
   ```

2. Strip two leading directory components (equivalent to '`--strip-components=2`'):

   ```
   $ tar --transform='s,/*[^/]*/[^/]*/,,' -x -f arch.tar
   ```

3. Convert each file name to lower case:

   ```
   $ tar --transform 's/.*/\L&/' -x -f arch.tar
   ```

4. Prepend '`/prefix/`' to each file name:

   ```
   $ tar --transform 's,^,/prefix/,' -x -f arch.tar
   ```

5. Archive the '`/lib`' directory, prepending '`/usr/local`' to each archive member:

   ```
   $ tar --transform 's,^,/usr/local/,S' -c -f arch.tar /lib
   ```

Notice the use of flags in the last example. The '`/lib`' directory often contains many symbolic links to files within it. It may look, for example, like this:

```
$ ls -l
drwxr-xr-x root/root           0 2008-07-08 16:20 /lib/
-rwxr-xr-x root/root 1250840 2008-05-25 07:44 /lib/libc-2.3.2.so
lrwxrwxrwx root/root           0 2008-06-24 17:12 /lib/libc.so.6 -> libc-2.3.2.so
...
```

Using the expression 's,^,/usr/local/,' would mean adding '/usr/local' to both regular archive members and to link targets. In this case, '/lib/libc.so.6' would become:

```
/usr/local/lib/libc.so.6 -> /usr/local/libc-2.3.2.so
```

This is definitely not desired. To avoid this, the 'S' flag is used, which excludes symbolic link targets from filename transformations. The result is:

```
$ tar --transform 's,^,/usr/local/,S', -c -v -f arch.tar \
        --show-transformed /lib
drwxr-xr-x root/root           0 2008-07-08 16:20 /usr/local/lib/
-rwxr-xr-x root/root 1250840 2008-05-25 07:44 /usr/local/lib/libc-2.3.2.so
lrwxrwxrwx root/root           0 2008-06-24 17:12 /usr/local/lib/libc.so.6 \
    -> libc-2.3.2.so
```

Unlike '--strip-components', '--transform' can be used in any GNU tar operation mode. For example, the following command adds files to the archive while replacing the leading 'usr/' component with 'var/':

```
$ tar -cf arch.tar --transform='s,^usr/,var/,' /
```

To test '--transform' effect we suggest using '--show-transformed-names' option:

```
$ tar -cf arch.tar --transform='s,^usr/,var/,' \
        --verbose --show-transformed-names /
```

If both '--strip-components' and '--transform' are used together, then '--transform' is applied first, and the required number of components is then stripped from its result.

You can use as many '--transform' options in a single command line as you want. The specified expressions will then be applied in order of their appearance. For example, the following two invocations are equivalent:

```
$ tar -cf arch.tar --transform='s,/usr/var,/var/' \
                        --transform='s,/usr/local,/usr/,'
$ tar -cf arch.tar \
                --transform='s,/usr/var,/var/;s,/usr/local,/usr/,'
```

6.8 Operating Only on New Files

The '--after-date=date' ('--newer=date', '-N date') option causes tar to only work on files whose data modification or status change times are newer than the date given. If date starts with '/' or '.', it is taken to be a file name; the data modification time of that file is used as the date. If you use this option when creating or appending to an archive, the archive will only include new files. If you use '--after-date' when extracting an archive, tar will only extract files newer than the date you specify.

If you only want `tar` to make the date comparison based on modification of the file's data (rather than status changes), then use the '`--newer-mtime=date`' option.

You may use these options with any operation. Note that these options differ from the '`--update`' ('`-u`') operation in that they allow you to specify a particular date against which `tar` can compare when deciding whether or not to archive the files.

'`--after-date=date`'
'`--newer=date`'
'`-N date`'   Only store files newer than *date*.

> Acts on files only if their data modification or status change times are later than *date*. Use in conjunction with any operation.

> If *date* starts with '`/`' or '`.`', it is taken to be a file name; the data modification time of that file is used as the date.

'`--newer-mtime=date`'

> Acts like '`--after-date`', but only looks at data modification times.

These options limit `tar` to operate only on files which have been modified after the date specified. A file's status is considered to have changed if its contents have been modified, or if its owner, permissions, and so forth, have been changed. (For more information on how to specify a date, see Chapter 7 [Date input formats], page 123; remember that the entire date argument must be quoted if it contains any spaces.)

Gurus would say that '`--after-date`' tests both the data modification time (`mtime`, the time the contents of the file were last modified) and the status change time (`ctime`, the time the file's status was last changed: owner, permissions, etc.) fields, while '`--newer-mtime`' tests only the `mtime` field.

To be precise, '`--after-date`' checks *both* `mtime` and `ctime` and processes the file if either one is more recent than *date*, while '`--newer-mtime`' only checks `mtime` and disregards `ctime`. Neither does it use `atime` (the last time the contents of the file were looked at).

Date specifiers can have embedded spaces. Because of this, you may need to quote date arguments to keep the shell from parsing them as separate arguments. For example, the following command will add to the archive all the files modified less than two days ago:

```
$ tar -cf foo.tar --newer-mtime '2 days ago'
```

When any of these options is used with the option '`--verbose`' (see [verbose tutorial], page 8) GNU `tar` will try to convert the specified date back to its textual representation and compare that with the one given with the option. If the two dates differ, `tar` will print a warning saying what date it will use. This is to help user ensure he is using the right date. For example:

```
$ tar -c -f archive.tar --after-date='10 days ago' .
tar: Option --after-date: Treating date '10 days ago' as 2006-06-11
13:19:37.232434
```

Please Note: '`--after-date`' and '`--newer-mtime`' should not be used for incremental backups. See Section 5.2 [Incremental Dumps], page 84, for proper way of creating incremental backups.

6.9 Descending into Directories

Usually, `tar` will recursively explore all directories (either those given on the command line or through the '`--files-from`' option) for the various files they contain. However, you may not always want `tar` to act this way.

The '`--no-recursion`' option inhibits `tar`'s recursive descent into specified directories. If you specify '`--no-recursion`', you can use the `find` (see section "find" in *GNU Find Manual*) utility for hunting through levels of directories to construct a list of file names which you could then pass to `tar`. `find` allows you to be more selective when choosing which files to archive; see Section 6.3 [files], page 99, for more information on using `find` with `tar`.

'`--no-recursion`'
> Prevents `tar` from recursively descending directories.

'`--recursion`'
> Requires `tar` to recursively descend directories. This is the default.

When you use '`--no-recursion`', GNU `tar` grabs directory entries themselves, but does not descend on them recursively. Many people use `find` for locating files they want to back up, and since `tar` *usually* recursively descends on directories, they have to use the '`-not -type d`' test in their `find` invocation (see section "Type test" in *Finding Files*), as they usually do not want all the files in a directory. They then use the '`--files-from`' option to archive the files located via `find`.

The problem when restoring files archived in this manner is that the directories themselves are not in the archive; so the '`--same-permissions`' ('`--preserve-permissions`', '`-p`') option does not affect them—while users might really like it to. Specifying '`--no-recursion`' is a way to tell `tar` to grab only the directory entries given to it, adding no new files on its own. To summarize, if you use `find` to create a list of files to be stored in an archive, use it as follows:

```
$ find dir tests | \
    tar -cf archive -T - --no-recursion
```

The '`--no-recursion`' option also applies when extracting: it causes `tar` to extract only the matched directory entries, not the files under those directories.

The '`--no-recursion`' option also affects how globbing patterns are interpreted (see [controlling pattern-matching], page 107).

The '`--no-recursion`' and '`--recursion`' options apply to later options and operands, and can be overridden by later occurrences of '`--no-recursion`' and '`--recursion`'. For example:

```
$ tar -cf jams.tar --no-recursion grape --recursion grape/concord
```
creates an archive with one entry for 'grape', and the recursive contents of 'grape/concord', but no entries under 'grape' other than 'grape/concord'.

6.10 Crossing File System Boundaries

`tar` will normally automatically cross file system boundaries in order to archive files which are part of a directory tree. You can change this behavior by running `tar` and specifying '`--one-file-system`'. This option only affects files that are archived because they are in a directory that is being archived; `tar` will still archive files explicitly named on the command line or through '`--files-from`', regardless of where they reside.

'`--one-file-system`'
> Prevents `tar` from crossing file system boundaries when archiving. Use in conjunction with any write operation.

The '`--one-file-system`' option causes `tar` to modify its normal behavior in archiving the contents of directories. If a file in a directory is not on the same file system as the directory itself, then `tar` will not archive that file. If the file is a directory itself, `tar` will not archive anything beneath it; in other words, `tar` will not cross mount points.

This option is useful for making full or incremental archival backups of a file system. If this option is used in conjunction with '`--verbose`' ('`-v`'), files that are excluded are mentioned by name on the standard error.

6.10.1 Changing the Working Directory

To change the working directory in the middle of a list of file names, either on the command line or in a file specified using '`--files-from`' ('`-T`'), use '`--directory`' ('`-C`'). This will change the working directory to the specified directory after that point in the list.

'`--directory=directory`'
'`-C directory`'
> Changes the working directory in the middle of a command line.

For example,
```
$ tar -c -f jams.tar grape prune -C food cherry
```
will place the files 'grape' and 'prune' from the current directory into the archive 'jams.tar', followed by the file 'cherry' from the directory 'food'. This option is especially useful when you have several widely separated files that you want to store in the same archive.

Note that the file 'cherry' is recorded in the archive under the precise name 'cherry', *not* 'food/cherry'. Thus, the archive will contain three files that all appear to have come from the same directory; if the archive is extracted with plain '`tar --extract`', all three files will be written in the current directory.

Contrast this with the command,

```
$ tar -c -f jams.tar grape prune -C food red/cherry
```

which records the third file in the archive under the name 'red/cherry' so that, if the archive is extracted using 'tar --extract', the third file will be written in a subdirectory named 'red'.

You can use the '--directory' option to make the archive independent of the original name of the directory holding the files. The following command places the files '/etc/passwd', '/etc/hosts', and '/lib/libc.a' into the archive 'foo.tar':

```
$ tar -c -f foo.tar -C /etc passwd hosts -C /lib libc.a
```

However, the names of the archive members will be exactly what they were on the command line: 'passwd', 'hosts', and 'libc.a'. They will not appear to be related by file name to the original directories where those files were located.

Note that '--directory' options are interpreted consecutively. If '--directory' specifies a relative file name, it is interpreted relative to the then current directory, which might not be the same as the original current working directory of **tar**, due to a previous '--directory' option.

When using '--files-from' (see Section 6.3 [files], page 99), you can put various **tar** options (including '-C') in the file list. Notice, however, that in this case the option and its argument may not be separated by whitespace. If you use short option, its argument must either follow the option letter immediately, without any intervening whitespace, or occupy the next line. Otherwise, if you use long option, separate its argument by an equal sign.

For instance, the file list for the above example will be:

```
-C/etc
passwd
hosts
--directory=/lib
libc.a
```

To use it, you would invoke **tar** as follows:

```
$ tar -c -f foo.tar --files-from list
```

The interpretation of '--directory' is disabled by '--null' option.

6.10.2 Absolute File Names

By default, GNU **tar** drops a leading '/' on input or output, and complains about file names containing a '..' component. There is an option that turns off this behavior:

'--absolute-names'
'-P'   Do not strip leading slashes from file names, and permit file names containing a '..' file name component.

When **tar** extracts archive members from an archive, it strips any leading slashes ('/') from the member name. This causes absolute member names in the archive to be treated as relative file names. This allows you to have such members extracted wherever you want, instead of being restricted to extracting the member in the exact directory named in the archive. For example, if the archive member has the name '`/etc/passwd`', `tar` will extract it as if the name were really '`etc/passwd`'.

File names containing '`..`' can cause problems when extracting, so `tar` normally warns you about such files when creating an archive, and rejects attempts to extracts such files.

Other `tar` programs do not do this. As a result, if you create an archive whose member names start with a slash, they will be difficult for other people with a non-GNU `tar` program to use. Therefore, GNU `tar` also strips leading slashes from member names when putting members into the archive. For example, if you ask `tar` to add the file '`/bin/ls`' to an archive, it will do so, but the member name will be '`bin/ls`'[5].

Symbolic links containing '`..`' or leading '`/`' can also cause problems when extracting, so `tar` normally extracts them last; it may create empty files as placeholders during extraction.

If you use the '`--absolute-names`' ('`-P`') option, `tar` will do none of these transformations.

To archive or extract files relative to the root directory, specify the '`--absolute-names`' ('`-P`') option.

Normally, `tar` acts on files relative to the working directory—ignoring superior directory names when archiving, and ignoring leading slashes when extracting.

When you specify '`--absolute-names`' ('`-P`'), `tar` stores file names including all superior directory names, and preserves leading slashes. If you only invoked `tar` from the root directory you would never need the '`--absolute-names`' option, but using this option may be more convenient than switching to root.

'`--absolute-names`'

>   Preserves full file names (including superior directory names) when archiving and extracting files.

`tar` prints out a message about removing the '`/`' from file names. This message appears once per GNU `tar` invocation. It represents something which ought to be told; ignoring what it means can cause very serious surprises, later.

Some people, nevertheless, do not want to see this message. Wanting to play really dangerously, one may of course redirect `tar` standard error to the sink. For example, under `sh`:

---

[5] A side effect of this is that when '`--create`' is used with '`--verbose`' the resulting output is not, generally speaking, the same as the one you'd get running `tar --list` command. This may be important if you use some scripts for comparing both outputs. See [listing member and file names], page 15, for the information on how to handle this case.

```
$ tar -c -f archive.tar /home 2> /dev/null
```

Another solution, both nicer and simpler, would be to change to the '/' directory first, and then avoid absolute notation. For example:

```
$ tar -c -f archive.tar -C / home
```

See Section 10.2.2 [Integrity], page 180, for some of the security-related implications of using this option.

7 Date input formats

First, a quote:

> Our units of temporal measurement, from seconds on up to months, are so complicated, asymmetrical and disjunctive so as to make coherent mental reckoning in time all but impossible. Indeed, had some tyrannical god contrived to enslave our minds to time, to make it all but impossible for us to escape subjection to sodden routines and unpleasant surprises, he could hardly have done better than handing down our present system. It is like a set of trapezoidal building blocks, with no vertical or horizontal surfaces, like a language in which the simplest thought demands ornate constructions, useless particles and lengthy circumlocutions. Unlike the more successful patterns of language and science, which enable us to face experience boldly or at least level-headedly, our system of temporal calculation silently and persistently encourages our terror of time.
>
> ... It is as though architects had to measure length in feet, width in meters and height in ells; as though basic instruction manuals demanded a knowledge of five different languages. It is no wonder then that we often look into our own immediate past or future, last Tuesday or a week from Sunday, with feelings of helpless confusion.
>
> ...
>
> —Robert Grudin, *Time and the Art of Living*.

This section describes the textual date representations that GNU programs accept. These are the strings you, as a user, can supply as arguments to the various programs. The C interface (via the `parse_datetime` function) is not described here.

7.1 General date syntax

A *date* is a string, possibly empty, containing many items separated by whitespace. The whitespace may be omitted when no ambiguity arises. The empty string means the beginning of today (i.e., midnight). Order of the items is immaterial. A date string may contain many flavors of items:

- calendar date items
- time of day items
- time zone items
- combined date and time of day items
- day of the week items
- relative items
- pure numbers.

We describe each of these item types in turn, below.

A few ordinal numbers may be written out in words in some contexts. This is most useful for specifying day of the week items or relative items (see below). Among the most commonly used ordinal numbers, the word 'last' stands for −1, 'this' stands for 0, and 'first' and 'next' both stand for 1. Because the word 'second' stands for the unit of time there is no way to write the ordinal number 2, but for convenience 'third' stands for 3, 'fourth' for 4, 'fifth' for 5, 'sixth' for 6, 'seventh' for 7, 'eighth' for 8, 'ninth' for 9, 'tenth' for 10, 'eleventh' for 11 and 'twelfth' for 12.

When a month is written this way, it is still considered to be written numerically, instead of being "spelled in full"; this changes the allowed strings.

In the current implementation, only English is supported for words and abbreviations like 'AM', 'DST', 'EST', 'first', 'January', 'Sunday', 'tomorrow', and 'year'.

The output of the date command is not always acceptable as a date string, not only because of the language problem, but also because there is no standard meaning for time zone items like 'IST'. When using date to generate a date string intended to be parsed later, specify a date format that is independent of language and that does not use time zone items other than 'UTC' and 'Z'. Here are some ways to do this:

```
$ LC_ALL=C TZ=UTC0 date
Mon Mar  1 00:21:42 UTC 2004
$ TZ=UTC0 date +'%Y-%m-%d %H:%M:%SZ'
2004-03-01 00:21:42Z
$ date --rfc-3339=ns  # --rfc-3339 is a GNU extension.
2004-02-29 16:21:42.692722128-08:00
$ date --rfc-2822  # a GNU extension
Sun, 29 Feb 2004 16:21:42 -0800
$ date +'%Y-%m-%d %H:%M:%S %z'  # %z is a GNU extension.
2004-02-29 16:21:42 -0800
$ date +'@%s.%N'  # %s and %N are GNU extensions.
@1078100502.692722128
```

Alphabetic case is completely ignored in dates. Comments may be introduced between round parentheses, as long as included parentheses are properly nested. Hyphens not followed by a digit are currently ignored. Leading zeros on numbers are ignored.

Invalid dates like '2005-02-29' or times like '24:00' are rejected. In the typical case of a host that does not support leap seconds, a time like '23:59:60' is rejected even if it corresponds to a valid leap second.

7.2 Calendar date items

A *calendar date item* specifies a day of the year. It is specified differently, depending on whether the month is specified numerically or literally. All these strings specify the same calendar date:

```
1972-09-24    # ISO 8601.
```

```
72-9-24              # Assume 19xx for 69 through 99,
                     # 20xx for 00 through 68.
72-09-24             # Leading zeros are ignored.
9/24/72              # Common U.S. writing.
24 September 1972
24 Sept 72           # September has a special abbreviation.
24 Sep 72            # Three-letter abbreviations always allowed.
Sep 24, 1972
24-sep-72
24sep72
```

The year can also be omitted. In this case, the last specified year is used, or the current year if none. For example:

```
9/24
sep 24
```

Here are the rules.

For numeric months, the ISO 8601 format '`year-month-day`' is allowed, where *year* is any positive number, *month* is a number between 01 and 12, and *day* is a number between 01 and 31. A leading zero must be present if a number is less than ten. If *year* is 68 or smaller, then 2000 is added to it; otherwise, if *year* is less than 100, then 1900 is added to it. The construct '`month/day/year`', popular in the United States, is accepted. Also '`month/day`', omitting the year.

Literal months may be spelled out in full: '`January`', '`February`', '`March`', '`April`', '`May`', '`June`', '`July`', '`August`', '`September`', '`October`', '`November`' or '`December`'. Literal months may be abbreviated to their first three letters, possibly followed by an abbreviating dot. It is also permitted to write '`Sept`' instead of '`September`'.

When months are written literally, the calendar date may be given as any of the following:

```
day month year
day month
month day year
day-month-year
```

Or, omitting the year:

```
month day
```

7.3 Time of day items

A *time of day item* in date strings specifies the time on a given day. Here are some examples, all of which represent the same time:

```
20:02:00.000000
20:02
8:02pm
20:02-0500           # In EST (U.S. Eastern Standard Time).
```

More generally, the time of day may be given as '*hour*:*minute*:*second*', where *hour* is a number between 0 and 23, *minute* is a number between 0 and 59, and *second* is a number between 0 and 59 possibly followed by '.' or ',' and a fraction containing one or more digits. Alternatively, ':*second*' can be omitted, in which case it is taken to be zero. On the rare hosts that support leap seconds, *second* may be 60.

If the time is followed by 'am' or 'pm' (or 'a.m.' or 'p.m.'), *hour* is restricted to run from 1 to 12, and ':*minute*' may be omitted (taken to be zero). 'am' indicates the first half of the day, 'pm' indicates the second half of the day. In this notation, 12 is the predecessor of 1: midnight is '12am' while noon is '12pm'. (This is the zero-oriented interpretation of '12am' and '12pm', as opposed to the old tradition derived from Latin which uses '12m' for noon and '12pm' for midnight.)

The time may alternatively be followed by a time zone correction, expressed as '*shhmm*', where *s* is '+' or '-', *hh* is a number of zone hours and *mm* is a number of zone minutes. The zone minutes term, *mm*, may be omitted, in which case the one- or two-digit correction is interpreted as a number of hours. You can also separate *hh* from *mm* with a colon. When a time zone correction is given this way, it forces interpretation of the time relative to Coordinated Universal Time (UTC), overriding any previous specification for the time zone or the local time zone. For example, '+0530' and '+05:30' both stand for the time zone 5.5 hours ahead of UTC (e.g., India). This is the best way to specify a time zone correction by fractional parts of an hour. The maximum zone correction is 24 hours.

Either 'am'/'pm' or a time zone correction may be specified, but not both.

7.4 Time zone items

A *time zone item* specifies an international time zone, indicated by a small set of letters, e.g., 'UTC' or 'Z' for Coordinated Universal Time. Any included periods are ignored. By following a non-daylight-saving time zone by the string 'DST' in a separate word (that is, separated by some white space), the corresponding daylight saving time zone may be specified. Alternatively, a non-daylight-saving time zone can be followed by a time zone correction, to add the two values. This is normally done only for 'UTC'; for example, 'UTC+05:30' is equivalent to '+05:30'.

Time zone items other than 'UTC' and 'Z' are obsolescent and are not recommended, because they are ambiguous; for example, 'EST' has a different meaning in Australia than in the United States. Instead, it's better to use unambiguous numeric time zone corrections like '-0500', as described in the previous section.

If neither a time zone item nor a time zone correction is supplied, time stamps are interpreted using the rules of the default time zone (see Section 7.10 [Specifying time zone rules], page 129).

7.5 Combined date and time of day items

The ISO 8601 date and time of day extended format consists of an ISO 8601 date, a 'T' character separator, and an ISO 8601 time of day. This format is also recognized if the 'T' is replaced by a space.

In this format, the time of day should use 24-hour notation. Fractional seconds are allowed, with either comma or period preceding the fraction. ISO 8601 fractional minutes and hours are not supported. Typically, hosts support nanosecond timestamp resolution; excess precision is silently discarded.

Here are some examples:

```
2012-09-24T20:02:00.052-0500
2012-12-31T23:59:59,999999999+1100
1970-01-01 00:00Z
```

7.6 Day of week items

The explicit mention of a day of the week will forward the date (only if necessary) to reach that day of the week in the future.

Days of the week may be spelled out in full: 'Sunday', 'Monday', 'Tuesday', 'Wednesday', 'Thursday', 'Friday' or 'Saturday'. Days may be abbreviated to their first three letters, optionally followed by a period. The special abbreviations 'Tues' for 'Tuesday', 'Wednes' for 'Wednesday' and 'Thur' or 'Thurs' for 'Thursday' are also allowed.

A number may precede a day of the week item to move forward supplementary weeks. It is best used in expression like 'third monday'. In this context, 'last *day*' or 'next *day*' is also acceptable; they move one week before or after the day that *day* by itself would represent.

A comma following a day of the week item is ignored.

7.7 Relative items in date strings

Relative items adjust a date (or the current date if none) forward or backward. The effects of relative items accumulate. Here are some examples:

```
1 year
1 year ago
3 years
2 days
```

The unit of time displacement may be selected by the string 'year' or 'month' for moving by whole years or months. These are fuzzy units, as years and months are not all of equal duration. More precise units are 'fortnight' which is worth 14 days, 'week' worth 7 days, 'day' worth 24 hours, 'hour' worth 60 minutes, 'minute' or 'min' worth 60 seconds, and 'second' or 'sec' worth one second. An 's' suffix on these units is accepted and ignored.

The unit of time may be preceded by a multiplier, given as an optionally signed number. Unsigned numbers are taken as positively signed. No number at all implies 1 for a multiplier. Following a relative item by the string 'ago' is equivalent to preceding the unit by a multiplier with value −1.

The string 'tomorrow' is worth one day in the future (equivalent to 'day'), the string 'yesterday' is worth one day in the past (equivalent to 'day ago').

The strings 'now' or 'today' are relative items corresponding to zero-valued time displacement, these strings come from the fact a zero-valued time displacement represents the current time when not otherwise changed by previous items. They may be used to stress other items, like in '12:00 today'. The string 'this' also has the meaning of a zero-valued time displacement, but is preferred in date strings like 'this thursday'.

When a relative item causes the resulting date to cross a boundary where the clocks were adjusted, typically for daylight saving time, the resulting date and time are adjusted accordingly.

The fuzz in units can cause problems with relative items. For example, '2003-07-31 -1 month' might evaluate to 2003-07-01, because 2003-06-31 is an invalid date. To determine the previous month more reliably, you can ask for the month before the 15th of the current month. For example:

```
$ date -R
Thu, 31 Jul 2003 13:02:39 -0700
$ date --date='-1 month' +'Last month was %B?'
Last month was July?
$ date --date="$(date +%Y-%m-15) -1 month" +'Last month was %B!'
Last month was June!
```

Also, take care when manipulating dates around clock changes such as daylight saving leaps. In a few cases these have added or subtracted as much as 24 hours from the clock, so it is often wise to adopt universal time by setting the TZ environment variable to 'UTC0' before embarking on calendrical calculations.

7.8 Pure numbers in date strings

The precise interpretation of a pure decimal number depends on the context in the date string.

If the decimal number is of the form *yyyymmdd* and no other calendar date item (see Section 7.2 [Calendar date items], page 124) appears before it in the date string, then *yyyy* is read as the year, *mm* as the month number and *dd* as the day of the month, for the specified calendar date.

If the decimal number is of the form *hhmm* and no other time of day item appears before it in the date string, then *hh* is read as the hour of the day and *mm* as the minute of the hour, for the specified time of day. *mm* can also be omitted.

If both a calendar date and a time of day appear to the left of a number in the date string, but no relative item, then the number overrides the year.

7.9 Seconds since the Epoch

If you precede a number with '@', it represents an internal time stamp as a count of seconds. The number can contain an internal decimal point (either '.' or ','); any excess precision not supported by the internal representation is truncated toward minus infinity. Such a number cannot be combined with any other date item, as it specifies a complete time stamp.

Internally, computer times are represented as a count of seconds since an epoch—a well-defined point of time. On GNU and POSIX systems, the epoch is 1970-01-01 00:00:00 UTC, so '@0' represents this time, '@1' represents 1970-01-01 00:00:01 UTC, and so forth. GNU and most other POSIX-compliant systems support such times as an extension to POSIX, using negative counts, so that '@-1' represents 1969-12-31 23:59:59 UTC.

Traditional Unix systems count seconds with 32-bit two's-complement integers and can represent times from 1901-12-13 20:45:52 through 2038-01-19 03:14:07 UTC. More modern systems use 64-bit counts of seconds with nanosecond subcounts, and can represent all the times in the known lifetime of the universe to a resolution of 1 nanosecond.

On most hosts, these counts ignore the presence of leap seconds. For example, on most hosts '@915148799' represents 1998-12-31 23:59:59 UTC, '@915148800' represents 1999-01-01 00:00:00 UTC, and there is no way to represent the intervening leap second 1998-12-31 23:59:60 UTC.

7.10 Specifying time zone rules

Normally, dates are interpreted using the rules of the current time zone, which in turn are specified by the TZ environment variable, or by a system default if TZ is not set. To specify a different set of default time zone rules that apply just to one date, start the date with a string of the form 'TZ="*rule*"'. The two quote characters ('"') must be present in the date, and any quotes or backslashes within *rule* must be escaped by a backslash.

For example, with the GNU date command you can answer the question "What time is it in New York when a Paris clock shows 6:30am on October 31, 2004?" by using a date beginning with 'TZ="Europe/Paris"' as shown in the following shell transcript:

```
$ export TZ="America/New_York"
$ date --date='TZ="Europe/Paris" 2004-10-31 06:30'
Sun Oct 31 01:30:00 EDT 2004
```

In this example, the '--date' operand begins with its own TZ setting, so the rest of that operand is processed according to 'Europe/Paris' rules, treating the string '2004-10-31 06:30' as if it were in Paris. However, since the output of the date command is processed according to the overall time zone rules, it uses New York time. (Paris was normally six hours ahead of New York in 2004, but this example refers to a brief Halloween period when the gap was five hours.)

A TZ value is a rule that typically names a location in the 'tz' database. A recent catalog of location names appears in the TWiki Date and Time Gateway. A few non-GNU hosts require a colon before a location name in a TZ setting, e.g., 'TZ=":America/New_York"'.

The 'tz' database includes a wide variety of locations ranging from 'Arctic/Longyearbyen' to 'Antarctica/South_Pole', but if you are at sea and have your own private time zone, or if you are using a non-GNU host that does not support the 'tz' database, you may need to use a POSIX rule instead. Simple POSIX rules like 'UTC0' specify a time zone without daylight saving time; other rules can specify simple daylight saving regimes. See section "Specifying the Time Zone with TZ" in *The GNU C Library*.

7.11 Authors of parse_datetime

parse_datetime started life as getdate, as originally implemented by Steven M. Bellovin (smb@research.att.com) while at the University of North Carolina at Chapel Hill. The code was later tweaked by a couple of people on Usenet, then completely overhauled by Rich $alz (rsalz@bbn.com) and Jim Berets (jberets@bbn.com) in August, 1990. Various revisions for the GNU system were made by David MacKenzie, Jim Meyering, Paul Eggert and others, including renaming it to get_date to avoid a conflict with the alternative Posix function getdate, and a later rename to parse_datetime. The Posix function getdate can parse more locale-specific dates using strptime, but relies on an environment variable and external file, and lacks the thread-safety of parse_datetime.

This chapter was originally produced by François Pinard (pinard@iro.umontreal.ca) from the 'parse_datetime.y' source code, and then edited by K. Berry (kb@cs.umb.edu).

8 Controlling the Archive Format

Due to historical reasons, there are several formats of tar archives. All of them are based on the same principles, but have some subtle differences that often make them incompatible with each other.

GNU tar is able to create and handle archives in a variety of formats. The most frequently used formats are (in alphabetical order):

gnu   Format used by GNU `tar` versions up to 1.13.25. This format derived from an early POSIX standard, adding some improvements such as sparse file handling and incremental archives. Unfortunately these features were implemented in a way incompatible with other archive formats.

           Archives in 'gnu' format are able to hold file names of unlimited length.

oldgnu   Format used by GNU `tar` of versions prior to 1.12.

v7   Archive format, compatible with the V7 implementation of tar. This format imposes a number of limitations. The most important of them are:

           1. The maximum length of a file name is limited to 99 characters.

           2. The maximum length of a symbolic link is limited to 99 characters.

           3. It is impossible to store special files (block and character devices, fifos etc.)

           4. Maximum value of user or group ID is limited to 2097151 (7777777 octal)

           5. V7 archives do not contain symbolic ownership information (user and group name of the file owner).

           This format has traditionally been used by Automake when producing Makefiles. This practice will change in the future, in the meantime, however this means that projects containing file names more than 99 characters long will not be able to use GNU `tar` 1.28 and Automake prior to 1.9.

ustar   Archive format defined by POSIX.1-1988 specification. It stores symbolic ownership information. It is also able to store special files. However, it imposes several restrictions as well:

           1. The maximum length of a file name is limited to 256 characters, provided that the file name can be split at a directory separator in two parts, first of them being at most 155 bytes long. So, in most cases the maximum file name length will be shorter than 256 characters.

2. The maximum length of a symbolic link name is limited to 100 characters.

3. Maximum size of a file the archive is able to accommodate is 8GB

4. Maximum value of UID/GID is 2097151.

5. Maximum number of bits in device major and minor numbers is 21.

star   Format used by Jörg Schilling `star` implementation. GNU `tar` is able to read '`star`' archives but currently does not produce them.

posix   Archive format defined by POSIX.1-2001 specification. This is the most flexible and feature-rich format. It does not impose any restrictions on file sizes or file name lengths. This format is quite recent, so not all tar implementations are able to handle it properly. However, this format is designed in such a way that any tar implementation able to read '`ustar`' archives will be able to read most '`posix`' archives as well, with the only exception that any additional information (such as long file names etc.) will in such case be extracted as plain text files along with the files it refers to.

                This archive format will be the default format for future versions of GNU `tar`.

The following table summarizes the limitations of each of these formats:

Format	UID	File Size	File Name	Devn
gnu	1.8e19	Unlimited	Unlimited	63
oldgnu	1.8e19	Unlimited	Unlimited	63
v7	2097151	8GB	99	n/a
ustar	2097151	8GB	256	21
posix	Unlimited	Unlimited	Unlimited	Unlimited

The default format for GNU `tar` is defined at compilation time. You may check it by running `tar --help`, and examining the last lines of its output. Usually, GNU `tar` is configured to create archives in '`gnu`' format, however, future version will switch to '`posix`'.

8.1 Using Less Space through Compression

8.1.1 Creating and Reading Compressed Archives

GNU `tar` is able to create and read compressed archives. It supports a wide variety of compression programs, namely: `gzip`, `bzip2`, `lzip`, `lzma`, `lzop`, `xz` and traditional `compress`. The latter is supported mostly for backward compatibility, and we recommend against using it, because it is by far less effective than the other compression programs[1].

Creating a compressed archive is simple: you just specify a *compression option* along with the usual archive creation commands. The compression option is '-z' ('--gzip') to create a `gzip` compressed archive, '-j' ('--bzip2') to create a `bzip2` compressed archive, '--lzip' to create an lzip compressed archive, '-J' ('--xz') to create an XZ archive, '--lzma' to create an LZMA compressed archive, '--lzop' to create an LSOP archive, and '-Z' ('--compress') to use `compress` program. For example:

```
$ tar czf archive.tar.gz .
```

You can also let GNU `tar` select the compression program based on the suffix of the archive file name. This is done using '--auto-compress' ('-a') command line option. For example, the following invocation will use `bzip2` for compression:

```
$ tar caf archive.tar.bz2 .
```

whereas the following one will use `lzma`:

```
$ tar caf archive.tar.lzma .
```

For a complete list of file name suffixes recognized by GNU `tar`, see [auto-compress], page 135.

Reading compressed archive is even simpler: you don't need to specify any additional options as GNU `tar` recognizes its format automatically. Thus, the following commands will list and extract the archive created in previous example:

```
# List the compressed archive
$ tar tf archive.tar.gz
# Extract the compressed archive
$ tar xf archive.tar.gz
```

The format recognition algorithm is based on *signatures*, a special byte sequences in the beginning of file, that are specific for certain compression formats. If this approach fails, `tar` falls back to using archive name suffix to determine its format (see [auto-compress], page 135, for a list of recognized suffixes).

Some compression programs are able to handle different compression formats. GNU `tar` uses this, if the principal decompressor for the given format is not available. For example, if `compress` is not installed, `tar` will try to use `gzip`. As of version 1.28 the following alternatives are tried[2]:

Format	Main decompressor	Alternatives
compress	compress	gzip
lzma	lzma	xz
bzip2	bzip2	lbzip2

---

[1] It also had patent problems in the past.

[2] To verbosely trace the decompressor selection, use the '--warning=decompress-program' option (see Section 3.9 [warnings], page 56).

The only case when you have to specify a decompression option while reading the archive is when reading from a pipe or from a tape drive that does not support random access. However, in this case GNU `tar` will indicate which option you should use. For example:

```
$ cat archive.tar.gz | tar tf -
tar: Archive is compressed.  Use -z option
tar: Error is not recoverable: exiting now
```

If you see such diagnostics, just add the suggested option to the invocation of GNU `tar`:

```
$ cat archive.tar.gz | tar tzf -
```

Notice also, that there are several restrictions on operations on compressed archives. First of all, compressed archives cannot be modified, i.e., you cannot update ('--update', alias '-u') them or delete ('--delete') members from them or add ('--append', alias '-r') members to them. Likewise, you cannot append another `tar` archive to a compressed archive using '--concatenate' ('-A'). Secondly, multi-volume archives cannot be compressed.

The following options allow to select a particular compressor program:

'-z'
'--gzip'
'--ungzip'
      Filter the archive through `gzip`.

'-J'
'--xz'   Filter the archive through `xz`.

'-j'
'--bzip2' Filter the archive through `bzip2`.

'--lzip'   Filter the archive through `lzip`.

'--lzma'   Filter the archive through `lzma`.

'--lzop'   Filter the archive through `lzop`.

'-Z'
'--compress'
'--uncompress'
      Filter the archive through `compress`.

When any of these options is given, GNU `tar` searches the compressor binary in the current path and invokes it. The name of the compressor program is specified at compilation time using a corresponding '--with-*compname*' option to `configure`, e.g. '--with-bzip2' to select a specific `bzip2` binary. See Section 8.1.1.1 [lbzip2], page 136, for a detailed discussion.

The output produced by `tar --help` shows the actual compressor names along with each of these options.

You can use any of these options on physical devices (tape drives, etc.) and remote files as well as on normal files; data to or from such devices or remote files is reblocked by another copy of the `tar` program to enforce the specified (or default) record size. The default compression parameters are used. Most compression programs let you override these by setting a program-specific environment variable. For example, with `gzip` you can set GZIP:

```
$ GZIP='-9 -n' tar czf archive.tar.gz subdir
```

Another way would be to use the '`-I`' option instead (see below), e.g.:

```
$ tar -cf archive.tar.gz -I 'gzip -9 -n' subdir
```

Finally, the third, traditional, way to do this is to use a pipe:

```
$ tar cf - subdir | gzip -9 -n > archive.tar.gz
```

Compressed archives are easily corrupted, because compressed files have little redundancy. The adaptive nature of the compression scheme means that the compression tables are implicitly spread all over the archive. If you lose a few blocks, the dynamic construction of the compression tables becomes unsynchronized, and there is little chance that you could recover later in the archive.

Other compression options provide better control over creating compressed archives. These are:

'`--auto-compress`'

'`-a`'   Select a compression program to use by the archive file name suffix. The following suffixes are recognized:

Suffix	Compression program
'`.gz`'	gzip
'`.tgz`'	gzip
'`.taz`'	gzip
'`.Z`'	compress
'`.taZ`'	compress
'`.bz2`'	bzip2
'`.tz2`'	bzip2
'`.tbz2`'	bzip2
'`.tbz`'	bzip2
'`.lz`'	lzip
'`.lzma`'	lzma
'`.tlz`'	lzma
'`.lzo`'	lzop
'`.xz`'	xz

'`--use-compress-program=command`'

'`-I=command`'

Use external compression program *command*. Use this option if you are not happy with the compression program associated with the suffix at compile time or if you have a compression program that GNU `tar` does not support. The *command* argument is a valid command invocation, as you would type it at the command line prompt, with any additional options as needed. Enclose it in quotes if it contains white space (see Section 3.11 [external], page 59, for more detail).

The *command* should follow two conventions:

First, when invoked without additional options, it should read data from standard input, compress it and output it on standard output.

Secondly, if invoked with the additional '-d' option, it should do exactly the opposite, i.e., read the compressed data from the standard input and produce uncompressed data on the standard output.

The latter requirement means that you must not use the '-d' option as a part of the *command* itself.

The '--use-compress-program' option, in particular, lets you implement your own filters, not necessarily dealing with compression/decompression. For example, suppose you wish to implement PGP encryption on top of compression, using **gpg** (see section "gpg —- encryption and signing tool" in *GNU Privacy Guard Manual*). The following script does that:

```
#! /bin/sh
case $1 in
-d) gpg --decrypt - | gzip -d -c;;
'') gzip -c | gpg -s;;
*)  echo "Unknown option $1">&2; exit 1;;
esac
```

Suppose you name it 'gpgz' and save it somewhere in your PATH. Then the following command will create a compressed archive signed with your private key:

```
$ tar -cf foo.tar.gpgz -Igpgz .
```

Likewise, the command below will list its contents:

```
$ tar -tf foo.tar.gpgz -Igpgz .
```

8.1.1.1 Using lbzip2 with GNU tar.

Lbzip2 is a multithreaded utility for handling 'bzip2' compression, written by Laszlo Ersek. It makes use of multiple processors to speed up its operation and in general works considerably faster than **bzip2**. For a detailed description of **lbzip2** see http://freshmeat.net/projects/lbzip2 and lbzip2: parallel bzip2 utility.

Recent versions of **lbzip2** are mostly command line compatible with **bzip2**, which makes it possible to automatically invoke it via the '--bzip2' GNU **tar** command line option. To do so, GNU **tar** must be configured with the '--with-bzip2' command line option, like this:

```
$ ./configure --with-bzip2=lbzip2 [other-options]
```

Once configured and compiled this way, **tar** --help will show the following:

```
$ tar --help | grep -- --bzip2
  -j, --bzip2                    filter the archive through lbzip2
```

which means that running `tar --bzip2` will invoke `lbzip2`.

8.1.2 Archiving Sparse Files

Files in the file system occasionally have *holes*. A *hole* in a file is a section of the file's contents which was never written. The contents of a hole reads as all zeros. On many operating systems, actual disk storage is not allocated for holes, but they are counted in the length of the file. If you archive such a file, `tar` could create an archive longer than the original. To have `tar` attempt to recognize the holes in a file, use '`--sparse`' ('`-S`'). When you use this option, then, for any file using less disk space than would be expected from its length, `tar` searches the file for consecutive stretches of zeros. It then records in the archive for the file where the consecutive stretches of zeros are, and only archives the "real contents" of the file. On extraction (using '`--sparse`' is not needed on extraction) any such files have holes created wherever the continuous stretches of zeros were found. Thus, if you use '`--sparse`', `tar` archives won't take more space than the original.

'`-S`'

'`--sparse`'

> This option instructs `tar` to test each file for sparseness before attempting to archive it. If the file is found to be sparse it is treated specially, thus allowing to decrease the amount of space used by its image in the archive.

> This option is meaningful only when creating or updating archives. It has no effect on extraction.

Consider using '`--sparse`' when performing file system backups, to avoid archiving the expanded forms of files stored sparsely in the system.

Even if your system has no sparse files currently, some may be created in the future. If you use '`--sparse`' while making file system backups as a matter of course, you can be assured the archive will never take more space on the media than the files take on disk (otherwise, archiving a disk filled with sparse files might take hundreds of tapes). See Section 5.2 [Incremental Dumps], page 84.

However, be aware that '`--sparse`' option presents a serious drawback. Namely, in order to determine if the file is sparse `tar` has to read it before trying to archive it, so in total the file is read **twice**. So, always bear in mind that the time needed to process all files with this option is roughly twice the time needed to archive them without it.

When using '`POSIX`' archive format, GNU `tar` is able to store sparse files using in three distinct ways, called *sparse formats*. A sparse format is identified by its *number*, consisting, as usual of two decimal numbers, delimited by a dot. By default, format '`1.0`' is used. If, for some reason, you wish to use an earlier format, you can select it using '--sparse-version' option.

'--sparse-version=*version*'

>Select the format to store sparse files in. Valid *version* values are: '0.0', '0.1' and '1.0'. See [Sparse Formats], page 202, for a detailed description of each format.

Using '--sparse-format' option implies '--sparse'.

8.2 Handling File Attributes

When tar reads files, it updates their access times. To avoid this, use the '--atime-preserve[=METHOD]' option, which can either reset the access time retroactively or avoid changing it in the first place.

'--atime-preserve'
'--atime-preserve=replace'
'--atime-preserve=system'

>Preserve the access times of files that are read. This works only for files that you own, unless you have superuser privileges.

>'--atime-preserve=replace' works on most systems, but it also restores the data modification time and updates the status change time. Hence it doesn't interact with incremental dumps nicely (see Section 5.2 [Incremental Dumps], page 84), and it can set access or data modification times incorrectly if other programs access the file while tar is running.

>'--atime-preserve=system' avoids changing the access time in the first place, if the operating system supports this. Unfortunately, this may or may not work on any given operating system or file system. If tar knows for sure it won't work, it complains right away.

>Currently '--atime-preserve' with no operand defaults to '--atime-preserve=replace', but this is intended to change to '--atime-preserve=system' when the latter is better-supported.

'-m'
'--touch'   Do not extract data modification time.

>When this option is used, tar leaves the data modification times of the files it extracts as the times when the files were extracted, instead of setting it to the times recorded in the archive.

>This option is meaningless with '--list' ('-t').

'--same-owner'

>Create extracted files with the same ownership they have in the archive.

This is the default behavior for the superuser, so this option
is meaningful only for non-root users, when `tar` is executed on
those systems able to give files away. This is considered as a
security flaw by many people, at least because it makes quite
difficult to correctly account users for the disk space they occupy.
Also, the `suid` or `sgid` attributes of files are easily and silently
lost when files are given away.

When writing an archive, `tar` writes the user ID and user name
separately. If it can't find a user name (because the user ID
is not in '`/etc/passwd`'), then it does not write one. When
restoring, it tries to look the name (if one was written) up in
'`/etc/passwd`'. If it fails, then it uses the user ID stored in the
archive instead.

'`--no-same-owner`'
'`-o`'   Do not attempt to restore ownership when extracting. This is
                the default behavior for ordinary users, so this option has an
                effect only for the superuser.

'`--numeric-owner`'
                The '`--numeric-owner`' option allows (ANSI) archives to be
                written without user/group name information or such informa-
                tion to be ignored when extracting. It effectively disables the
                generation and/or use of user/group name information. This
                option forces extraction using the numeric ids from the archive,
                ignoring the names.

                This is useful in certain circumstances, when restoring a backup
                from an emergency floppy with different passwd/group files for
                example. It is otherwise impossible to extract files with the
                right ownerships if the password file in use during the extraction
                does not match the one belonging to the file system(s) being ex-
                tracted. This occurs, for example, if you are restoring your files
                after a major crash and had booted from an emergency floppy
                with no password file or put your disk into another machine to
                do the restore.

                The numeric ids are *always* saved into `tar` archives. The iden-
                tifying names are added at create time when provided by the
                system, unless '`--format=oldgnu`' is used. Numeric ids could
                be used when moving archives between a collection of machines
                using a centralized management for attribution of numeric ids
                to users and groups. This is often made through using the NIS
                capabilities.

                When making a `tar` file for distribution to other sites, it is some-
                times cleaner to use a single owner for all files in the distribu-
                tion, and nicer to specify the write permission bits of the files as
                stored in the archive independently of their actual value on the

file system. The way to prepare a clean distribution is usually to have some Makefile rule creating a directory, copying all needed files in that directory, then setting ownership and permissions as wanted (there are a lot of possible schemes), and only then making a `tar` archive out of this directory, before cleaning everything out. Of course, we could add a lot of options to GNU `tar` for fine tuning permissions and ownership. This is not the good way, I think. GNU `tar` is already crowded with options and moreover, the approach just explained gives you a great deal of control already.

'`-p`'
'`--same-permissions`'
'`--preserve-permissions`'

Extract all protection information.

This option causes `tar` to set the modes (access permissions) of extracted files exactly as recorded in the archive. If this option is not used, the current `umask` setting limits the permissions on extracted files. This option is by default enabled when `tar` is executed by a superuser.

This option is meaningless with '`--list`' ('`-t`').

'`--preserve`'

Same as both '`--same-permissions`' and '`--same-order`'.

This option is deprecated, and will be removed in GNU `tar` version 1.23.

8.3 Making tar Archives More Portable

Creating a `tar` archive on a particular system that is meant to be useful later on many other machines and with other versions of `tar` is more challenging than you might think. `tar` archive formats have been evolving since the first versions of Unix. Many such formats are around, and are not always compatible with each other. This section discusses a few problems, and gives some advice about making `tar` archives more portable.

One golden rule is simplicity. For example, limit your `tar` archives to contain only regular files and directories, avoiding other kind of special files. Do not attempt to save sparse files or contiguous files as such. Let's discuss a few more problems, in turn.

8.3.1 Portable Names

Use portable file and member names. A name is portable if it contains only ASCII letters and digits, '`/`', '`.`', '`_`', and '`-`'; it cannot be empty, start with '`-`' or '`//`', or contain '`/-`'. Avoid deep directory nesting. For portability to old Unix hosts, limit your file name components to 14 characters or less.

If you intend to have your `tar` archives to be read under MSDOS, you should not rely on case distinction for file names, and you might use the GNU `doschk` program for helping you further diagnosing illegal MSDOS names, which are even more limited than System V's.

8.3.2 Symbolic Links

Normally, when `tar` archives a symbolic link, it writes a block to the archive naming the target of the link. In that way, the `tar` archive is a faithful record of the file system contents. When '--dereference' ('-h') is used with '--create' ('-c'), `tar` archives the files symbolic links point to, instead of the links themselves.

When creating portable archives, use '--dereference' ('-h'): some systems do not support symbolic links, and moreover, your distribution might be unusable if it contains unresolved symbolic links.

When reading from an archive, the '--dereference' ('-h') option causes `tar` to follow an already-existing symbolic link when `tar` writes or reads a file named in the archive. Ordinarily, `tar` does not follow such a link, though it may remove the link before writing a new file. See [Dealing with Old Files], page 72.

The '--dereference' option is unsafe if an untrusted user can modify directories while `tar` is running. See Section 10.2 [Security], page 180.

8.3.3 Hard Links

Normally, when `tar` archives a hard link, it writes a block to the archive naming the target of the link (a '1' type block). In that way, the actual file contents is stored in file only once. For example, consider the following two files:

```
$ ls -l
-rw-r--r-- 2 gray staff 4 2007-10-30 15:11 one
-rw-r--r-- 2 gray staff 4 2007-10-30 15:11 jeden
```

Here, 'jeden' is a link to 'one'. When archiving this directory with a verbose level 2, you will get an output similar to the following:

```
$ tar cvvf ../archive.tar .
drwxr-xr-x gray/staff        0 2007-10-30 15:13 ./
-rw-r--r-- gray/staff        4 2007-10-30 15:11 ./jeden
hrw-r--r-- gray/staff        0 2007-10-30 15:11 ./one link to ./jeden
```

The last line shows that, instead of storing two copies of the file, `tar` stored it only once, under the name 'jeden', and stored file 'one' as a hard link to this file.

It may be important to know that all hard links to the given file are stored in the archive. For example, this may be necessary for exact reproduction of the file system. The following option does that:

'`--check-links`'
'`-l`'   Check the number of links dumped for each processed file. If
               this number does not match the total number of hard links for
               the file, print a warning message.

For example, trying to archive only file '`jeden`' with this option produces
the following diagnostics:

```
$ tar -c -f ../archive.tar -l jeden
tar: Missing links to 'jeden'.
```

Although creating special records for hard links helps keep a faithful
record of the file system contents and makes archives more compact, it
may present some difficulties when extracting individual members from the
archive. For example, trying to extract file '`one`' from the archive created in
previous examples produces, in the absense of file '`jeden`':

```
$ tar xf archive.tar ./one
tar: ./one: Cannot hard link to './jeden': No such file or directory
tar: Error exit delayed from previous errors
```

The reason for this behavior is that **tar** cannot seek back in the archive
to the previous member (in this case, '`one`'), to extract it[3]. If you wish to
avoid such problems at the cost of a bigger archive, use the following option:

'`--hard-dereference`'
               Dereference hard links and store the files they refer to.

For example, trying this option on our two sample files, we get two copies
in the archive, each of which can then be extracted independently of the
other:

```
$ tar -c -vv -f ../archive.tar --hard-dereference .
drwxr-xr-x gray/staff        0 2007-10-30 15:13 ./
-rw-r--r-- gray/staff        4 2007-10-30 15:11 ./jeden
-rw-r--r-- gray/staff        4 2007-10-30 15:11 ./one
```

8.3.4 Old V7 Archives

Certain old versions of **tar** cannot handle additional information recorded
by newer **tar** programs. To create an archive in V7 format (not ANSI),
which can be read by these old versions, specify the '`--format=v7`' option in
conjunction with the '`--create`' ('`-c`') (**tar** also accepts '`--portability`'
or '`--old-archive`' for this option). When you specify it, **tar** leaves out
information about directories, pipes, fifos, contiguous files, and device files,
and specifies file ownership by group and user IDs instead of group and user
names.

When updating an archive, do not use '`--format=v7`' unless the archive
was created using this option.

In most cases, a *new* format archive can be read by an *old* **tar** program
without serious trouble, so this option should seldom be needed. On the

---

[3] There are plans to fix this in future releases.

other hand, most modern `tars` are able to read old format archives, so it might be safer for you to always use '`--format=v7`' for your distributions. Notice, however, that '`ustar`' format is a better alternative, as it is free from many of '`v7`''s drawbacks.

8.3.5 Ustar Archive Format

The archive format defined by the POSIX.1-1988 specification is called `ustar`. Although it is more flexible than the V7 format, it still has many restrictions (see Chapter 8 [Formats], page 131, for the detailed description of `ustar` format). Along with V7 format, `ustar` format is a good choice for archives intended to be read with other implementations of `tar`.

To create an archive in `ustar` format, use the '`--format=ustar`' option in conjunction with '`--create`' ('`-c`').

8.3.6 GNU **and old** GNU `tar` **format**

GNU `tar` was based on an early draft of the POSIX 1003.1 `ustar` standard. GNU extensions to `tar`, such as the support for file names longer than 100 characters, use portions of the `tar` header record which were specified in that POSIX draft as unused. Subsequent changes in POSIX have allocated the same parts of the header record for other purposes. As a result, GNU `tar` format is incompatible with the current POSIX specification, and with `tar` programs that follow it.

In the majority of cases, `tar` will be configured to create this format by default. This will change in future releases, since we plan to make '`POSIX`' format the default.

To force creation a GNU `tar` archive, use option '`--format=gnu`'.

8.3.7 GNU `tar` **and** POSIX `tar`

Starting from version 1.14 GNU `tar` features full support for POSIX.1-2001 archives.

A POSIX conformant archive will be created if `tar` was given '`--format=posix`' ('`--format=pax`') option. No special option is required to read and extract from a POSIX archive.

8.3.7.1 Controlling Extended Header Keywords

'`--pax-option=`*keyword-list*'
>   Handle keywords in PAX extended headers. This option is equivalent to '`-o`' option of the `pax` utility.

Keyword-list is a comma-separated list of keyword options, each keyword option taking one of the following forms:

`delete=`*pattern*

> When used with one of archive-creation commands, this option instructs `tar` to omit from extended header records that it produces any keywords matching the string *pattern*.
>
> When used in extract or list mode, this option instructs tar to ignore any keywords matching the given *pattern* in the extended header records. In both cases, matching is performed using the pattern matching notation described in POSIX 1003.2, 3.13 (see Section 6.5 [wildcards], page 106). For example:
>
> ```
> --pax-option delete=security.*
> ```
>
> would suppress security-related information.

`exthdr.name=`*string*

> This keyword allows user control over the name that is written into the ustar header blocks for the extended headers. The name is obtained from *string* after making the following substitutions:

Meta-character	Replaced By
%d	The directory name of the file, equivalent to the result of the `dirname` utility on the translated file name.
%f	The name of the file with the directory information stripped, equivalent to the result of the `basename` utility on the translated file name.
%p	The process ID of the `tar` process.
%%	A '%' character.

> Any other '%' characters in *string* produce undefined results.
>
> If no option 'exthdr.name=string' is specified, `tar` will use the following default value:
>
> ```
> %d/PaxHeaders.%p/%f
> ```

`exthdr.mtime=`*value*

> This keyword defines the value of the 'mtime' field that is written into the ustar header blocks for the extended headers. By default, the 'mtime' field is set to the modification time of the archive member described by that extended headers.

`globexthdr.name=`*string*

> This keyword allows user control over the name that is written into the ustar header blocks for global extended header records. The name is obtained from the contents of *string*, after making the following substitutions:

Meta-character	Replaced By

%n   An integer that represents the sequence
                               number of the global extended header
                               record in the archive, starting at 1.

%p   The process ID of the `tar` process.

%%   A '%' character.

Any other '%' characters in *string* produce undefined results.

If no option '`globexthdr.name=string`' is specified, `tar` will
use the following default value:

    $TMPDIR/GlobalHead.%p.%n

where '`$TMPDIR`' represents the value of the *TMPDIR* environment variable. If *TMPDIR* is not set, `tar` uses '`/tmp`'.

`globexthdr.mtime=value`

This keyword defines the value of the '`mtime`' field that is written
into the ustar header blocks for the global extended headers. By
default, the '`mtime`' field is set to the time when `tar` was invoked.

`keyword=value`

When used with one of archive-creation commands, these key-
word/value pairs will be included at the beginning of the archive
in a global extended header record. When used with one of
archive-reading commands, `tar` will behave as if it has encountered these keyword/value pairs at the beginning of the archive
in a global extended header record.

`keyword:=value`

When used with one of archive-creation commands, these key-
word/value pairs will be included as records at the beginning of
an extended header for each file. This is effectively equivalent to
keyword=value form except that it creates no global extended
header records.

When used with one of archive-reading commands, `tar` will behave as if these keyword/value pairs were included as records at
the end of each extended header; thus, they will override any
global or file-specific extended header record keywords of the
same names. For example, in the command:

    tar --format=posix --create \
        --file archive --pax-option gname:=user .

the group name will be forced to a new value for all files stored
in the archive.

In any of the forms described above, the *value* may be a string enclosed
in curly braces. In that case, the string between the braces is understood
either as a textual time representation, as described in Chapter 7 [Date input
formats], page 123, or a name of the existing file, starting with '/' or '.'. In
the latter case, the modification time of that file is used.

For example, to set all modification times to the current date, you use the following option:

```
--pax-option='mtime:={now}'
```

Note quoting of the option's argument.

As another example, here is the option that ensures that any two archives created using it, will be binary equivalent if they have the same contents:

```
--pax-option=exthdr.name=%d/PaxHeaders/%f,atime:=0
```

8.3.8 Checksumming Problems

SunOS and HP-UX **tar** fail to accept archives created using GNU **tar** and containing non-ASCII file names, that is, file names having characters with the eighth bit set, because they use signed checksums, while GNU **tar** uses unsigned checksums while creating archives, as per POSIX standards. On reading, GNU **tar** computes both checksums and accepts either of them. It is somewhat worrying that a lot of people may go around doing backup of their files using faulty (or at least non-standard) software, not learning about it until it's time to restore their missing files with an incompatible file extractor, or vice versa.

GNU **tar** computes checksums both ways, and accepts either of them on read, so GNU tar can read Sun tapes even with their wrong checksums. GNU **tar** produces the standard checksum, however, raising incompatibilities with Sun. That is to say, GNU **tar** has not been modified to *produce* incorrect archives to be read by buggy **tar**'s. I've been told that more recent Sun **tar** now read standard archives, so maybe Sun did a similar patch, after all?

The story seems to be that when Sun first imported **tar** sources on their system, they recompiled it without realizing that the checksums were computed differently, because of a change in the default signing of **char**'s in their compiler. So they started computing checksums wrongly. When they later realized their mistake, they merely decided to stay compatible with it, and with themselves afterwards. Presumably, but I do not really know, HP-UX has chosen their **tar** archives to be compatible with Sun's. The current standards do not favor Sun **tar** format. In any case, it now falls on the shoulders of SunOS and HP-UX users to get a **tar** able to read the good archives they receive.

8.3.9 Large or Negative Values

(This message will disappear, once this node revised.)

The above sections suggest to use 'oldest possible' archive format if in doubt. However, sometimes it is not possible. If you attempt to archive a file whose metadata cannot be represented using required format, GNU **tar** will print error message and ignore such a file. You will than have to switch to a format that is able to handle such values. The format summary table (see Chapter 8 [Formats], page 131) will help you to do so.

In particular, when trying to archive files larger than 8GB or with time-stamps not in the range 1970-01-01 00:00:00 through 2242-03-16 12:56:31 UTC, you will have to chose between GNU and POSIX archive formats. When considering which format to choose, bear in mind that the GNU format uses two's-complement base-256 notation to store values that do not fit into standard ustar range. Such archives can generally be read only by a GNU `tar` implementation. Moreover, they sometimes cannot be correctly restored on another hosts even by GNU `tar`. For example, using two's complement representation for negative time stamps that assumes a signed 32-bit `time_t` generates archives that are not portable to hosts with differing `time_t` representations.

On the other hand, POSIX archives, generally speaking, can be extracted by any tar implementation that understands older ustar format. The only exception are files larger than 8GB.

8.3.10 How to Extract GNU-Specific Data Using Other tar Implementations

In previous sections you became acquainted with various quirks necessary to make your archives portable. Sometimes you may need to extract archives containing GNU-specific members using some third-party `tar` implementation or an older version of GNU `tar`. Of course your best bet is to have GNU `tar` installed, but if it is for some reason impossible, this section will explain how to cope without it.

When we speak about *GNU-specific* members we mean two classes of them: members split between the volumes of a multi-volume archive and sparse members. You will be able to always recover such members if the archive is in PAX format. In addition split members can be recovered from archives in old GNU format. The following subsections describe the required procedures in detail.

8.3.10.1 Extracting Members Split Between Volumes

If a member is split between several volumes of an old GNU format archive most third party `tar` implementation will fail to extract it. To extract it, use `tarcat` program (see Section 9.6.3 [Tarcat], page 173). This program is available from GNU tar home page. It concatenates several archive volumes into a single valid archive. For example, if you have three volumes named from 'vol-1.tar' to 'vol-3.tar', you can do the following to extract them using a third-party `tar`:

```
$ tarcat vol-1.tar vol-2.tar vol-3.tar | tar xf -
```

You could use this approach for most (although not all) PAX format archives as well. However, extracting split members from a PAX archive is a much easier task, because PAX volumes are constructed in such a way that each part of a split member is extracted to a different file by `tar` implementations that are not aware of GNU extensions. More specifically, the very first part retains its original name, and all subsequent parts are named using the pattern:

```
%d/GNUFileParts.%p/%f.%n
```

where symbols preceeded by '%' are *macro characters* that have the following meaning:

Meta-character	Replaced By
%d	The directory name of the file, equivalent to the result of the `dirname` utility on its full name.
%f	The file name of the file, equivalent to the result of the `basename` utility on its full name.
%p	The process ID of the `tar` process that created the archive.
%n	Ordinal number of this particular part.

For example, if the file 'var/longfile' was split during archive creation between three volumes, and the creator `tar` process had process ID '27962', then the member names will be:

```
var/longfile
var/GNUFileParts.27962/longfile.1
var/GNUFileParts.27962/longfile.2
```

When you extract your archive using a third-party `tar`, these files will be created on your disk, and the only thing you will need to do to restore your file in its original form is concatenate them in the proper order, for example:

```
$ cd var
$ cat GNUFileParts.27962/longfile.1 \
  GNUFileParts.27962/longfile.2 >> longfile
$ rm -f GNUFileParts.27962
```

Notice, that if the `tar` implementation you use supports PAX format archives, it will probably emit warnings about unknown keywords during extraction. They will look like this:

```
Tar file too small
Unknown extended header keyword 'GNU.volume.filename' ignored.
Unknown extended header keyword 'GNU.volume.size' ignored.
Unknown extended header keyword 'GNU.volume.offset' ignored.
```

You can safely ignore these warnings.

If your `tar` implementation is not PAX-aware, you will get more warnings and more files generated on your disk, e.g.:

```
$ tar xf vol-1.tar
var/PaxHeaders.27962/longfile: Unknown file type 'x', extracted as
normal file
Unexpected EOF in archive
$ tar xf vol-2.tar
tmp/GlobalHead.27962.1: Unknown file type 'g', extracted as normal file
GNUFileParts.27962/PaxHeaders.27962/sparsefile.1: Unknown file type
'x', extracted as normal file
```

Ignore these warnings. The 'PaxHeaders.*' directories created will contain files with *extended header keywords* describing the extracted files. You can delete them, unless they describe sparse members. Read further to learn more about them.

8.3.10.2 Extracting Sparse Members

Any `tar` implementation will be able to extract sparse members from a PAX archive. However, the extracted files will be *condensed*, i.e., any zero blocks will be removed from them. When we restore such a condensed file to its original form, by adding zero blocks (or *holes*) back to their original locations, we call this process *expanding* a compressed sparse file.

To expand a file, you will need a simple auxiliary program called `xsparse`. It is available in source form from GNU tar home page.

Let's begin with archive members in *sparse format version 1.0*[4], which are the easiest to expand. The condensed file will contain both file map and file data, so no additional data will be needed to restore it. If the original file name was '*dir/name*', then the condensed file will be named '*dir/GNUSparseFile.n/name*', where *n* is a decimal number[5].

To expand a version 1.0 file, run `xsparse` as follows:

```
$ xsparse 'cond-file'
```

where 'cond-file' is the name of the condensed file. The utility will deduce the name for the resulting expanded file using the following algorithm:

1. If 'cond-file' does not contain any directories, '../cond-file' will be used;

2. If 'cond-file' has the form '*dir/t/name*', where both *t* and *name* are simple names, with no '/' characters in them, the output file name will be '*dir/name*'.

3. Otherwise, if 'cond-file' has the form '*dir/name*', the output file name will be '*name*'.

In the unlikely case when this algorithm does not suit your needs, you can explicitly specify output file name as a second argument to the command:

```
$ xsparse 'cond-file' 'out-file'
```

---

[4] See [PAX 1], page 204.

[5] Technically speaking, *n* is a *process ID* of the `tar` process which created the archive (see Section 8.3.7.1 [PAX keywords], page 143).

It is often a good idea to run **xsparse** in *dry run* mode first. In this mode, the command does not actually expand the file, but verbosely lists all actions it would be taking to do so. The dry run mode is enabled by '**-n**' command line argument:

```
$ xsparse -n /home/gray/GNUSparseFile.6058/sparsefile
Reading v.1.0 sparse map
Expanding file '/home/gray/GNUSparseFile.6058/sparsefile' to
'/home/gray/sparsefile'
Finished dry run
```

To actually expand the file, you would run:

```
$ xsparse /home/gray/GNUSparseFile.6058/sparsefile
```

The program behaves the same way all UNIX utilities do: it will keep quiet unless it has simething important to tell you (e.g. an error condition or something). If you wish it to produce verbose output, similar to that from the dry run mode, use '**-v**' option:

```
$ xsparse -v /home/gray/GNUSparseFile.6058/sparsefile
Reading v.1.0 sparse map
Expanding file '/home/gray/GNUSparseFile.6058/sparsefile' to
'/home/gray/sparsefile'
Done
```

Additionally, if your **tar** implementation has extracted the *extended headers* for this file, you can instruct **xstar** to use them in order to verify the integrity of the expanded file. The option '**-x**' sets the name of the extended header file to use. Continuing our example:

```
$ xsparse -v -x /home/gray/PaxHeaders.6058/sparsefile \
   /home/gray/GNUSparseFile.6058/sparsefile
Reading extended header file
Found variable GNU.sparse.major = 1
Found variable GNU.sparse.minor = 0
Found variable GNU.sparse.name = sparsefile
Found variable GNU.sparse.realsize = 217481216
Reading v.1.0 sparse map
Expanding file '/home/gray/GNUSparseFile.6058/sparsefile' to
'/home/gray/sparsefile'
Done
```

An *extended header* is a special **tar** archive header that precedes an archive member and contains a set of *variables*, describing the member properties that cannot be stored in the standard **ustar** header. While optional for expanding sparse version 1.0 members, the use of extended headers is mandatory when expanding sparse members in older sparse formats: v.0.0 and v.0.1 (The sparse formats are described in detail in [Sparse Formats], page 202.) So, for these formats, the question is: how to obtain extended headers from the archive?

If you use a **tar** implementation that does not support PAX format, extended headers for each member will be extracted as a separate file. If we represent the member name as '*dir/name*', then the extended header file will be named '*dir*/PaxHeaders.*n*/*name*', where *n* is an integer number.

Things become more difficult if your `tar` implementation does support PAX headers, because in this case you will have to manually extract the headers. We recommend the following algorithm:

1. Consult the documentation of your `tar` implementation for an option that prints *block numbers* along with the archive listing (analogous to GNU `tar`'s '-R' option). For example, `star` has '-block-number'.

2. Obtain verbose listing using the '`block number`' option, and find block numbers of the sparse member in question and the member immediately following it. For example, running `star` on our archive we obtain:

```
$ star -t -v -block-number -f arc.tar
...
star: Unknown extended header keyword 'GNU.sparse.size' ignored.
star: Unknown extended header keyword 'GNU.sparse.numblocks' ignored.
star: Unknown extended header keyword 'GNU.sparse.name' ignored.
star: Unknown extended header keyword 'GNU.sparse.map' ignored.
block        56:  425984 -rw-r--r--  gray/users Jun 25 14:46 2006 GNUSparseFile.
block       897:   65391 -rw-r--r--  gray/users Jun 24 20:06 2006 README
...
```

(as usual, ignore the warnings about unknown keywords.)

3. Let *size* be the size of the sparse member, *Bs* be its block number and *Bn* be the block number of the next member. Compute:

```
N = Bs - Bn - size/512 - 2
```

This number gives the size of the extended header part in tar *blocks*. In our example, this formula gives: `897 - 56 - 425984 / 512 - 2 = 7`.

4. Use `dd` to extract the headers:

```
dd if=archive of=hname bs=512 skip=Bs count=N
```

where *archive* is the archive name, *hname* is a name of the file to store the extended header in, *Bs* and *N* are computed in previous steps.

In our example, this command will be

```
$ dd if=arc.tar of=xhdr bs=512 skip=56 count=7
```

Finally, you can expand the condensed file, using the obtained header:

```
$ xsparse -v -x xhdr GNUSparseFile.6058/sparsefile
Reading extended header file
Found variable GNU.sparse.size = 217481216
Found variable GNU.sparse.numblocks = 208
Found variable GNU.sparse.name = sparsefile
Found variable GNU.sparse.map = 0,2048,1050624,2048,...
Expanding file 'GNUSparseFile.28124/sparsefile' to 'sparsefile'
Done
```

8.4 Comparison of `tar` and `cpio`

(This message will disappear, once this node revised.)

The `cpio` archive formats, like `tar`, do have maximum file name lengths. The binary and old ASCII formats have a maximum file length of 256, and the new ASCII and CRC ASCII formats have a max file length of 1024. GNU cpio can read and write archives with arbitrary file name lengths, but other cpio implementations may crash unexplainedly trying to read them.

tar handles symbolic links in the form in which it comes in BSD; cpio doesn't handle symbolic links in the form in which it comes in System V prior to SVR4, and some vendors may have added symlinks to their system without enhancing cpio to know about them. Others may have enhanced it in a way other than the way I did it at Sun, and which was adopted by AT&T (and which is, I think, also present in the cpio that Berkeley picked up from AT&T and put into a later BSD release—I think I gave them my changes).

(SVR4 does some funny stuff with tar; basically, its cpio can handle tar format input, and write it on output, and it probably handles symbolic links. They may not have bothered doing anything to enhance tar as a result.)

cpio handles special files; traditional tar doesn't.

tar comes with V7, System III, System V, and BSD source; cpio comes only with System III, System V, and later BSD (4.3-tahoe and later).

tar's way of handling multiple hard links to a file can handle file systems that support 32-bit i-numbers (e.g., the BSD file system); cpios way requires you to play some games (in its "binary" format, i-numbers are only 16 bits, and in its "portable ASCII" format, they're 18 bits—it would have to play games with the "file system ID" field of the header to make sure that the file system ID/i-number pairs of different files were always different), and I don't know which cpios, if any, play those games. Those that don't might get confused and think two files are the same file when they're not, and make hard links between them.

tars way of handling multiple hard links to a file places only one copy of the link on the tape, but the name attached to that copy is the *only* one you can use to retrieve the file; cpios way puts one copy for every link, but you can retrieve it using any of the names.

What type of check sum (if any) is used, and how is this calculated.

See the attached manual pages for tar and cpio format. tar uses a checksum which is the sum of all the bytes in the tar header for a file; cpio uses no checksum.

If anyone knows why cpio was made when tar was present at the unix scene,

It wasn't. cpio first showed up in PWB/UNIX 1.0; no generally-available version of UNIX had tar at the time. I don't know whether any version that was generally available *within AT&T* had tar, or, if so, whether the people within AT&T who did cpio knew about it.

On restore, if there is a corruption on a tape tar will stop at that point, while cpio will skip over it and try to restore the rest of the files.

The main difference is just in the command syntax and header format.

tar is a little more tape-oriented in that everything is blocked to start
on a record boundary.

> Is there any differences between the ability to recover crashed
> archives between the two of them. (Is there any chance of recover-
> ing crashed archives at all.)

Theoretically it should be easier under tar since the blocking lets you
find a header with some variation of 'dd skip=nn'. However, modern cpio's
and variations have an option to just search for the next file header after
an error with a reasonable chance of resyncing. However, lots of tape driver
software won't allow you to continue past a media error which should be the
only reason for getting out of sync unless a file changed sizes while you were
writing the archive.

> If anyone knows why cpio was made when tar was present at the
> unix scene, please tell me about this too.

Probably because it is more media efficient (by not blocking everything
and using only the space needed for the headers where tar always uses 512
bytes per file header) and it knows how to archive special files.

You might want to look at the freely available alternatives. The major
ones are afio, GNU tar, and pax, each of which have their own extensions
with some backwards compatibility.

Sparse files were tarred as sparse files (which you can easily test, because
the resulting archive gets smaller, and GNU cpio can no longer read it).

9 Tapes and Other Archive Media

(This message will disappear, once this node revised.)

A few special cases about tape handling warrant more detailed description. These special cases are discussed below.

Many complexities surround the use of **tar** on tape drives. Since the creation and manipulation of archives located on magnetic tape was the original purpose of **tar**, it contains many features making such manipulation easier.

Archives are usually written on dismountable media—tape cartridges, mag tapes, or floppy disks.

The amount of data a tape or disk holds depends not only on its size, but also on how it is formatted. A 2400 foot long reel of mag tape holds 40 megabytes of data when formatted at 1600 bits per inch. The physically smaller EXABYTE tape cartridge holds 2.3 gigabytes.

Magnetic media are re-usable—once the archive on a tape is no longer needed, the archive can be erased and the tape or disk used over. Media quality does deteriorate with use, however. Most tapes or disks should be discarded when they begin to produce data errors. EXABYTE tape cartridges should be discarded when they generate an *error count* (number of non-usable bits) of more than 10k.

Magnetic media are written and erased using magnetic fields, and should be protected from such fields to avoid damage to stored data. Sticking a floppy disk to a filing cabinet using a magnet is probably not a good idea.

9.1 Device Selection and Switching

(This message will disappear, once this node revised.)

'-f [*hostname*:]*file*'
'--file=[*hostname*:]*file*'
           Use archive file or device *file* on *hostname*.

This option is used to specify the file name of the archive **tar** works on.

If the file name is '-', **tar** reads the archive from standard input (when listing or extracting), or writes it to standard output (when creating). If the '-' file name is given when updating an archive, **tar** will read the original archive from its standard input, and will write the entire new archive to its standard output.

If the file name contains a ':', it is interpreted as '**hostname:file name**'. If the *hostname* contains an *at* sign ('**@**'), it is treated as '**user@hostname:file name**'. In either case, **tar** will invoke the command **rsh** (or **remsh**) to start up an **/usr/libexec/rmt** on the remote machine. If you give an alternate login name, it will be given to the **rsh**. Naturally, the remote machine must have an executable **/usr/libexec/rmt**. This program is free software from the University of California, and a copy of the source code can be found with the sources for `tar`; it's compiled and installed by default. The exact path to this utility is determined when configuring the package. It is '*prefix*`/libexec/rmt`', where *prefix* stands for your installation prefix. This location may also be overridden at runtime by using the '`--rmt-command=`*command*' option (See Section 3.4.2 [Option Summary], page 29, for detailed description of this option. See Section 9.2 [Remote Tape Server], page 157, for the description of `rmt` command).

If this option is not given, but the environment variable `TAPE` is set, its value is used; otherwise, old versions of `tar` used a default archive name (which was picked when `tar` was compiled). The default is normally set up to be the *first* tape drive or other transportable I/O medium on the system.

Starting with version 1.11.5, GNU `tar` uses standard input and standard output as the default device, and I will not try anymore supporting automatic device detection at installation time. This was failing really in too many cases, it was hopeless. This is now completely left to the installer to override standard input and standard output for default device, if this seems preferable. Further, I think *most* actual usages of `tar` are done with pipes or disks, not really tapes, cartridges or diskettes.

Some users think that using standard input and output is running after trouble. This could lead to a nasty surprise on your screen if you forget to specify an output file name—especially if you are going through a network or terminal server capable of buffering large amounts of output. We had so many bug reports in that area of configuring default tapes automatically, and so many contradicting requests, that we finally consider the problem to be portably intractable. We could of course use something like '`/dev/tape`' as a default, but this is *also* running after various kind of trouble, going from hung processes to accidental destruction of real tapes. After having seen all this mess, using standard input and output as a default really sounds like the only clean choice left, and a very useful one too.

GNU `tar` reads and writes archive in records, I suspect this is the main reason why block devices are preferred over character devices. Most probably, block devices are more efficient too. The installer could also check for '`DEFTAPE`' in '`<sys/mtio.h>`'.

'`--force-local`'

> Archive file is local even if it contains a colon.

'`--rsh-command=`*command*'

> Use remote *command* instead of `rsh`. This option exists so that people who use something other than the standard `rsh` (e.g., a Kerberized `rsh`) can access a remote device.

> When this command is not used, the shell command found when the `tar` program was installed is used instead. This is the first found of '`/usr/ucb/rsh`', '`/usr/bin/remsh`', '`/usr/bin/rsh`', '`/usr/bsd/rsh`' or '`/usr/bin/nsh`'. The installer may have

overridden this by defining the environment variable RSH *at installation time.*

'-[0-7][lmh]'

Specify drive and density.

'-M'
'--multi-volume'

Create/list/extract multi-volume archive.

This option causes tar to write a *multi-volume* archive—one that may be larger than will fit on the medium used to hold it. See Section 9.6.1 [Multi-Volume Archives], page 169.

'-L *num*'
'--tape-length=*size*[*suf*]'

Change tape after writing *size* units of data. Unless *suf* is given, *size* is treated as kilobytes, i.e. 'size x 1024' bytes. The following suffixes alter this behavior:

Suffix	Units	Byte Equivalent
b	Blocks	*size* x 512
B	Kilobytes	*size* x 1024
c	Bytes	*size*
G	Gigabytes	*size* x 1024^3
K	Kilobytes	*size* x 1024
k	Kilobytes	*size* x 1024
M	Megabytes	*size* x 1024^2
P	Petabytes	*size* x 1024^5
T	Terabytes	*size* x 1024^4
w	Words	*size* x 2

Table 9.1: Size Suffixes

This option might be useful when your tape drivers do not properly detect end of physical tapes. By being slightly conservative on the maximum tape length, you might avoid the problem entirely.

'-F *command*'
'--info-script=*command*'
'--new-volume-script=*command*'

Execute *command* at end of each tape. This implies '--multi-volume' ('-M'). See [info-script], page 170, for a detailed description of this option.

9.2 Remote Tape Server

In order to access the tape drive on a remote machine, tar uses the remote tape server written at the University of California at Berkeley. The remote

tape server must be installed as '*prefix*/libexec/rmt' on any machine
whose tape drive you want to use. `tar` calls `rmt` by running an `rsh` or
`remsh` to the remote machine, optionally using a different login name if one
is supplied.

A copy of the source for the remote tape server is provided. Its source
code can be freely distributed. It is compiled and installed by default.

Unless you use the '--absolute-names' ('-P') option, GNU `tar` will not
allow you to create an archive that contains absolute file names (a file name
beginning with '/'.) If you try, `tar` will automatically remove the leading
'/' from the file names it stores in the archive. It will also type a warning
message telling you what it is doing.

When reading an archive that was created with a different `tar` program,
GNU `tar` automatically extracts entries in the archive which have absolute
file names as if the file names were not absolute. This is an important feature.
A visitor here once gave a `tar` tape to an operator to restore; the operator
used Sun `tar` instead of GNU `tar`, and the result was that it replaced large
portions of our '/bin' and friends with versions from the tape; needless to
say, we were unhappy about having to recover the file system from backup
tapes.

For example, if the archive contained a file '/usr/bin/computoy', GNU
`tar` would extract the file to 'usr/bin/computoy', relative to the current
directory. If you want to extract the files in an archive to the same absolute
names that they had when the archive was created, you should do a 'cd
/' before extracting the files from the archive, or you should either use the
'--absolute-names' option, or use the command 'tar -C / ...'.

Some versions of Unix (Ultrix 3.1 is known to have this problem), can
claim that a short write near the end of a tape succeeded, when it actually
failed. This will result in the -M option not working correctly. The best
workaround at the moment is to use a significantly larger blocking factor
than the default 20.

In order to update an archive, `tar` must be able to backspace the archive
in order to reread or rewrite a record that was just read (or written). This is
currently possible only on two kinds of files: normal disk files (or any other
file that can be backspaced with 'lseek'), and industry-standard 9-track
magnetic tape (or any other kind of tape that can be backspaced with the
`MTIOCTOP ioctl`).

This means that the '--append', '--concatenate', and '--delete' commands will not work on any other kind of file. Some media simply cannot
be backspaced, which means these commands and options will never be able
to work on them. These non-backspacing media include pipes and cartridge
tape drives.

Some other media can be backspaced, and `tar` will work on them once
`tar` is modified to do so.

Archives created with the '--multi-volume', '--label', and '--incremental' ('-G') options may not be readable by other version of tar. In particular, restoring a file that was split over a volume boundary will require some careful work with dd, if it can be done at all. Other versions of tar may also create an empty file whose name is that of the volume header. Some versions of tar may create normal files instead of directories archived with the '--incremental' ('-G') option.

9.3 Some Common Problems and their Solutions

errors from system:
permission denied
no such file or directory
not owner

errors from tar:
directory checksum error
header format error

errors from media/system:
i/o error
device busy

9.4 Blocking

Block and *record* terminology is rather confused, and it is also confusing to the expert reader. On the other hand, readers who are new to the field have a fresh mind, and they may safely skip the next two paragraphs, as the remainder of this manual uses those two terms in a quite consistent way.

John Gilmore, the writer of the public domain tar from which GNU tar was originally derived, wrote (June 1995):

> The nomenclature of tape drives comes from IBM, where I believe they were invented for the IBM 650 or so. On IBM mainframes, what is recorded on tape are tape blocks. The logical organization of data is into records. There are various ways of putting records into blocks, including F (fixed sized records), V (variable sized records), FB (fixed blocked: fixed size records, *n* to a block), VB (variable size records, *n* to a block), VSB (variable spanned blocked: variable sized records that can occupy more than one block), etc. The JCL 'DD RECFORM=' parameter specified this to the operating system.
>
> The Unix man page on tar was totally confused about this. When I wrote PD TAR, I used the historically correct terminology (tar writes data records, which are grouped into blocks). It appears that the bogus terminology made it into POSIX (no surprise here), and now

François has migrated that terminology back into the source code too.

The term *physical block* means the basic transfer chunk from or to a device, after which reading or writing may stop without anything being lost. In this manual, the term *block* usually refers to a disk physical block, *assuming* that each disk block is 512 bytes in length. It is true that some disk devices have different physical blocks, but `tar` ignore these differences in its own format, which is meant to be portable, so a `tar` block is always 512 bytes in length, and *block* always mean a `tar` block. The term *logical block* often represents the basic chunk of allocation of many disk blocks as a single entity, which the operating system treats somewhat atomically; this concept is only barely used in GNU `tar`.

The term *physical record* is another way to speak of a physical block, those two terms are somewhat interchangeable. In this manual, the term *record* usually refers to a tape physical block, *assuming* that the `tar` archive is kept on magnetic tape. It is true that archives may be put on disk or used with pipes, but nevertheless, `tar` tries to read and write the archive one *record* at a time, whatever the medium in use. One record is made up of an integral number of blocks, and this operation of putting many disk blocks into a single tape block is called *reblocking*, or more simply, *blocking*. The term *logical record* refers to the logical organization of many characters into something meaningful to the application. The term *unit record* describes a small set of characters which are transmitted whole to or by the application, and often refers to a line of text. Those two last terms are unrelated to what we call a *record* in GNU `tar`.

When writing to tapes, `tar` writes the contents of the archive in chunks known as *records*. To change the default blocking factor, use the '`--blocking-factor=512-size`' ('`-b 512-size`') option. Each record will then be composed of *512-size* blocks. (Each `tar` block is 512 bytes. See [Standard], page 193.) Each file written to the archive uses at least one full record. As a result, using a larger record size can result in more wasted space for small files. On the other hand, a larger record size can often be read and written much more efficiently.

Further complicating the problem is that some tape drives ignore the blocking entirely. For these, a larger record size can still improve performance (because the software layers above the tape drive still honor the blocking), but not as dramatically as on tape drives that honor blocking.

When reading an archive, `tar` can usually figure out the record size on itself. When this is the case, and a non-standard record size was used when the archive was created, `tar` will print a message about a non-standard blocking factor, and then operate normally[1]. On some tape devices, however, `tar` cannot figure out the record size itself. On most of those, you can

---

[1] If this message is not needed, you can turn it off using the '`--warning=no-record-size`' option.

specify a blocking factor (with '--blocking-factor') larger than the actual blocking factor, and then use the '--read-full-records' ('-B') option. (If you specify a blocking factor with '--blocking-factor' and don't use the '--read-full-records' option, then `tar` will not attempt to figure out the recording size itself.) On some devices, you must always specify the record size exactly with '--blocking-factor' when reading, because `tar` cannot figure it out. In any case, use '--list' ('-t') before doing any extractions to see whether `tar` is reading the archive correctly.

`tar` blocks are all fixed size (512 bytes), and its scheme for putting them into records is to put a whole number of them (one or more) into each record. `tar` records are all the same size; at the end of the file there's a block containing all zeros, which is how you tell that the remainder of the last record(s) are garbage.

In a standard `tar` file (no options), the block size is 512 and the record size is 10240, for a blocking factor of 20. What the '--blocking-factor' option does is sets the blocking factor, changing the record size while leaving the block size at 512 bytes. 20 was fine for ancient 800 or 1600 bpi reel-to-reel tape drives; most tape drives these days prefer much bigger records in order to stream and not waste tape. When writing tapes for myself, some tend to use a factor of the order of 2048, say, giving a record size of around one megabyte.

If you use a blocking factor larger than 20, older `tar` programs might not be able to read the archive, so we recommend this as a limit to use in practice. GNU `tar`, however, will support arbitrarily large record sizes, limited only by the amount of virtual memory or the physical characteristics of the tape device.

9.4.1 Format Variations

(This message will disappear, once this node revised.)

Format parameters specify how an archive is written on the archive media. The best choice of format parameters will vary depending on the type and number of files being archived, and on the media used to store the archive.

To specify format parameters when accessing or creating an archive, you can use the options described in the following sections. If you do not specify any format parameters, `tar` uses default parameters. You cannot modify a compressed archive. If you create an archive with the '--blocking-factor' option specified (see Section 9.4.2 [Blocking Factor], page 161), you must specify that blocking-factor when operating on the archive. See Chapter 8 [Formats], page 131, for other examples of format parameter considerations.

9.4.2 The Blocking Factor of an Archive

(This message will disappear, once this node revised.)

The data in an archive is grouped into blocks, which are 512 bytes. Blocks are read and written in whole number multiples called *records*. The number of blocks in a record (i.e., the size of a record in units of 512 bytes) is called the *blocking factor*. The '`--blocking-factor=512-size`' ('`-b 512-size`') option specifies the blocking factor of an archive. The default blocking factor is typically 20 (i.e., 10240 bytes), but can be specified at installation. To find out the blocking factor of an existing archive, use '`tar --list --file=archive-name`'. This may not work on some devices.

Records are separated by gaps, which waste space on the archive media. If you are archiving on magnetic tape, using a larger blocking factor (and therefore larger records) provides faster throughput and allows you to fit more data on a tape (because there are fewer gaps). If you are archiving on cartridge, a very large blocking factor (say 126 or more) greatly increases performance. A smaller blocking factor, on the other hand, may be useful when archiving small files, to avoid archiving lots of nulls as `tar` fills out the archive to the end of the record. In general, the ideal record size depends on the size of the inter-record gaps on the tape you are using, and the average size of the files you are archiving. See Section 2.6 [create], page 10, for information on writing archives.

Archives with blocking factors larger than 20 cannot be read by very old versions of `tar`, or by some newer versions of `tar` running on old machines with small address spaces. With GNU `tar`, the blocking factor of an archive is limited only by the maximum record size of the device containing the archive, or by the amount of available virtual memory.

Also, on some systems, not using adequate blocking factors, as sometimes imposed by the device drivers, may yield unexpected diagnostics. For example, this has been reported:

```
Cannot write to /dev/dlt: Invalid argument
```

In such cases, it sometimes happen that the `tar` bundled by the system is aware of block size idiosyncrasies, while GNU `tar` requires an explicit specification for the block size, which it cannot guess. This yields some people to consider GNU `tar` is misbehaving, because by comparison, *the bundle* `tar` *works OK*. Adding `-b 256`, for example, might resolve the problem.

If you use a non-default blocking factor when you create an archive, you must specify the same blocking factor when you modify that archive. Some archive devices will also require you to specify the blocking factor when reading that archive, however this is not typically the case. Usually, you can use '`--list`' ('`-t`') without specifying a blocking factor—`tar` reports a non-default record size and then lists the archive members as it would normally. To extract files from an archive with a non-standard blocking factor (particularly if you're not sure what the blocking factor is), you can usually use the '`--read-full-records`' ('`-B`') option while specifying a blocking factor larger then the blocking factor of the archive (i.e., '`tar --extract --read-full-records --blocking-factor=300`'). See Section 2.7 [list], page 15, for more information on the '`--list`' ('`-t`') operation. See Section 4.4.1 [Reading], page 71, for a more detailed explanation of that option.

'--blocking-factor=*number*'
'-b *number*'
>   Specifies the blocking factor of an archive. Can be used with
>   any operation, but is usually not necessary with '--list' ('-t').

Device blocking

'-b *blocks*'
'--blocking-factor=*blocks*'
>   Set record size to *blocks* * 512 bytes.
>
>   This option is used to specify a *blocking factor* for the archive.
>   When reading or writing the archive, tar, will do reads and
>   writes of the archive in records of *block* * 512 bytes. This is true
>   even when the archive is compressed. Some devices requires that
>   all write operations be a multiple of a certain size, and so, tar
>   pads the archive out to the next record boundary.
>
>   The default blocking factor is set when tar is compiled, and
>   is typically 20. Blocking factors larger than 20 cannot be read
>   by very old versions of tar, or by some newer versions of tar
>   running on old machines with small address spaces.
>
>   With a magnetic tape, larger records give faster throughput and
>   fit more data on a tape (because there are fewer inter-record
>   gaps). If the archive is in a disk file or a pipe, you may want to
>   specify a smaller blocking factor, since a large one will result in
>   a large number of null bytes at the end of the archive.
>
>   When writing cartridge or other streaming tapes, a much larger
>   blocking factor (say 126 or more) will greatly increase perfor-
>   mance. However, you must specify the same blocking factor
>   when reading or updating the archive.
>
>   Apparently, Exabyte drives have a physical block size of 8K
>   bytes. If we choose our blocksize as a multiple of 8k bytes,
>   then the problem seems to disappear. Id est, we are using block
>   size of 112 right now, and we haven't had the problem since we
>   switched. . .
>
>   With GNU tar the blocking factor is limited only by the maxi-
>   mum record size of the device containing the archive, or by the
>   amount of available virtual memory.
>
>   However, deblocking or reblocking is virtually avoided in a spe-
>   cial case which often occurs in practice, but which requires all
>   the following conditions to be simultaneously true:
>
>   * the archive is subject to a compression option,
>   * the archive is not handled through standard input or out-
>   put, nor redirected nor piped,
>   * the archive is directly handled to a local disk, instead of any
>   special device,

- '--blocking-factor' is not explicitly specified on the tar invocation.

If the output goes directly to a local disk, and not through stdout, then the last write is not extended to a full record size. Otherwise, reblocking occurs. Here are a few other remarks on this topic:

- gzip will complain about trailing garbage if asked to uncompress a compressed archive on tape, there is an option to turn the message off, but it breaks the regularity of simply having to use 'prog -d' for decompression. It would be nice if gzip was silently ignoring any number of trailing zeros. I'll ask Jean-loup Gailly, by sending a copy of this message to him.

- compress does not show this problem, but as Jean-loup pointed out to Michael, 'compress -d' silently adds garbage after the result of decompression, which tar ignores because it already recognized its end-of-file indicator. So this bug may be safely ignored.

- 'gzip -d -q' will be silent about the trailing zeros indeed, but will still return an exit status of 2 which tar reports in turn. tar might ignore the exit status returned, but I hate doing that, as it weakens the protection tar offers users against other possible problems at decompression time. If gzip was silently skipping trailing zeros *and* also avoiding setting the exit status in this innocuous case, that would solve this situation.

- tar should become more solid at not stopping to read a pipe at the first null block encountered. This inelegantly breaks the pipe. tar should rather drain the pipe out before exiting itself.

'-i'
'--ignore-zeros'

        Ignore blocks of zeros in archive (means EOF).

        The '--ignore-zeros' ('-i') option causes tar to ignore blocks of zeros in the archive. Normally a block of zeros indicates the end of the archive, but when reading a damaged archive, or one which was created by concatenating several archives together, this option allows tar to read the entire archive. This option is not on by default because many versions of tar write garbage after the zeroed blocks.

        Note that this option causes tar to read to the end of the archive file, which may sometimes avoid problems when multiple files are stored on a single physical tape.

'-B'
'--read-full-records'
>   Reblock as we read (for reading 4.2BSD pipes).

>   If '--read-full-records' is used, tar will not panic if an at-
>   tempt to read a record from the archive does not return a full
>   record. Instead, tar will keep reading until it has obtained a
>   full record.

>   This option is turned on by default when tar is reading an
>   archive from standard input, or from a remote machine. This
>   is because on BSD Unix systems, a read of a pipe will return
>   however much happens to be in the pipe, even if it is less than
>   tar requested. If this option was not used, tar would fail as
>   soon as it read an incomplete record from the pipe.

>   This option is also useful with the commands for updating an
>   archive.

Tape blocking

When handling various tapes or cartridges, you have to take care of selecting a proper blocking, that is, the number of disk blocks you put together
as a single tape block on the tape, without intervening tape gaps. A *tape
gap* is a small landing area on the tape with no information on it, used for
decelerating the tape to a full stop, and for later regaining the reading or
writing speed. When the tape driver starts reading a record, the record has
to be read whole without stopping, as a tape gap is needed to stop the tape
motion without losing information.

Using higher blocking (putting more disk blocks per tape block) will use
the tape more efficiently as there will be less tape gaps. But reading such
tapes may be more difficult for the system, as more memory will be required
to receive at once the whole record. Further, if there is a reading error on a
huge record, this is less likely that the system will succeed in recovering the
information. So, blocking should not be too low, nor it should be too high.
tar uses by default a blocking of 20 for historical reasons, and it does not really matter when reading or writing to disk. Current tape technology would
easily accommodate higher blockings. Sun recommends a blocking of 126
for Exabytes and 96 for DATs. We were told that for some DLT drives, the
blocking should be a multiple of 4Kb, preferably 64Kb (*-b 128*) or 256 for
decent performance. Other manufacturers may use different recommenda-
tions for the same tapes. This might also depends of the buffering techniques
used inside modern tape controllers. Some imposes a minimum blocking, or
a maximum blocking. Others request blocking to be some exponent of two.

So, there is no fixed rule for blocking. But blocking at read time should
ideally be the same as blocking used at write time. At one place I know,
with a wide variety of equipment, they found it best to use a blocking of 32
to guarantee that their tapes are fully interchangeable.

I was also told that, for recycled tapes, prior erasure (by the same drive unit that will be used to create the archives) sometimes lowers the error rates observed at rewriting time.

I might also use '--number-blocks' instead of '--block-number', so '--block' will then expand to '--blocking-factor' unambiguously.

9.5 Many Archives on One Tape

Most tape devices have two entries in the '/dev' directory, or entries that come in pairs, which differ only in the minor number for this device. Let's take for example '/dev/tape', which often points to the only or usual tape device of a given system. There might be a corresponding '/dev/nrtape' or '/dev/ntape'. The simpler name is the *rewinding* version of the device, while the name having 'nr' in it is the *no rewinding* version of the same device.

A rewinding tape device will bring back the tape to its beginning point automatically when this device is opened or closed. Since **tar** opens the archive file before using it and closes it afterwards, this means that a simple:

```
$ tar cf /dev/tape directory
```

will reposition the tape to its beginning both prior and after saving *directory* contents to it, thus erasing prior tape contents and making it so that any subsequent write operation will destroy what has just been saved.

So, a rewinding device is normally meant to hold one and only one file. If you want to put more than one **tar** archive on a given tape, you will need to avoid using the rewinding version of the tape device. You will also have to pay special attention to tape positioning. Errors in positioning may overwrite the valuable data already on your tape. Many people, burnt by past experiences, will only use rewinding devices and limit themselves to one file per tape, precisely to avoid the risk of such errors. Be fully aware that writing at the wrong position on a tape loses all information past this point and most probably until the end of the tape, and this destroyed information *cannot* be recovered.

To save *directory-1* as a first archive at the beginning of a tape, and leave that tape ready for a second archive, you should use:

```
$ mt -f /dev/nrtape rewind
$ tar cf /dev/nrtape directory-1
```

Tape marks are special magnetic patterns written on the tape media, which are later recognizable by the reading hardware. These marks are used after each file, when there are many on a single tape. An empty file (that is to say, two tape marks in a row) signal the logical end of the tape, after which no file exist. Usually, non-rewinding tape device drivers will react to the close request issued by **tar** by first writing two tape marks after your archive, and by backspacing over one of these. So, if you remove the tape at that time from the tape drive, it is properly terminated. But if you write another file at the current position, the second tape mark will be erased by the new information, leaving only one tape mark between files.

So, you may now save *directory-2* as a second archive after the first on the same tape by issuing the command:

```
$ tar cf /dev/nrtape directory-2
```

and so on for all the archives you want to put on the same tape.

Another usual case is that you do not write all the archives the same day, and you need to remove and store the tape between two archive sessions. In general, you must remember how many files are already saved on your tape. Suppose your tape already has 16 files on it, and that you are ready to write the 17th. You have to take care of skipping the first 16 tape marks before saving *directory-17*, say, by using these commands:

```
$ mt -f /dev/nrtape rewind
$ mt -f /dev/nrtape fsf 16
$ tar cf /dev/nrtape directory-17
```

In all the previous examples, we put aside blocking considerations, but you should do the proper things for that as well. See Section 9.4 [Blocking], page 159.

9.5.1 Tape Positions and Tape Marks

(This message will disappear, once this node revised.)

Just as archives can store more than one file from the file system, tapes can store more than one archive file. To keep track of where archive files (or any other type of file stored on tape) begin and end, tape archive devices write magnetic *tape marks* on the archive media. Tape drives write one tape mark between files, two at the end of all the file entries.

If you think of data as a series of records "rrrr"'s, and tape marks as "*"'s, a tape might look like the following:

```
rrrr*rrrrrr*rrrrr*rr*rrrrr**------------------------
```

Tape devices read and write tapes using a read/write *tape head*—a physical part of the device which can only access one point on the tape at a time. When you use **tar** to read or write archive data from a tape device, the device will begin reading or writing from wherever on the tape the tape head happens to be, regardless of which archive or what part of the archive the tape head is on. Before writing an archive, you should make sure that no data on the tape will be overwritten (unless it is no longer needed). Before reading an archive, you should make sure the tape head is at the beginning of the archive you want to read. You can do it manually via **mt** utility (see Section 9.5.2 [mt], page 168). The **restore** script does that automatically (see Section 5.6 [Scripted Restoration], page 94).

If you want to add new archive file entries to a tape, you should advance the tape to the end of the existing file entries, backspace over the last tape mark, and write the new archive file. If you were to add two archives to the example above, the tape might look like the following:

rrrr*rrrrrr*rrrrr*rr*rrrrr*rrr*rrrr**---------------

9.5.2 The `mt` Utility

(This message will disappear, once this node revised.)

See Section 9.4.2 [Blocking Factor], page 161.

You can use the `mt` utility to advance or rewind a tape past a specified number of archive files on the tape. This will allow you to move to the beginning of an archive before extracting or reading it, or to the end of all the archives before writing a new one.

The syntax of the `mt` command is:

```
mt [-f tapename] operation [number]
```

where *tapename* is the name of the tape device, *number* is the number of times an operation is performed (with a default of one), and *operation* is one of the following:

'eof'
'weof'   Writes *number* tape marks at the current position on the tape.

'fsf'   Moves tape position forward *number* files.

'bsf'   Moves tape position back *number* files.

'rewind'   Rewinds the tape. (Ignores *number*.)

'offline'
'rewoffl'   Rewinds the tape and takes the tape device off-line. (Ignores *number*.)

'status'   Prints status information about the tape unit.

If you don't specify a *tapename*, `mt` uses the environment variable `TAPE`; if `TAPE` is not set, `mt` will use the default device specified in your 'sys/mtio.h' file (`DEFTAPE` variable). If this is not defined, the program will display a descriptive error message and exit with code 1.

`mt` returns a 0 exit status when the operation(s) were successful, 1 if the command was unrecognized, and 2 if an operation failed.

9.6 Using Multiple Tapes

Often you might want to write a large archive, one larger than will fit on the actual tape you are using. In such a case, you can run multiple `tar` commands, but this can be inconvenient, particularly if you are using options like '--exclude=pattern' or dumping entire file systems. Therefore, `tar` provides a special mode for creating multi-volume archives.

Multi-volume archive is a single `tar` archive, stored on several media volumes of fixed size. Although in this section we will often call 'volume' a *tape*, there is absolutely no requirement for multi-volume archives to be stored on tapes. Instead, they can use whatever media type the user finds convenient, they can even be located on files.

When creating a multi-volume archive, GNU `tar` continues to fill current volume until it runs out of space, then it switches to next volume (usually the operator is queried to replace the tape on this point), and continues working on the new volume. This operation continues until all requested files are dumped. If GNU `tar` detects end of media while dumping a file, such a file is archived in split form. Some very big files can even be split across several volumes.

Each volume is itself a valid GNU `tar` archive, so it can be read without any special options. Consequently any file member residing entirely on one volume can be extracted or otherwise operated upon without needing the other volume. Sure enough, to extract a split member you would need all volumes its parts reside on.

Multi-volume archives suffer from several limitations. In particular, they cannot be compressed.

GNU `tar` is able to create multi-volume archives of two formats (see Chapter 8 [Formats], page 131): 'GNU' and 'POSIX'.

9.6.1 Archives Longer than One Tape or Disk

To create an archive that is larger than will fit on a single unit of the media, use the '--multi-volume' ('-M') option in conjunction with the '--create' option (see Section 2.6 [create], page 10). A *multi-volume* archive can be manipulated like any other archive (provided the '--multi-volume' option is specified), but is stored on more than one tape or file.

When you specify '--multi-volume', `tar` does not report an error when it comes to the end of an archive volume (when reading), or the end of the media (when writing). Instead, it prompts you to load a new storage volume. If the archive is on a magnetic tape, you should change tapes when you see the prompt; if the archive is on a floppy disk, you should change disks; etc.

'--multi-volume'
'-M'   Creates a multi-volume archive, when used in conjunction with
               '--create' ('-c'). To perform any other operation on a multi-
               volume archive, specify '--multi-volume' in conjunction with
               that operation. For example:
                   $ *tar --create --multi-volume --file=/dev/tape files*

The method `tar` uses to detect end of tape is not perfect, and fails on some operating systems or on some devices. If `tar` cannot detect the end of the tape itself, you can use '--tape-length' option to inform it about the capacity of the tape:

'--tape-length=*size* [*suf*]'
'-L *size* [*suf*]'
               Set maximum length of a volume. The *suf*, if given, specifies
               units in which *size* is expressed, e.g. '2M' mean 2 megabytes (see
               Table 9.1, for a list of allowed size suffixes). Without *suf*, units
               of 1024 bytes (kilobyte) are assumed.

This option selects '--multi-volume' automatically. For example:

```
$ tar --create --tape-length=41943040 --file=/dev/tape files
```

or, which is equivalent:

```
$ tar --create --tape-length=4G --file=/dev/tape files
```

When GNU tar comes to the end of a storage media, it asks you to change the volume. The built-in prompt for POSIX locale is[2]:

```
Prepare volume #n for 'archive' and hit return:
```

where *n* is the ordinal number of the volume to be created and *archive* is archive file or device name.

When prompting for a new tape, tar accepts any of the following responses:

?　　　　　　Request tar to explain possible responses.

q　　　　　　Request tar to exit immediately.

n file-name

　　　　　　Request tar to write the next volume on the file *file-name*.

!　　　　　　Request tar to run a subshell. This option can be disabled by giving '--restrict' command line option to tar[3].

y　　　　　　Request tar to begin writing the next volume.

(You should only type 'y' after you have changed the tape; otherwise tar will write over the volume it just finished.)

The volume number used by tar in its tape-changing prompt can be changed; if you give the '--volno-file=file-of-number' option, then *file-of-number* should be an non-existing file to be created, or else, a file already containing a decimal number. That number will be used as the volume number of the first volume written. When tar is finished, it will rewrite the file with the now-current volume number. (This does not change the volume number written on a tape label, as per Section 9.7 [label], page 173, it *only* affects the number used in the prompt.)

If you want more elaborate behavior than this, you can write a special *new volume script*, that will be responsible for changing the volume, and instruct tar to use it instead of its normal prompting procedure:

'--info-script=*command*'
'--new-volume-script=*command*'
'-F *command*'

　　　　　　Specify the command to invoke when switching volumes. The *command* can be used to eject cassettes, or to broadcast messages such as 'Someone please come change my tape' when performing unattended backups.

---

[2] If you run GNU tar under a different locale, the translation to the locale's language will be used.

[3] See [–restrict], page 42, for more information about this option.

The *command* can contain additional options, if such are needed. See Section 3.11 [external], page 59, for a detailed discussion of the way GNU `tar` runs external commands. It inherits `tar`'s shell environment. Additional data is passed to it via the following environment variables:

`TAR_VERSION`

> GNU `tar` version number.

`TAR_ARCHIVE`

> The name of the archive `tar` is processing.

`TAR_BLOCKING_FACTOR`

> Current blocking factor (see Section 9.4 [Blocking], page 159).

`TAR_VOLUME`

> Ordinal number of the volume `tar` is about to start.

`TAR_SUBCOMMAND`

> A short option describing the operation `tar` is executing. See Section 4.2.1 [Operations], page 62, for a complete list of subcommand options.

`TAR_FORMAT`

> Format of the archive being processed. See Chapter 8 [Formats], page 131, for a complete list of archive format names.

`TAR_FD`   File descriptor which can be used to communicate the new volume name to `tar`.

These variables can be used in the *command* itself, provided that they are properly quoted to prevent them from being expanded by the shell that invokes `tar`.

The volume script can instruct `tar` to use new archive name, by writing in to file descriptor `$TAR_FD` (see below for an example).

If the info script fails, `tar` exits; otherwise, it begins writing the next volume.

If you want `tar` to cycle through a series of files or tape drives, there are three approaches to choose from. First of all, you can give `tar` multiple '`--file`' options. In this case the specified files will be used, in sequence, as the successive volumes of the archive. Only when the first one in the sequence needs to be used again will `tar` prompt for a tape change (or run the info script). For example, suppose someone has two tape drives on a system named '`/dev/tape0`' and '`/dev/tape1`'. For having GNU `tar` to switch to the second drive when it needs to write the second tape, and then back to the first tape, etc., just do either of:

```
$ tar --create --multi-volume --file=/dev/tape0 --file=/dev/tape1 files
$ tar -cM -f /dev/tape0 -f /dev/tape1 files
```

The second method is to use the '`n`' response to the tape-change prompt.

Finally, the most flexible approach is to use a volume script, that writes new archive name to the file descriptor `$TAR_FD`. For example, the following volume script will create a series of archive files, named 'archive-vol', where archive is the name of the archive being created (as given by '--file' option) and vol is the ordinal number of the archive being created:

```
#! /bin/bash
# For this script it's advisable to use a shell, such as Bash,
# that supports a TAR_FD value greater than 9.

echo Preparing volume $TAR_VOLUME of $TAR_ARCHIVE.

name=`expr $TAR_ARCHIVE : '\(.*\)-.*'`
case $TAR_SUBCOMMAND in
-c)       ;;
-d|-x|-t) test -r ${name:-$TAR_ARCHIVE}-$TAR_VOLUME || exit 1
          ;;
*)        exit 1
esac

echo ${name:-$TAR_ARCHIVE}-$TAR_VOLUME >&$TAR_FD
```

The same script can be used while listing, comparing or extracting from the created archive. For example:

```
# Create a multi-volume archive:
$ tar -c -L1024 -f archive.tar -F new-volume .
# Extract from the created archive:
$ tar -x -f archive.tar -F new-volume .
```

Notice, that the first command had to use '-L' option, since otherwise GNU tar will end up writing everything to file 'archive.tar'.

You can read each individual volume of a multi-volume archive as if it were an archive by itself. For example, to list the contents of one volume, use '--list', without '--multi-volume' specified. To extract an archive member from one volume (assuming it is described that volume), use '--extract', again without '--multi-volume'.

If an archive member is split across volumes (i.e., its entry begins on one volume of the media and ends on another), you need to specify '--multi-volume' to extract it successfully. In this case, you should load the volume where the archive member starts, and use 'tar --extract --multi-volume'—tar will prompt for later volumes as it needs them. See Section 2.8.1 [extracting archives], page 17, for more information about extracting archives.

Multi-volume archives can be modified like any other archive. To add files to a multi-volume archive, you need to only mount the last volume of the archive media (and new volumes, if needed). For all other operations, you need to use the entire archive.

If a multi-volume archive was labeled using '--label=archive-label' (see Section 9.7 [label], page 173) when it was created, tar will not automatically label volumes which are added later. To label subsequent volumes, specify '--label=archive-label' again in conjunction with the '--append', '--update' or '--concatenate' operation.

Notice that multi-volume support is a GNU extension and the archives created in this mode should be read only using GNU `tar`. If you absolutely have to process such archives using a third-party `tar` implementation, read Section 8.3.10.1 [Split Recovery], page 147.

9.6.2 Tape Files

(This message will disappear, once this node revised.)

To give the archive a name which will be recorded in it, use the '`--label=volume-label`' ('`-V volume-label`') option. This will write a special block identifying *volume-label* as the name of the archive to the front of the archive which will be displayed when the archive is listed with '`--list`'. If you are creating a multi-volume archive with '`--multi-volume`' (see Section 9.6 [Using Multiple Tapes], page 168), then the volume label will have '`Volume nnn`' appended to the name you give, where *nnn* is the number of the volume of the archive. If you use the '`--label=volume-label`' option when reading an archive, it checks to make sure the label on the tape matches the one you gave. See Section 9.7 [label], page 173.

When `tar` writes an archive to tape, it creates a single tape file. If multiple archives are written to the same tape, one after the other, they each get written as separate tape files. When extracting, it is necessary to position the tape at the right place before running `tar`. To do this, use the `mt` command. For more information on the `mt` command and on the organization of tapes into a sequence of tape files, see Section 9.5.2 [mt], page 168.

People seem to often do:

```
--label="some-prefix `date +some-format`"
```

or such, for pushing a common date in all volumes or an archive set.

9.6.3 Concatenate Volumes into a Single Archive

Sometimes it is necessary to convert existing GNU `tar` multi-volume archive to a single `tar` archive. Simply concatenating all volumes into one will not work, since each volume carries an additional information at the beginning. GNU `tar` is shipped with the shell script `tarcat` designed for this purpose.

The script takes a list of files comprising a multi-volume archive and creates the resulting archive at the standard output. For example:

```
tarcat vol.1 vol.2 vol.3 | tar tf -
```

The script implements a simple heuristics to determine the format of the first volume file and to decide how to process the rest of the files. However, it makes no attempt to verify whether the files are given in order or even if they are valid `tar` archives. It uses `dd` and does not filter its standard error, so you will usually see lots of spurious messages.

9.7 Including a Label in the Archive

To avoid problems caused by misplaced paper labels on the archive media, you can include a *label* entry — an archive member which contains the name of the archive — in the archive itself. Use the '--label=*archive-label*' ('-V *archive-label*') option[4] in conjunction with the '--create' operation to include a label entry in the archive as it is being created.

'--label=*archive-label*'
'-V *archive-label*'

> Includes an *archive-label* at the beginning of the archive when the archive is being created, when used in conjunction with the '--create' operation. Checks to make sure the archive label matches the one specified (when used in conjunction with any other operation).

If you create an archive using both '--label=*archive-label*' ('-V *archive-label*') and '--multi-volume' ('-M'), each volume of the archive will have an archive label of the form '*archive-label* Volume *n*', where *n* is 1 for the first volume, 2 for the next, and so on. See Section 9.6 [Using Multiple Tapes], page 168, for information on creating multiple volume archives.

The volume label will be displayed by '--list' along with the file contents. If verbose display is requested, it will also be explicitly marked as in the example below:

```
$ tar --verbose --list --file=iamanarchive
V--------- 0/0               0 1992-03-07 12:01 iamalabel--Volume Header-
-
-rw-r--r-- ringo/user       40 1990-05-21 13:30 iamafilename
```

However, '--list' option will cause listing entire contents of the archive, which may be undesirable (for example, if the archive is stored on a tape). You can request checking only the volume label by specifying '--test-label' option. This option reads only the first block of an archive, so it can be used with slow storage devices. For example:

```
$ tar --test-label --file=iamanarchive
iamalabel
```

If '--test-label' is used with one or more command line arguments, tar compares the volume label with each argument. It exits with code 0 if a match is found, and with code 1 otherwise[5]. No output is displayed, unless you also used the '--verbose' option. For example:

```
$ tar --test-label --file=iamanarchive 'iamalabel'
⇒ 0
$ tar --test-label --file=iamanarchive 'alabel'
⇒ 1
```

---

[4] Until version 1.10, that option was called '--volume', but is not available under that name anymore.

[5] Note that GNU tar versions up to 1.23 indicated mismatch with an exit code 2 and printed a spurious diagnostics on stderr.

When used with the '--verbose' option, tar prints the actual volume label (if any), and a verbose diagnostics in case of a mismatch:

```
$ tar --test-label --verbose --file=iamanarchive 'iamalabel'
iamalabel
⇒ 0
$ tar --test-label --verbose --file=iamanarchive 'alabel'
iamalabel
tar: Archive label mismatch
⇒ 1
```

If you request any operation, other than '--create', along with using '--label' option, tar will first check if the archive label matches the one specified and will refuse to proceed if it does not. Use this as a safety precaution to avoid accidentally overwriting existing archives. For example, if you wish to add files to 'archive', presumably labeled with string 'My volume', you will get:

```
$ tar -rf archive --label 'My volume' .
tar: Archive not labeled to match 'My volume'
```

in case its label does not match. This will work even if 'archive' is not labeled at all.

Similarly, tar will refuse to list or extract the archive if its label doesn't match the *archive-label* specified. In those cases, *archive-label* argument is interpreted as a globbing-style pattern which must match the actual magnetic volume label. See Section 6.4 [exclude], page 101, for a precise description of how match is attempted[6]. If the switch '--multi-volume' ('-M') is being used, the volume label matcher will also suffix *archive-label* by ' Volume [1-9]*' if the initial match fails, before giving up. Since the volume numbering is automatically added in labels at creation time, it sounded logical to equally help the user taking care of it when the archive is being read.

You can also use '--label' to get a common information on all tapes of a series. For having this information different in each series created through a single script used on a regular basis, just manage to get some date string as part of the label. For example:

```
$ tar -cM -f /dev/tape -V "Daily backup for `date +%Y-%m-%d`"
$ tar --create --file=/dev/tape --multi-volume \
      --label="Daily backup for `date +%Y-%m-%d`"
```

Some more notes about volume labels:

• Each label has its own date and time, which corresponds to the time when GNU tar initially attempted to write it, often soon after the operator launches tar or types the carriage return telling that the next tape is ready.

---

[6] Previous versions of tar used full regular expression matching, or before that, only exact string matching, instead of wildcard matchers. We decided for the sake of simplicity to use a uniform matching device through tar.

- Comparing date labels to get an idea of tape throughput is unreliable. It gives correct results only if the delays for rewinding tapes and the operator switching them were negligible, which is usually not the case.

9.8 Verifying Data as It is Stored

'-W'
'--verify'
>   Attempt to verify the archive after writing.

This option causes `tar` to verify the archive after writing it. Each volume is checked after it is written, and any discrepancies are recorded on the standard error output.

Verification requires that the archive be on a back-space-able medium. This means pipes, some cartridge tape drives, and some other devices cannot be verified.

You can insure the accuracy of an archive by comparing files in the system with archive members. `tar` can compare an archive to the file system as the archive is being written, to verify a write operation, or can compare a previously written archive, to insure that it is up to date.

To check for discrepancies in an archive immediately after it is written, use the '--verify' ('-W') option in conjunction with the '--create' operation. When this option is specified, `tar` checks archive members against their counterparts in the file system, and reports discrepancies on the standard error.

To verify an archive, you must be able to read it from before the end of the last written entry. This option is useful for detecting data errors on some tapes. Archives written to pipes, some cartridge tape drives, and some other devices cannot be verified.

One can explicitly compare an already made archive with the file system by using the '--compare' ('--diff', '-d') option, instead of using the more automatic '--verify' option. See Section 4.2.6 [compare], page 69.

Note that these two options have a slightly different intent. The '--compare' option checks how identical are the logical contents of some archive with what is on your disks, while the '--verify' option is really for checking if the physical contents agree and if the recording media itself is of dependable quality. So, for the '--verify' operation, `tar` tries to defeat all in-memory cache pertaining to the archive, while it lets the speed optimization undisturbed for the '--compare' option. If you nevertheless use '--compare' for media verification, you may have to defeat the in-memory cache yourself, maybe by opening and reclosing the door latch of your recording unit, forcing some doubt in your operating system about the fact this is really the same volume as the one just written or read.

The '--verify' option would not be necessary if drivers were indeed able to detect dependably all write failures. This sometimes require many magnetic heads, some able to read after the writes occurred. One would not say that drivers unable to detect all cases are necessarily flawed, as long as programming is concerned.

The '--verify' ('-W') option will not work in conjunction with the '--multi-volume' ('-M') option or the '--append' ('-r'), '--update' ('-u') and '--delete' operations. See Section 4.2.1 [Operations], page 62, for more information on these operations.

Also, since tar normally strips leading '/' from file names (see Section 6.10.2 [absolute], page 120), a command like 'tar --verify -cf /tmp/foo.tar /etc' will work as desired only if the working directory is '/', as tar uses the archive's relative member names (e.g., 'etc/motd') when verifying the archive.

9.9 Write Protection

Almost all tapes and diskettes, and in a few rare cases, even disks can be *write protected*, to protect data on them from being changed. Once an archive is written, you should write protect the media to prevent the archive from being accidentally overwritten or deleted. (This will protect the archive from being changed with a tape or floppy drive—it will not protect it from magnet fields or other physical hazards.)

The write protection device itself is usually an integral part of the physical media, and can be a two position (write enabled/write disabled) switch, a notch which can be popped out or covered, a ring which can be removed from the center of a tape reel, or some other changeable feature.

10 Reliability and Security

The `tar` command reads and writes files as any other application does, and is subject to the usual caveats about reliability and security. This section contains some commonsense advice on the topic.

10.1 Reliability

Ideally, when `tar` is creating an archive, it reads from a file system that is not being modified, and encounters no errors or inconsistencies while reading and writing. If this is the case, the archive should faithfully reflect what was read. Similarly, when extracting from an archive, ideally `tar` ideally encounters no errors and the extracted files faithfully reflect what was in the archive.

However, when reading or writing real-world file systems, several things can go wrong; these include permissions problems, corruption of data, and race conditions.

10.1.1 Permissions Problems

If `tar` encounters errors while reading or writing files, it normally reports an error and exits with nonzero status. The work it does may therefore be incomplete. For example, when creating an archive, if `tar` cannot read a file then it cannot copy the file into the archive.

10.1.2 Data Corruption and Repair

If an archive becomes corrupted by an I/O error, this may corrupt the data in an extracted file. Worse, it may corrupt the file's metadata, which may cause later parts of the archive to become misinterpreted. An tar-format archive contains a checksum that most likely will detect errors in the metadata, but it will not detect errors in the data.

If data corruption is a concern, you can compute and check your own checksums of an archive by using other programs, such as `cksum`.

When attempting to recover from a read error or data corruption in an archive, you may need to skip past the questionable data and read the rest of the archive. This requires some expertise in the archive format and in other software tools.

10.1.3 Race conditions

If some other process is modifying the file system while `tar` is reading or writing files, the result may well be inconsistent due to race conditions. For example, if another process creates some files in a directory while `tar` is creating an archive containing the directory's files, `tar` may see some of the files but not others, or it may see a file that is in the process of being created. The resulting archive may not be a snapshot of the file system at any point in time. If an application such as a database system depends on an accurate

snapshot, restoring from the `tar` archive of a live file system may therefore
break that consistency and may break the application. The simplest way
to avoid the consistency issues is to avoid making other changes to the file
system while tar is reading it or writing it.

When creating an archive, several options are available to avoid race
conditions. Some hosts have a way of snapshotting a file system, or of
temporarily suspending all changes to a file system, by (say) suspending
the only virtual machine that can modify a file system; if you use these
facilities and have `tar -c` read from a snapshot when creating an archive,
you can avoid inconsistency problems. More drastically, before starting `tar`
you could suspend or shut down all processes other than `tar` that have access
to the file system, or you could unmount the file system and then mount it
read-only.

When extracting from an archive, one approach to avoid race conditions
is to create a directory that no other process can write to, and extract into
that.

10.2 Security

In some cases `tar` may be used in an adversarial situation, where an untrusted user is attempting to gain information about or modify otherwise-
inaccessible files. Dealing with untrusted data (that is, data generated by
an untrusted user) typically requires extra care, because even the smallest
mistake in the use of `tar` is more likely to be exploited by an adversary than
by a race condition.

10.2.1 Privacy

Standard privacy concerns apply when using `tar`. For example, suppose you
are archiving your home directory into a file '`/archive/myhome.tar`'. Any
secret information in your home directory, such as your SSH secret keys,
are copied faithfully into the archive. Therefore, if your home directory
contains any file that should not be read by some other user, the archive
itself should be not be readable by that user. And even if the archive's
data are inaccessible to untrusted users, its metadata (such as size or last-
modified date) may reveal some information about your home directory;
if the metadata are intended to be private, the archive's parent directory
should also be inaccessible to untrusted users.

One precaution is to create '`/archive`' so that it is not accessible to any
user, unless that user also has permission to access all the files in your home
directory.

Similarly, when extracting from an archive, take care that the permissions
of the extracted files are not more generous than what you want. Even if
the archive itself is readable only to you, files extracted from it have their
own permissions that may differ.

10.2.2 Integrity

When creating archives, take care that they are not writable by a untrusted user; otherwise, that user could modify the archive, and when you later extract from the archive you will get incorrect data.

When `tar` extracts from an archive, by default it writes into files relative to the working directory. If the archive was generated by an untrusted user, that user therefore can write into any file under the working directory. If the working directory contains a symbolic link to another directory, the untrusted user can also write into any file under the referenced directory. When extracting from an untrusted archive, it is therefore good practice to create an empty directory and run `tar` in that directory.

When extracting from two or more untrusted archives, each one should be extracted independently, into different empty directories. Otherwise, the first archive could create a symbolic link into an area outside the working directory, and the second one could follow the link and overwrite data that is not under the working directory. For example, when restoring from a series of incremental dumps, the archives should have been created by a trusted process, as otherwise the incremental restores might alter data outside the working directory.

If you use the '`--absolute-names`' ('`-P`') option when extracting, `tar` respects any file names in the archive, even file names that begin with '`/`' or contain '`..`'. As this lets the archive overwrite any file in your system that you can write, the '`--absolute-names`' ('`-P`') option should be used only for trusted archives.

Conversely, with the '`--keep-old-files`' ('`-k`') and '`--skip-old-files`' options, `tar` refuses to replace existing files when extracting. The difference between the two options is that the former treats existing files as errors whereas the latter just silently ignores them.

Finally, with the '`--no-overwrite-dir`' option, `tar` refuses to replace the permissions or ownership of already-existing directories. These options may help when extracting from untrusted archives.

10.2.3 Dealing with Live Untrusted Data

Extra care is required when creating from or extracting into a file system that is accessible to untrusted users. For example, superusers who invoke `tar` must be wary about its actions being hijacked by an adversary who is reading or writing the file system at the same time that `tar` is operating.

When creating an archive from a live file system, `tar` is vulnerable to denial-of-service attacks. For example, an adversarial user could create the illusion of an indefinitely-deep directory hierarchy '`d/e/f/g/...`' by creating directories one step ahead of `tar`, or the illusion of an indefinitely-long file by creating a sparse file but arranging for blocks to be allocated just before `tar` reads them. There is no easy way for `tar` to distinguish these scenarios from legitimate uses, so you may need to monitor `tar`, just as you'd need to monitor any other system service, to detect such attacks.

While a superuser is extracting from an archive into a live file system, an untrusted user might replace a directory with a symbolic link, in hopes that `tar` will follow the symbolic link and extract data into files that the untrusted user does not have access to. Even if the archive was generated by the superuser, it may contain a file such as 'd/etc/passwd' that the untrusted user earlier created in order to break in; if the untrusted user replaces the directory 'd/etc' with a symbolic link to '/etc' while `tar` is running, `tar` will overwrite '/etc/passwd'. This attack can be prevented by extracting into a directory that is inaccessible to untrusted users.

Similar attacks via symbolic links are also possible when creating an archive, if the untrusted user can modify an ancestor of a top-level argument of `tar`. For example, an untrusted user that can modify '/home/eve' can hijack a running instance of 'tar -cf - /home/eve/Documents/yesterday' by replacing '/home/eve/Documents' with a symbolic link to some other location. Attacks like these can be prevented by making sure that untrusted users cannot modify any files that are top-level arguments to `tar`, or any ancestor directories of these files.

10.2.4 Security Rules of Thumb

This section briefly summarizes rules of thumb for avoiding security pitfalls.

- Protect archives at least as much as you protect any of the files being archived.

- Extract from an untrusted archive only into an otherwise-empty directory. This directory and its parent should be accessible only to trusted users. For example:

  ```
  $ chmod go-rwx .
  $ mkdir -m go-rwx dir
  $ cd dir
  $ tar -xvf /archives/got-it-off-the-net.tar.gz
  ```

  As a corollary, do not do an incremental restore from an untrusted archive.

- Do not let untrusted users access files extracted from untrusted archives without checking first for problems such as setuid programs.

- Do not let untrusted users modify directories that are ancestors of top-level arguments of `tar`. For example, while you are executing 'tar -cf /archive/u-home.tar /u/home', do not let an untrusted user modify '/', '/archive', or '/u'.

- Pay attention to the diagnostics and exit status of `tar`.

- When archiving live file systems, monitor running instances of `tar` to detect denial-of-service attacks.

- Avoid unusual options such as '`--absolute-names`' ('`-P`'), '`--dereference`' ('`-h`'), '`--overwrite`', '`--recursive-unlink`', and '`--remove-files`' unless you understand their security implications.

Appendix A Changes

This appendix lists some important user-visible changes between version
GNU `tar` 1.28 and previous versions. An up-to-date version of this document
is available at the GNU tar documentation page.

Use of globbing patterns when listing and extracting.

> Previous versions of GNU tar assumed shell-style globbing when
> extracting from or listing an archive. For example:
>
> ```
> $ tar xf foo.tar '*.c'
> ```
>
> would extract all files whose names end in '`.c`'. This behavior
> was not documented and was incompatible with traditional tar
> implementations. Therefore, starting from version 1.15.91, GNU
> tar no longer uses globbing by default. For example, the above
> invocation is now interpreted as a request to extract from the
> archive the file named '`*.c`'.
>
> To facilitate transition to the new behavior for those users who
> got used to the previous incorrect one, `tar` will print a warning if
> it finds out that a requested member was not found in the archive
> and its name looks like a globbing pattern. For example:
>
> ```
> $ tar xf foo.tar  '*.c'
> tar: Pattern matching characters used in file names. Please,
> tar: use --wildcards to enable pattern matching, or --no-wildcards to
> tar: suppress this warning.
> tar: *.c: Not found in archive
> tar: Error exit delayed from previous errors
> ```
>
> To treat member names as globbing patterns, use the
> '`--wildcards`' option. If you want to tar to mimic the
> behavior of versions prior to 1.15.91, add this option to your
> `TAR_OPTIONS` variable.
>
> See Section 6.5 [wildcards], page 106, for the detailed discussion
> of the use of globbing patterns by GNU `tar`.

Use of short option '`-o`'.

> Earlier versions of GNU `tar` understood '`-o`' command line op-
> tion as a synonym for '`--old-archive`'.
>
> GNU `tar` starting from version 1.13.90 understands this option
> as a synonym for '`--no-same-owner`'. This is compatible with
> UNIX98 `tar` implementations.
>
> However, to facilitate transition, '`-o`' option retains its old se-
> mantics when it is used with one of archive-creation commands.
> Users are encouraged to use '`--format=oldgnu`' instead.
>
> It is especially important, since versions of GNU Automake up
> to and including 1.8.4 invoke tar with this option to produce
> distribution tarballs. See Chapter 8 [Formats], page 131, for the
> detailed discussion of this issue and its implications.

See section "Changing Automake's Behavior" in *GNU Automake*, for a description on how to use various archive formats with `automake`.

Future versions of GNU `tar` will understand '-o' only as a synonym for '--no-same-owner'.

Use of short option '-l'

Earlier versions of GNU `tar` understood '-l' option as a synonym for '--one-file-system'. Since such usage contradicted to UNIX98 specification and harmed compatibility with other implementations, it was declared deprecated in version 1.14. However, to facilitate transition to its new semantics, it was supported by versions 1.15 and 1.15.90. The present use of '-l' as a short variant of '--check-links' was introduced in version 1.15.91.

Use of options '--portability' and '--old-archive'

These options are deprecated. Please use '--format=v7' instead.

Use of option '--posix'

This option is deprecated. Please use '--format=posix' instead.

Appendix B Configuring Help Summary

Running `tar --help` displays the short `tar` option summary (see Section 3.5 [help], page 49). This summary is organized by *groups* of semantically close options. The options within each group are printed in the following order: a short option, eventually followed by a list of corresponding long option names, followed by a short description of the option. For example, here is an excerpt from the actual `tar --help` output:

```
Main operation mode:

 -A, --catenate, --concatenate   append tar files to an archive
 -c, --create                    create a new archive
 -d, --diff, --compare           find differences between archive and
                                 file system
     --delete                    delete from the archive
```

The exact visual representation of the help output is configurable via `ARGP_HELP_FMT` environment variable. The value of this variable is a comma-separated list of *format variable* assignments. There are two kinds of format variables. An *offset variable* keeps the offset of some part of help output text from the leftmost column on the screen. A *boolean* variable is a flag that toggles some output feature on or off. Depending on the type of the corresponding variable, there are two kinds of assignments:

Offset assignment

> The assignment to an offset variable has the following syntax:
>
> > `variable=value`
>
> where *variable* is the variable name, and *value* is a numeric value to be assigned to the variable.

Boolean assignment

> To assign `true` value to a variable, simply put this variable name. To assign `false` value, prefix the variable name with 'no-'. For example:
>
> > ```
> > # Assign true value:
> > dup-args
> > # Assign false value:
> > no-dup-args
> > ```

Following variables are declared:

`boolean dup-args`   [Help Output]

> If true, arguments for an option are shown with both short and long options, even when a given option has both forms, for example:
>
> > `-f ARCHIVE, --file=ARCHIVE use archive file or device ARCHIVE`

If false, then if an option has both short and long forms, the argument is only shown with the long one, for example:

```
     -f, --file=ARCHIVE            use archive file or device ARCHIVE
```

and a message indicating that the argument is applicable to both forms is printed below the options. This message can be disabled using **dup-args-note** (see below).

The default is false.

boolean dup-args-note   [Help Output]

If this variable is true, which is the default, the following notice is displayed at the end of the help output:

> Mandatory or optional arguments to long options are also mandatory or optional for any corresponding short options.

Setting **no-dup-args-note** inhibits this message. Normally, only one of variables **dup-args** or **dup-args-note** should be set.

offset short-opt-col   [Help Output]

Column in which short options start. Default is 2.

```
$ tar --help|grep ARCHIVE
  -f, --file=ARCHIVE   use archive file or device ARCHIVE
$ ARGP_HELP_FMT=short-opt-col=6 tar --help|grep ARCHIVE
      -f, --file=ARCHIVE   use archive file or device ARCHIVE
```

offset long-opt-col   [Help Output]

Column in which long options start. Default is 6. For example:

```
$ tar --help|grep ARCHIVE
  -f, --file=ARCHIVE   use archive file or device ARCHIVE
$ ARGP_HELP_FMT=long-opt-col=16 tar --help|grep ARCHIVE
  -f,              --file=ARCHIVE   use archive file or device ARCHIVE
```

offset doc-opt-col   [Help Output]

Column in which *doc options* start. A doc option isn't actually an option, but rather an arbitrary piece of documentation that is displayed in much the same manner as the options. For example, in the description of '--format' option:

```
  -H, --format=FORMAT         create archive of the given format.

  FORMAT is one of the following:

      gnu                GNU tar 1.13.x format
      oldgnu             GNU format as per tar <= 1.12
      pax                POSIX 1003.1-2001 (pax) format
      posix              same as pax
      ustar              POSIX 1003.1-1988 (ustar) format
      v7                 old V7 tar format
```

the format names are doc options. Thus, if you set *ARGP_HELP_FMT=doc-opt-col=6* the above part of the help output will look as follows:

```
        -H, --format=FORMAT          create archive of the given format.

    FORMAT is one of the following:

        gnu                          GNU tar 1.13.x format
        oldgnu                       GNU format as per tar <= 1.12
        pax                          POSIX 1003.1-2001 (pax) format
        posix                        same as pax
        ustar                        POSIX 1003.1-1988 (ustar) format
        v7                           old V7 tar format
```

offset opt-doc-col   [Help Output]

Column in which option description starts. Default is 29.

```
    $ tar --help|grep ARCHIVE
      -f, --file=ARCHIVE        use archive file or device ARCHIVE
    $ ARGP_HELP_FMT=opt-doc-col=19 tar --help|grep ARCHIVE
      -f, --file=ARCHIVE   use archive file or device ARCHIVE
    $ ARGP_HELP_FMT=opt-doc-col=9 tar --help|grep ARCHIVE
      -f, --file=ARCHIVE
              use archive file or device ARCHIVE
```

Notice, that the description starts on a separate line if opt-doc-col value is too small.

offset header-col   [Help Output]

Column in which *group headers* are printed. A group header is a descriptive text preceding an option group. For example, in the following text:

```
    Main operation mode:

      -A, --catenate, --concatenate   append tar files to
                                      an archive
      -c, --create                 create a new archive
```

'Main operation mode:' is the group header.

The default value is 1.

offset usage-indent   [Help Output]

Indentation of wrapped usage lines. Affects '--usage' output. Default is 12.

offset rmargin   [Help Output]

Right margin of the text output. Used for wrapping.

Appendix C Fixing Snapshot Files

Various situations can cause device numbers to change: upgrading your kernel version, reconfiguring your hardware, loading kernel modules in a different order, using virtual volumes that are assembled dynamically (such as with LVM or RAID), hot-plugging drives (e.g. external USB or Firewire drives), etc. In the majority of cases this change is unnoticed by the users. However, it influences `tar` incremental backups: the device number is stored in tar snapshot files (see [Snapshot Files], page 205) and is used to determine whether the file has changed since the last backup. If the device numbers change for some reason, by default the next backup you run will be a full backup.

To minimize the impact in these cases, GNU `tar` comes with the `tar-snapshot-edit` utility for inspecting and updating device numbers in snapshot files. (The utility, written by Dustin J. Mitchell, is also available from the GNU tar home page.)

To obtain a summary of the device numbers found in the snapshot file, run

```
$ tar-snapshot-edit snapfile
```

where *snapfile* is the name of the snapshot file (you can supply as many files as you wish in a single command line). You can then compare the numbers across snapshot files, or against those currently in use on the live filesystem (using `ls -l` or `stat`).

Assuming the device numbers have indeed changed, it's often possible to simply tell GNU `tar` to ignore the device number when processing the incremental snapshot files for these backups, using the '`--no-check-device`' option (see [device numbers], page 85).

Alternatively, you can use the `tar-edit-snapshot` script's '`-r`' option to update all occurrences of the given device number in the snapshot file(s). It takes a single argument of the form '*olddev-newdev*', where *olddev* is the device number used in the snapshot file, and *newdev* is the corresponding new device number. Both numbers may be specified in hex (e.g., '`0xfe01`'), decimal (e.g., '`65025`'), or as a major:minor number pair (e.g., '`254:1`'). To change several device numbers at once, specify them in a single comma-separated list, as in '`-r 0x3060-0x4500,0x307-0x4600`'.

Before updating the snapshot file, it is a good idea to create a backup copy of it. This is accomplished by '`-b`' option. The name of the backup file is obtained by appending '`~`' to the original file name.

An example session:

```
$ tar-snapshot-edit root_snap.0 boot_snap.0
File: root_snap.0
  Detected snapshot file version: 2

  Device 0x0000 occurs 1 times.
  Device 0x0003 occurs 1 times.
```

```
        Device 0x0005 occurs 1 times.
        Device 0x0013 occurs 1 times.
        Device 0x6801 occurs 1 times.
        Device 0x6803 occurs 6626 times.
        Device 0xfb00 occurs 1 times.

    File: boot_snap.0
        Detected snapshot file version: 2

        Device 0x6801 occurs 3 times.
    $ tar-snapshot-edit -b -r 0x6801-0x6901,0x6803-0x6903 root_snap.0 boot_snap.0
    File: root_snap.0
        Detected snapshot file version: 2

        Updated 6627 records.

    File: boot_snap.0
        Detected snapshot file version: 2

        Updated 3 records.
```

Appendix D Tar Internals

Basic Tar Format

(This message will disappear, once this node revised.)

While an archive may contain many files, the archive itself is a single ordinary file. Like any other file, an archive file can be written to a storage device such as a tape or disk, sent through a pipe or over a network, saved on the active file system, or even stored in another archive. An archive file is not easy to read or manipulate without using the **tar** utility or Tar mode in GNU Emacs.

Physically, an archive consists of a series of file entries terminated by an end-of-archive entry, which consists of two 512 blocks of zero bytes. A file entry usually describes one of the files in the archive (an *archive member*), and consists of a file header and the contents of the file. File headers contain file names and statistics, checksum information which **tar** uses to detect file corruption, and information about file types.

Archives are permitted to have more than one member with the same member name. One way this situation can occur is if more than one version of a file has been stored in the archive. For information about adding new versions of a file to an archive, see Section 4.2.3 [update], page 66.

In addition to entries describing archive members, an archive may contain entries which **tar** itself uses to store information. See Section 9.7 [label], page 173, for an example of such an archive entry.

A **tar** archive file contains a series of blocks. Each block contains **BLOCKSIZE** bytes. Although this format may be thought of as being on magnetic tape, other media are often used.

Each file archived is represented by a header block which describes the file, followed by zero or more blocks which give the contents of the file. At the end of the archive file there are two 512-byte blocks filled with binary zeros as an end-of-file marker. A reasonable system should write such end-of-file marker at the end of an archive, but must not assume that such a block exists when reading an archive. In particular GNU **tar** always issues a warning if it does not encounter it.

The blocks may be *blocked* for physical I/O operations. Each record of n blocks (where n is set by the '--blocking-factor=*512-size*' ('-b *512-size*') option to **tar**) is written with a single '**write ()**' operation. On magnetic tapes, the result of such a write is a single record. When writing an archive, the last record of blocks should be written at the full size, with blocks after the zero block containing all zeros. When reading an archive, a reasonable system should properly handle an archive whose last record is shorter than the rest, or which contains garbage records after a zero block.

The header block is defined in C as follows. In the GNU **tar** distribution, this is part of file '**src/tar.h**':

```
/* tar Header Block, from POSIX 1003.1-1990. */

/* POSIX header. */

struct posix_header
{                                    /* byte offset */
  char name[100];                    /*   0 */
  char mode[8];                      /* 100 */
  char uid[8];                       /* 108 */
  char gid[8];                       /* 116 */
  char size[12];                     /* 124 */
  char mtime[12];                    /* 136 */
  char chksum[8];                    /* 148 */
  char typeflag;                     /* 156 */
  char linkname[100];                /* 157 */
  char magic[6];                     /* 257 */
  char version[2];                   /* 263 */
  char uname[32];                    /* 265 */
  char gname[32];                    /* 297 */
  char devmajor[8];                  /* 329 */
  char devminor[8];                  /* 337 */
  char prefix[155];                  /* 345 */
                                     /* 500 */
};

#define TMAGIC    "ustar"           /* ustar and a null */
#define TMAGLEN   6
#define TVERSION  "00"              /* 00 and no null */
#define TVERSLEN  2

/* Values used in typeflag field. */
#define REGTYPE   '0'               /* regular file */
#define AREGTYPE  '\0'              /* regular file */
#define LNKTYPE   '1'               /* link */
#define SYMTYPE   '2'               /* reserved */
#define CHRTYPE   '3'               /* character special */
#define BLKTYPE   '4'               /* block special */
#define DIRTYPE   '5'               /* directory */
#define FIFOTYPE  '6'               /* FIFO special */
#define CONTTYPE  '7'               /* reserved */

#define XHDTYPE   'x'                  /* Extended header referring to the
                          next file in the archive */
#define XGLTYPE   'g'               /* Global extended header */

/* Bits used in the mode field, values in octal. */
#define TSUID     04000            /* set UID on execution */
#define TSGID     02000            /* set GID on execution */
#define TSVTX     01000            /* reserved */
                                   /* file permissions */
#define TUREAD    00400            /* read by owner */
```

```
#define TUWRITE    00200          /* write by owner */
#define TUEXEC     00100          /* execute/search by owner */
#define TGREAD     00040          /* read by group */
#define TGWRITE    00020          /* write by group */
#define TGEXEC     00010          /* execute/search by group */
#define TOREAD     00004          /* read by other */
#define TOWRITE    00002          /* write by other */
#define TOEXEC     00001          /* execute/search by other */
```

```
/* tar Header Block, GNU extensions. */
```

```
/* In GNU tar, SYMTYPE is for to symbolic links, and CONTTYPE is for
   contiguous files, so maybe disobeying the "reserved" comment in POSIX
   header description.  I suspect these were meant to be used this way, and
   should not have really been "reserved" in the published standards. */
```

```
/* *BEWARE* *BEWARE* *BEWARE* that the following information is still
   boiling, and may change.  Even if the OLDGNU format description should be
   accurate, the so-called GNU format is not yet fully decided.  It is
   surely meant to use only extensions allowed by POSIX, but the sketch
   below repeats some ugliness from the OLDGNU format, which should rather
   go away.  Sparse files should be saved in such a way that they do *not*
   require two passes at archive creation time.  Huge files get some POSIX
   fields to overflow, alternate solutions have to be sought for this. */
```

```
/* Descriptor for a single file hole. */
```

```
struct sparse
{                                /* byte offset */
  char offset[12];               /*  0 */
  char numbytes[12];             /* 12 */
                                 /* 24 */
};
```

```
/* Sparse files are not supported in POSIX ustar format.  For sparse files
   with a POSIX header, a GNU extra header is provided which holds overall
   sparse information and a few sparse descriptors.  When an old GNU header
   replaces both the POSIX header and the GNU extra header, it holds some
   sparse descriptors too.  Whether POSIX or not, if more sparse descriptors
   are still needed, they are put into as many successive sparse headers as
   necessary.  The following constants tell how many sparse descriptors fit
   in each kind of header able to hold them. */
```

```
#define SPARSES_IN_EXTRA_HEADER  16
#define SPARSES_IN_OLDGNU_HEADER 4
#define SPARSES_IN_SPARSE_HEADER 21
```

```
/* Extension header for sparse files, used immediately after the GNU extra
   header, and used only if all sparse information cannot fit into that
   extra header.  There might even be many such extension headers, one after
   the other, until all sparse information has been recorded. */
```

```
struct sparse_header
{                                      /* byte offset */
  struct sparse sp[SPARSES_IN_SPARSE_HEADER];
                                       /*   0 */
  char isextended;                     /* 504 */
                                       /* 505 */
};
```

/* The old GNU format header conflicts with POSIX format in such a way that
   POSIX archives may fool old GNU tar's, and POSIX tar's might well be
   fooled by old GNU tar archives. An old GNU format header uses the space
   used by the prefix field in a POSIX header, and cumulates information
   normally found in a GNU extra header. With an old GNU tar header, we
   never see any POSIX header nor GNU extra header. Supplementary sparse
   headers are allowed, however. */

```
struct oldgnu_header
{                                      /* byte offset */
  char unused_pad1[345];               /*   0 */
  char atime[12];                      /* 345 Incr. archive: atime of the file */
  char ctime[12];                      /* 357 Incr. archive: ctime of the file */
  char offset[12];                     /* 369 Multivolume archive: the offset of
                      the start of this volume */
  char longnames[4];                   /* 381 Not used */
  char unused_pad2;                    /* 385 */
  struct sparse sp[SPARSES_IN_OLDGNU_HEADER];
                                       /* 386 */
  char isextended;                     /* 482 Sparse file: Extension sparse header
                      follows */
  char realsize[12];                   /* 483 Sparse file: Real size*/
                                       /* 495 */
};
```

/* OLDGNU_MAGIC uses both magic and version fields, which are contiguous.
   Found in an archive, it indicates an old GNU header format, which will be
   hopefully become obsolescent. With OLDGNU_MAGIC, uname and gname are
   valid, though the header is not truly POSIX conforming. */
```
#define OLDGNU_MAGIC "ustar  "  /* 7 chars and a null */
```

/* The standards committee allows only capital A through capital Z for
   user-defined expansion. Other letters in use include:

   'A' Solaris Access Control List
   'E' Solaris Extended Attribute File
   'I' Inode only, as in 'star'
   'N' Obsolete GNU tar, for file names that do not fit into the main header.
   'X' POSIX 1003.1-2001 eXtended (VU version) */

/* This is a dir entry that contains the names of files that were in the
   dir at the time the dump was made. */
```
#define GNUTYPE_DUMPDIR 'D'
```

```
/* Identifies the *next* file on the tape as having a long linkname. */
#define GNUTYPE_LONGLINK 'K'

/* Identifies the *next* file on the tape as having a long name. */
#define GNUTYPE_LONGNAME 'L'

/* This is the continuation of a file that began on another volume. */
#define GNUTYPE_MULTIVOL 'M'

/* This is for sparse files. */
#define GNUTYPE_SPARSE 'S'

/* This file is a tape/volume header.  Ignore it on extraction. */
#define GNUTYPE_VOLHDR 'V'

/* Solaris extended header */
#define SOLARIS_XHDTYPE 'X'

/* Jörg Schilling star header */

struct star_header
{                              /* byte offset */
  char name[100];              /*   0 */
  char mode[8];                /* 100 */
  char uid[8];                 /* 108 */
  char gid[8];                 /* 116 */
  char size[12];               /* 124 */
  char mtime[12];              /* 136 */
  char chksum[8];              /* 148 */
  char typeflag;               /* 156 */
  char linkname[100];          /* 157 */
  char magic[6];               /* 257 */
  char version[2];             /* 263 */
  char uname[32];              /* 265 */
  char gname[32];              /* 297 */
  char devmajor[8];            /* 329 */
  char devminor[8];            /* 337 */
  char prefix[131];            /* 345 */
  char atime[12];              /* 476 */
  char ctime[12];              /* 488 */
                               /* 500 */
};

#define SPARSES_IN_STAR_HEADER      4
#define SPARSES_IN_STAR_EXT_HEADER  21

struct star_in_header
{
  char fill[345];      /*   0  Everything that is before t_prefix */
  char prefix[1];      /* 345  t_name prefix */
  char fill2;          /* 346 */
  char fill3[8];       /* 347 */
```

```
    char isextended;        /* 355 */
    struct sparse sp[SPARSES_IN_STAR_HEADER]; /* 356 */
    char realsize[12];      /* 452  Actual size of the file */
    char offset[12];        /* 464  Offset of multivolume contents */
    char atime[12];         /* 476 */
    char ctime[12];         /* 488 */
    char mfill[8];          /* 500 */
    char xmagic[4];         /* 508  "tar" */
};

struct star_ext_header
{
  struct sparse sp[SPARSES_IN_STAR_EXT_HEADER];
  char isextended;
};
```

All characters in header blocks are represented by using 8-bit characters in the local variant of ASCII. Each field within the structure is contiguous; that is, there is no padding used within the structure. Each character on the archive medium is stored contiguously.

Bytes representing the contents of files (after the header block of each file) are not translated in any way and are not constrained to represent characters in any character set. The **tar** format does not distinguish text files from binary files, and no translation of file contents is performed.

The **name**, **linkname**, **magic**, **uname**, and **gname** are null-terminated character strings. All other fields are zero-filled octal numbers in ASCII. Each numeric field of width w contains w minus 1 digits, and a null.

The **name** field is the file name of the file, with directory names (if any) preceding the file name, separated by slashes.

The **mode** field provides nine bits specifying file permissions and three bits to specify the Set UID, Set GID, and Save Text (*sticky*) modes. Values for these bits are defined above. When special permissions are required to create a file with a given mode, and the user restoring files from the archive does not hold such permissions, the mode bit(s) specifying those special permissions are ignored. Modes which are not supported by the operating system restoring files from the archive will be ignored. Unsupported modes should be faked up when creating or updating an archive; e.g., the group permission could be copied from the *other* permission.

The **uid** and **gid** fields are the numeric user and group ID of the file owners, respectively. If the operating system does not support numeric user or group IDs, these fields should be ignored.

The **size** field is the size of the file in bytes; linked files are archived with this field specified as zero.

The **mtime** field is the data modification time of the file at the time it was archived. It is the ASCII representation of the octal value of the last time the file's contents were modified, represented as an integer number of seconds since January 1, 1970, 00:00 Coordinated Universal Time.

The `chksum` field is the ASCII representation of the octal value of the simple sum of all bytes in the header block. Each 8-bit byte in the header is added to an unsigned integer, initialized to zero, the precision of which shall be no less than seventeen bits. When calculating the checksum, the `chksum` field is treated as if it were all blanks.

The `typeflag` field specifies the type of file archived. If a particular implementation does not recognize or permit the specified type, the file will be extracted as if it were a regular file. As this action occurs, `tar` issues a warning to the standard error.

The `atime` and `ctime` fields are used in making incremental backups; they store, respectively, the particular file's access and status change times.

The `offset` is used by the '`--multi-volume`' ('`-M`') option, when making a multi-volume archive. The offset is number of bytes into the file that we need to restart at to continue the file on the next tape, i.e., where we store the location that a continued file is continued at.

The following fields were added to deal with sparse files. A file is *sparse* if it takes in unallocated blocks which end up being represented as zeros, i.e., no useful data. A test to see if a file is sparse is to look at the number blocks allocated for it versus the number of characters in the file; if there are fewer blocks allocated for the file than would normally be allocated for a file of that size, then the file is sparse. This is the method `tar` uses to detect a sparse file, and once such a file is detected, it is treated differently from non-sparse files.

Sparse files are often `dbm` files, or other database-type files which have data at some points and emptiness in the greater part of the file. Such files can appear to be very large when an '`ls -l`' is done on them, when in truth, there may be a very small amount of important data contained in the file. It is thus undesirable to have `tar` think that it must back up this entire file, as great quantities of room are wasted on empty blocks, which can lead to running out of room on a tape far earlier than is necessary. Thus, sparse files are dealt with so that these empty blocks are not written to the tape. Instead, what is written to the tape is a description, of sorts, of the sparse file: where the holes are, how big the holes are, and how much data is found at the end of the hole. This way, the file takes up potentially far less room on the tape, and when the file is extracted later on, it will look exactly the way it looked beforehand. The following is a description of the fields used to handle a sparse file:

The `sp` is an array of `struct sparse`. Each `struct sparse` contains two 12-character strings which represent an offset into the file and a number of bytes to be written at that offset. The offset is absolute, and not relative to the offset in preceding array element.

The header can hold four of these **struct sparse** at the moment; if more are needed, they are not stored in the header.

The **isextended** flag is set when an **extended_header** is needed to deal with a file. Note that this means that this flag can only be set when dealing with a sparse file, and it is only set in the event that the description of the file will not fit in the allotted room for sparse structures in the header. In other words, an extended_header is needed.

The **extended_header** structure is used for sparse files which need more sparse structures than can fit in the header. The header can fit 4 such structures; if more are needed, the flag **isextended** gets set and the next block is an **extended_header**.

Each **extended_header** structure contains an array of 21 sparse structures, along with a similar **isextended** flag that the header had. There can be an indeterminate number of such **extended_headers** to describe a sparse file.

REGTYPE
AREGTYPE   These flags represent a regular file. In order to be compatible with older versions of **tar**, a **typeflag** value of **AREGTYPE** should be silently recognized as a regular file. New archives should be created using **REGTYPE**. Also, for backward compatibility, **tar** treats a regular file whose name ends with a slash as a directory.

LNKTYPE   This flag represents a file linked to another file, of any type, previously archived. Such files are identified in Unix by each file having the same device and inode number. The linked-to name is specified in the **linkname** field with a trailing null.

SYMTYPE   This represents a symbolic link to another file. The linked-to name is specified in the **linkname** field with a trailing null.

CHRTYPE
BLKTYPE   These represent character special files and block special files respectively. In this case the **devmajor** and **devminor** fields will contain the major and minor device numbers respectively. Operating systems may map the device specifications to their own local specification, or may ignore the entry.

DIRTYPE   This flag specifies a directory or sub-directory. The directory name in the **name** field should end with a slash. On systems where disk allocation is performed on a directory basis, the **size** field will contain the maximum number of bytes (which may be rounded to the nearest disk block allocation unit) which the directory may hold. A **size** field of zero indicates no such limiting. Systems which do not support limiting in this manner should ignore the **size** field.

FIFOTYPE   This specifies a FIFO special file. Note that the archiving of a FIFO file archives the existence of this file and not its contents.

CONTTYPE   This specifies a contiguous file, which is the same as a normal file except that, in operating systems which support it, all its space is allocated contiguously on the disk. Operating systems which do not allow contiguous allocation should silently treat this type as a normal file.

A ... Z   These are reserved for custom implementations. Some of these are used in the GNU modified format, as described below.

Other values are reserved for specification in future revisions of the P1003 standard, and should not be used by any `tar` program.

The `magic` field indicates that this archive was output in the P1003 archive format. If this field contains `TMAGIC`, the `uname` and `gname` fields will contain the ASCII representation of the owner and group of the file respectively. If found, the user and group IDs are used rather than the values in the `uid` and `gid` fields.

For references, see ISO/IEC 9945-1:1990 or IEEE Std 1003.1-1990, pages 169-173 (section 10.1) for *Archive/Interchange File Format*; and IEEE Std 1003.2-1992, pages 380-388 (section 4.48) and pages 936-940 (section E.4.48) for *pax - Portable archive interchange*.

GNU Extensions to the Archive Format

(This message will disappear, once this node revised.)

The GNU format uses additional file types to describe new types of files in an archive. These are listed below.

GNUTYPE_DUMPDIR

'D'   This represents a directory and a list of files created by the '--incremental' ('-G') option. The `size` field gives the total size of the associated list of files. Each file name is preceded by either a 'Y' (the file should be in this archive) or an 'N'. (The file is a directory, or is not stored in the archive.) Each file name is terminated by a null. There is an additional null after the last file name.

GNUTYPE_MULTIVOL

'M'   This represents a file continued from another volume of a multi-volume archive created with the '--multi-volume' ('-M') option. The original type of the file is not given here. The `size` field gives the maximum size of this piece of the file (assuming the volume does not end before the file is written out). The `offset` field gives the offset from the beginning of the file where this part of the file begins. Thus `size` plus `offset` should equal the original size of the file.

GNUTYPE_SPARSE

'S'   This flag indicates that we are dealing with a sparse file. Note that archiving a sparse file requires special operations to find holes in the file, which mark the positions of these holes, along with the number of bytes of data to be found after the hole.

GNUTYPE_VOLHDR
'V'   This file type is used to mark the volume header that was given with the '--label=archive-label' ('-V archive-label') option when the archive was created. The name field contains the name given after the '--label=archive-label' ('-V archive-label') option. The size field is zero. Only the first file in each volume of an archive should have this type.

You may have trouble reading a GNU format archive on a non-GNU system if the options '--incremental' ('-G'), '--multi-volume' ('-M'), '--sparse' ('-S'), or '--label=archive-label' ('-V archive-label') were used when writing the archive. In general, if tar does not use the GNU-added fields of the header, other versions of tar should be able to read the archive. Otherwise, the tar program will give an error, the most likely one being a checksum error.

Storing Sparse Files

The notion of sparse file, and the ways of handling it from the point of view of GNU tar user have been described in detail in Section 8.1.2 [sparse], page 137. This chapter describes the internal format GNU tar uses to store such files.

The support for sparse files in GNU tar has a long history. The earliest version featuring this support that I was able to find was 1.09, released in November, 1990. The format introduced back then is called *old GNU sparse format* and in spite of the fact that its design contained many flaws, it was the only format GNU tar supported until version 1.14 (May, 2004), which introduced initial support for sparse archives in PAX archives (see Section 8.3.7 [posix], page 143). This format was not free from design flaws, either and it was subsequently improved in versions 1.15.2 (November, 2005) and 1.15.92 (June, 2006).

In addition to GNU sparse format, GNU tar is able to read and extract sparse files archived by star.

The following subsections describe each format in detail.

Old GNU Format

The format introduced in November 1990 (v. 1.09) was designed on top of standard ustar headers in such an unfortunate way that some of its fields overwrote fields required by POSIX.

An old GNU sparse header is designated by type 'S' (GNUTYPE_SPARSE) and has the following layout:

Offset	Size	Name	Data type	Contents

0	345		N/A	Not used.
345	12	atime	Number	`atime` of the file.
357	12	ctime	Number	`ctime` of the file .
369	12	offset	Number	For multivolume archives: the offset of the start of this volume.
381	4		N/A	Not used.
385	1		N/A	Not used.
386	96	sp	`sparse_ header`	(4 entries) File map.
482	1	isextended	Bool	`1` if an extension sparse header follows, `0` otherwise.
483	12	realsize	Number	Real size of the file.

Each of `sparse_header` object at offset 386 describes a single data chunk. It has the following structure:

Offset	**Size**	**Data type**	**Contents**
0	12	Number	Offset of the beginning of the chunk.
12	12	Number	Size of the chunk.

If the member contains more than four chunks, the `isextended` field of the header has the value `1` and the main header is followed by one or more *extension headers*. Each such header has the following structure:

Offset	**Size**	**Name**	**Data type**	**Contents**
0	21	sp	`sparse_ header`	(21 entries) File map.
504	1	isextended	Bool	`1` if an extension sparse header follows, or `0` otherwise.

A header with `isextended=0` ends the map.

PAX Format, Versions 0.0 and 0.1

There are two formats available in this branch. The version `0.0` is the initial version of sparse format used by `tar` versions 1.14–1.15.1. The sparse file map is kept in extended (`x`) PAX header variables:

`GNU.sparse.size`
> Real size of the stored file;

`GNU.sparse.numblocks`
> Number of blocks in the sparse map;

`GNU.sparse.offset`
> Offset of the data block;

`GNU.sparse.numbytes`
> Size of the data block.

The latter two variables repeat for each data block, so the overall structure is like this:

```
GNU.sparse.size=size
GNU.sparse.numblocks=numblocks
repeat numblocks times
  GNU.sparse.offset=offset
  GNU.sparse.numbytes=numbytes
end repeat
```

This format presented the following two problems:

1. Whereas the POSIX specification allows a variable to appear multiple times in a header, it requires that only the last occurrence be meaningful. Thus, multiple occurrences of GNU.sparse.offset and GNU.sparse.numbytes are conflicting with the POSIX specs.

2. Attempting to extract such archives using a third-party's tar results in extraction of sparse files in *condensed form*. If the tar implementation in question does not support POSIX format, it will also extract a file containing extension header attributes. This file can be used to expand the file to its original state. However, posix-aware tars will usually ignore the unknown variables, which makes restoring the file more difficult. See [extracting sparse v.0.x], page 150, for the detailed description of how to restore such members using non-GNU tars.

GNU tar 1.15.2 introduced sparse format version 0.1, which attempted to solve these problems. As its predecessor, this format stores sparse map in the extended POSIX header. It retains GNU.sparse.size and GNU.sparse.numblocks variables, but instead of GNU.sparse.offset/GNU.sparse.numbytes pairs it uses a single variable:

GNU.sparse.map

>   Map of non-null data chunks. It is a string consisting of comma-separated values "*offset,size*[,*offset-1,size-1*...]"

To address the 2nd problem, the name field in ustar is replaced with a special name, constructed using the following pattern:

```
%d/GNUSparseFile.%p/%f
```

The real name of the sparse file is stored in the variable GNU.sparse.name. Thus, those tar implementations that are not aware of GNU extensions will at least extract the files into separate directories, giving the user a possibility to expand it afterwards. See [extracting sparse v.0.x], page 150, for the detailed description of how to restore such members using non-GNU tars.

The resulting GNU.sparse.map string can be *very* long. Although POSIX does not impose any limit on the length of a x header variable, this possibly can confuse some tars.

PAX Format, Version 1.0

The version 1.0 of sparse format was introduced with GNU `tar` 1.15.92. Its main objective was to make the resulting file extractable with little effort even by non-posix aware `tar` implementations. Starting from this version, the extended header preceding a sparse member always contains the following variables that identify the format being used:

`GNU.sparse.major`
>   Major version

`GNU.sparse.minor`
>   Minor version

The `name` field in `ustar` header contains a special name, constructed using the following pattern:

>   `%d/GNUSparseFile.%p/%f`

The real name of the sparse file is stored in the variable `GNU.sparse.name`. The real size of the file is stored in the variable `GNU.sparse.realsize`.

The sparse map itself is stored in the file data block, preceding the actual file data. It consists of a series of octal numbers of arbitrary length, delimited by newlines. The map is padded with nulls to the nearest block boundary.

The first number gives the number of entries in the map. Following are map entries, each one consisting of two numbers giving the offset and size of the data block it describes.

The format is designed in such a way that non-posix aware `tars` and `tars` not supporting `GNU.sparse.*` keywords will extract each sparse file in its condensed form with the file map prepended and will place it into a separate directory. Then, using a simple program it would be possible to expand the file to its original form even without GNU `tar`. See Section 8.3.10.2 [Sparse Recovery], page 149, for the detailed information on how to extract sparse members without GNU `tar`.

Format of the Incremental Snapshot Files

A *snapshot file* (or *directory file*) is created during incremental backups (see Section 5.2 [Incremental Dumps], page 84). It contains the status of the file system at the time of the dump and is used to determine which files were modified since the last backup.

GNU `tar` version 1.28 supports three snapshot file formats. The first format, called *format 0*, is the one used by GNU `tar` versions up to and including 1.15.1. The second format, called *format 1* is an extended version of this format, that contains more metadata and allows for further extensions. It was used by alpha release version 1.15.90. For alpha version 1.15.91 and stable releases version 1.16 up through 1.28, the *format 2* is used.

GNU `tar` is able to read all three formats, but will create snapshots only in format 2.

This appendix describes all three formats in detail.

0. 'Format 0' snapshot file begins with a line containing a decimal number that represents a UNIX timestamp of the beginning of the last archivation. This line is followed by directory metadata descriptions, one per line. Each description has the following format:

    `[nfs]dev inode name`

   where:

   nfs   A single plus character ('+'), if this directory is located on an NFS-mounted partition, otherwise empty.

   (That is, for non-NFS directories, the first character on the description line contains the start of the *dev* field.)

   dev   Device number of the directory;

   inode   I-node number of the directory;

   name   Name of the directory. Any special characters (white-space, backslashes, etc.) are quoted.

1. 'Format 1' snapshot file begins with a line specifying the format of the file. This line has the following structure:

    `'GNU tar-'tar-version'-'incr-format-version`

   where *tar-version* is the version number of GNU tar implementation that created this snapshot, and *incr-format-version* is the version number of the snapshot format (in this case '1').

   Next line contains two decimal numbers, representing the time of the last backup. First number is the number of seconds, the second one is the number of nanoseconds, since the beginning of the epoch.

   Lines that follow contain directory metadata, one line per directory. Each line is formatted as follows:

    `[nfs]mtime-sec mtime-nsec dev inode name`

   where *mtime-sec* and *mtime-nsec* represent last modification time of this directory with nanosecond precision; *nfs*, *dev*, *inode* and *name* have the same meaning as with 'format 0'.

2. 'Format 2' snapshot file begins with a format identifier, as described for version 1, e.g.:

    `GNU tar-1.28-2`

   This line is followed by newline. Rest of file consists of records, separated by null (ASCII 0) characters. Thus, in contrast to the previous formats, format 2 snapshot is a binary file.

   First two records are decimal integers, representing the time of the last backup. First number is the number of seconds, the second one is the number of nanoseconds, since the beginning of the epoch. These are followed by arbitrary number of directory records.

Each *directory record* contains a set of metadata describing a particular directory. Parts of a directory record are delimited with ASCII 0 characters. The following table describes each part. The *Number* type in this table stands for a decimal integer in ASCII notation. (Negative values are preceded with a "-" character, while positive values have no leading punctuation.)

Field	Type	Description
nfs	Character	'1' if the directory is located on an NFS-mounted partition, or '0' otherwise;
timestamp_sec	Number	Modification time, seconds;
timestamp_nsec	Number	Modification time, nanoseconds;
dev	Number	Device number;
ino	Number	I-node number;
name	String	Directory name; in contrast to the previous versions it is not quoted;
contents	Dumpdir	Contents of the directory; See [Dumpdir], page 207, for a description of its format.

Dumpdirs stored in snapshot files contain only records of types 'Y', 'N' and 'D'.

The specific range of values allowed in each of the *Number* fields depends on the underlying C datatypes as determined when `tar` is compiled. To see the specific ranges allowed for a particular `tar` binary, you can use the '`--show-snapshot-field-ranges`' option:

```
$ tar --show-snapshot-field-ranges
This tar's snapshot file field ranges are
    (field name      => [ min, max ]):

    nfs              => [ 0, 1 ],
    timestamp_sec    => [ -9223372036854775808, 9223372036854775807 ],
    timestamp_nsec   => [ 0, 999999999 ],
    dev              => [ 0, 18446744073709551615 ],
    ino              => [ 0, 18446744073709551615 ],
```

(This example is from a GNU/Linux x86_64 system.)

Dumpdir

Incremental archives keep information about contents of each dumped directory in special data blocks called *dumpdirs*.

Dumpdir is a sequence of entries of the following form:

```
C filename \0
```

where *C* is one of the *control codes* described below, *filename* is the name of the file *C* operates upon, and '\0' represents a nul character (ASCII 0). The white space characters were added for readability, real dumpdirs do not contain them.

Each dumpdir ends with a single nul character.

The following table describes control codes and their meanings:

‘Y’   *filename* is contained in the archive.

‘N’   *filename* was present in the directory at the time the archive was made, yet it was not dumped to the archive, because it had not changed since the last backup.

‘D’   *filename* is a directory.

‘R’   This code requests renaming of the *filename* to the name specified with the ‘T’ command, that immediately follows it.

‘T’   Specify target file name for ‘R’ command (see below).

‘X’   Specify *temporary directory* name for a rename operation (see below).

Codes ‘Y’, ‘N’ and ‘D’ require *filename* argument to be a relative file name to the directory this dumpdir describes, whereas codes ‘R’, ‘T’ and ‘X’ require their argument to be an absolute file name.

The three codes ‘R’, ‘T’ and ‘X’ specify a *renaming operation*. In the simplest case it is:

```
R‘source’\0T‘dest’\0
```

which means "rename file ‘source’ to file ‘dest’".

However, there are cases that require using a *temporary directory*. For example, consider the following scenario:

1. Previous run dumped a directory ‘foo’ which contained the following three directories:

```
a
b
c
```

2. They were renamed *cyclically*, so that:

```
‘a’ became ‘b’
‘b’ became ‘c’
‘c’ became ‘a’
```

3. New incremental dump was made.

This case cannot be handled by three successive renames, since renaming ‘a’ to ‘b’ will destroy the existing directory. To correctly process it, GNU `tar` needs a temporary directory, so it creates the following dumpdir (newlines have been added for readability):

```
Xfoo\0
Rfoo/a\0T\0
Rfoo/b\0Tfoo/c\0
Rfoo/c\0Tfoo/a\0
R\0Tfoo/a\0
```

The first command, ‘Xfoo\0’, instructs the extractor to create a temporary directory in the directory ‘foo’. Second command, ‘Rfoo/aT\0’, says "rename file 'foo/a' to the temporary directory that has just been created" (empty file name after a command means use temporary directory). Third and fourth commands work as usual, and, finally, the last command, 'R\0Tfoo/a\0' tells tar to rename the temporary directory to 'foo/a'.

The exact placement of a dumpdir in the archive depends on the archive format (see Chapter 8 [Formats], page 131):

- PAX archives

  In PAX archives, dumpdir is stored in the extended header of the corresponding directory, in variable GNU.dumpdir.

- GNU and old GNU archives

  These formats implement special header type 'D', which is similar to ustar header '5' (directory), except that it precedes a data block containing the dumpdir.

Appendix E Genfile

This appendix describes genfile, an auxiliary program used in the GNU tar testsuite. If you are not interested in developing GNU tar, skip this appendix.

Initially, genfile was used to generate data files for the testsuite, hence its name. However, new operation modes were being implemented as the testsuite grew more sophisticated, and now genfile is a multi-purpose instrument.

There are three basic operation modes:

File Generation

This is the default mode. In this mode, genfile generates data files.

File Status

In this mode genfile displays status of specified files.

Synchronous Execution.

In this mode genfile executes the given program with '--checkpoint' option and executes a set of actions when specified checkpoints are reached.

E.1 Generate Mode

In this mode genfile creates a data file for the test suite. The size of the file is given with the '--length' ('-l') option. By default the file contents is written to the standard output, this can be changed using '--file' ('-f') command line option. Thus, the following two commands are equivalent:

```
genfile --length 100 > outfile
genfile --length 100 --file outfile
```

If '--length' is not given, genfile will generate an empty (zero-length) file.

The command line option '--seek=N' istructs genfile to skip the given number of bytes (N) in the output file before writing to it. It is similar to the 'seek=N' of the dd utility.

You can instruct genfile to create several files at one go, by giving it '--files-from' ('-T') option followed by a name of file containing a list of file names. Using dash ('-') instead of the file name causes genfile to read file list from the standard input. For example:

```
# Read file names from file 'file.list'
genfile --files-from file.list
# Read file names from standard input
genfile --files-from -
```

The list file is supposed to contain one file name per line. To use file lists separated by ASCII NUL character, use '--null' ('-0') command line option:

```
genfile --null --files-from file.list
```

The default data pattern for filling the generated file consists of first 256 letters of ASCII code, repeated enough times to fill the entire file. This behavior can be changed with '--pattern' option. This option takes a mandatory argument, specifying pattern name to use. Currently two patterns are implemented:

'--pattern=default'

The default pattern as described above.

'--pattern=zero'

Fills the file with zeroes.

If no file name was given, the program exits with the code 0. Otherwise, it exits with 0 only if it was able to create a file of the specified length.

Special option '--sparse' ('-s') instructs genfile to create a sparse file. Sparse files consist of *data fragments*, separated by *holes* or blocks of zeros. On many operating systems, actual disk storage is not allocated for holes, but they are counted in the length of the file. To create a sparse file, genfile should know where to put data fragments, and what data to use to fill them. So, when '--sparse' is given the rest of the command line specifies a so-called *file map*.

The file map consists of any number of *fragment descriptors*. Each descriptor is composed of two values: a number, specifying fragment offset from the end of the previous fragment or, for the very first fragment, from the beginning of the file, and *contents string*, i.e., a string of characters, specifying the pattern to fill the fragment with. File offset can be suffixed with the following quantifiers:

'k'
'K'   The number is expressed in kilobytes.

'm'
'M'   The number is expressed in megabytes.

'g'
'G'   The number is expressed in gigabytes.

For each letter in contents string genfile will generate a *block* of data, filled with this letter and will write it to the fragment. The size of block is given by '--block-size' option. It defaults to 512. Thus, if the string consists of *n* characters, the resulting file fragment will contain *n*block-size* of data.

Last fragment descriptor can have only file offset part. In this case genfile will create a hole at the end of the file up to the given offset.

For example, consider the following invocation:

```
genfile --sparse --file sparsefile 0 ABCD 1M EFGHI 2000K
```

It will create 3101184-bytes long file of the following structure:

Offset   Length   Contents

0	4*512=2048	Four 512-byte blocks, filled with letters 'A', 'B', 'C' and 'D'.
2048	1046528	Zero bytes
1050624	5*512=2560	Five blocks, filled with letters 'E', 'F', 'G', 'H', 'I'.
1053184	2048000	Zero bytes

The exit code of `genfile --status` command is 0 only if created file is actually sparse.

E.2 Status Mode

In status mode, `genfile` prints file system status for each file specified in the command line. This mode is toggled by '`--stat`' ('`-S`') command line option. An optional argument to this option specifies output *format*: a comma-separated list of `struct stat` fields to be displayed. This list can contain following identifiers:

name   The file name.

dev
st_dev   Device number in decimal.

ino
st_ino   Inode number.

mode[.*number*]
st_mode[.*number*]
                File mode in octal. Optional *number* specifies octal mask to be applied to the mode before outputting. For example, `--stat mode.777` will preserve lower nine bits of it. Notice, that you can use any punctuation character in place of '`.`'.

nlink
st_nlink   Number of hard links.

uid
st_uid   User ID of owner.

gid
st_gid   Group ID of owner.

size
st_size   File size in decimal.

blksize
st_blksize   The size in bytes of each file block.

blocks
st_blocks   Number of blocks allocated.

atime
st_atime   Time of last access.

mtime

st_mtime   Time of last modification

ctime

st_ctime   Time of last status change

sparse   A boolean value indicating whether the file is 'sparse'.

Modification times are displayed in UTC as UNIX timestamps, unless suffixed with 'H' (for "human-readable"), as in 'ctimeH', in which case usual `tar tv` output format is used.

The default output format is: 'name,dev,ino,mode, nlink,uid,gid,size,blksize,blocks,atime,mtime,ctime'.

For example, the following command will display file names and corresponding times of last access for each file in the current working directory:

```
genfile --stat=name,atime *
```

E.3 Exec Mode

This mode is designed for testing the behavior of `paxutils` commands when some of the files change during archiving. It is an experimental mode.

The 'Exec Mode' is toggled by '--run' command line option (or its alias '-r'). The non-optional arguments to `getopt` give the command line to be executed. Normally, it should contain at least the '--checkpoint' option.

A set of options is provided for defining checkpoint values and actions to be executed upon reaching them. Checkpoint values are introduced with the '--checkpoint' command line option. Argument to this option is the number of checkpoint in decimal.

Any number of *actions* may be specified after a checkpoint. Available actions are

'--cut *file*'
'--truncate *file*'

> Truncate *file* to the size specified by previous '--length' option (or 0, if it is not given).

'--append *file*'

> Append data to *file*. The size of data and its pattern are given by previous '--length' and 'pattern' options.

'--touch *file*'

> Update the access and modification times of *file*. These timestamps are changed to the current time, unless '--date' option was given, in which case they are changed to the specified time. Argument to '--date' option is a date specification in an almost arbitrary format (see Chapter 7 [Date input formats], page 123).

'--exec *command*'

> Execute given shell command.

'`--unlink` *file*'
> Unlink the *file*.

Option '`--verbose`' instructs `genfile` to print on standard output notifications about checkpoints being executed and to verbosely describe exit status of the command.

While the command is being executed its standard output remains connected to descriptor 1. All messages it prints to file descriptor 2, except checkpoint notifications, are forwarded to standard error.

`Genfile` exits with the exit status of the executed command.

For compatibility with previous `genfile` versions, the '`--run`' option takes an optional argument. If used this way, its argument supplies the command line to be executed. There should be no non-optional arguments in the `genfile` command line.

The actual command line is constructed by inserting the '`--checkpoint`' option between the command name and its first argument (if any). Due to this, the argument to '`--run`' may not use traditional `tar` option syntax, i.e., the following is wrong:

```
# Wrong!
genfile --run='tar cf foo bar'
```

Use the following syntax instead:

```
genfile --run='tar -cf foo bar' actions...
```

The above command line is equivalent to

```
genfile actions... -- tar -cf foo bar
```

Notice, that the use of compatibility mode is deprecated.

Appendix F Free Software Needs Free Documentation

The biggest deficiency in the free software community today is not in the software—it is the lack of good free documentation that we can include with the free software. Many of our most important programs do not come with free reference manuals and free introductory texts. Documentation is an essential part of any software package; when an important free software package does not come with a free manual and a free tutorial, that is a major gap. We have many such gaps today.

Consider Perl, for instance. The tutorial manuals that people normally use are non-free. How did this come about? Because the authors of those manuals published them with restrictive terms—no copying, no modification, source files not available—which exclude them from the free software world.

That wasn't the first time this sort of thing happened, and it was far from the last. Many times we have heard a GNU user eagerly describe a manual that he is writing, his intended contribution to the community, only to learn that he had ruined everything by signing a publication contract to make it non-free.

Free documentation, like free software, is a matter of freedom, not price. The problem with the non-free manual is not that publishers charge a price for printed copies—that in itself is fine. (The Free Software Foundation sells printed copies of manuals, too.) The problem is the restrictions on the use of the manual. Free manuals are available in source code form, and give you permission to copy and modify. Non-free manuals do not allow this.

The criteria of freedom for a free manual are roughly the same as for free software. Redistribution (including the normal kinds of commercial redistribution) must be permitted, so that the manual can accompany every copy of the program, both on-line and on paper.

Permission for modification of the technical content is crucial too. When people modify the software, adding or changing features, if they are conscientious they will change the manual too—so they can provide accurate and clear documentation for the modified program. A manual that leaves you no choice but to write a new manual to document a changed version of the program is not really available to our community.

Some kinds of limits on the way modification is handled are acceptable. For example, requirements to preserve the original author's copyright notice, the distribution terms, or the list of authors, are ok. It is also no problem to require modified versions to include notice that they were modified. Even entire sections that may not be deleted or changed are acceptable, as long as they deal with nontechnical topics (like this one). These kinds of restrictions are acceptable because they don't obstruct the community's normal use of the manual.

However, it must be possible to modify all the *technical* content of the manual, and then distribute the result in all the usual media, through all the usual channels. Otherwise, the restrictions obstruct the use of the manual, it is not free, and we need another manual to replace it.

Please spread the word about this issue. Our community continues to lose manuals to proprietary publishing. If we spread the word that free software needs free reference manuals and free tutorials, perhaps the next person who wants to contribute by writing documentation will realize, before it is too late, that only free manuals contribute to the free software community.

If you are writing documentation, please insist on publishing it under the GNU Free Documentation License or another free documentation license. Remember that this decision requires your approval—you don't have to let the publisher decide. Some commercial publishers will use a free license if you insist, but they will not propose the option; it is up to you to raise the issue and say firmly that this is what you want. If the publisher you are dealing with refuses, please try other publishers. If you're not sure whether a proposed license is free, write to `licensing@gnu.org`.

You can encourage commercial publishers to sell more free, copylefted manuals and tutorials by buying them, and particularly by buying copies from the publishers that paid for their writing or for major improvements. Meanwhile, try to avoid buying non-free documentation at all. Check the distribution terms of a manual before you buy it, and insist that whoever seeks your business must respect your freedom. Check the history of the book, and try reward the publishers that have paid or pay the authors to work on it.

The Free Software Foundation maintains a list of free documentation published by other publishers, at `http://www.fsf.org/doc/other-free-books.html`.

Appendix G GNU Free Documentation License

Version 1.3, 3 November 2008

Copyright © 2000-2002, 2007-2008, 2014 Free Software Foundation, Inc.

http://fsf.org/

Everyone is permitted to copy and distribute verbatim copies of this license document, but changing it is not allowed.

0. PREAMBLE

The purpose of this License is to make a manual, textbook, or other functional and useful document *free* in the sense of freedom: to assure everyone the effective freedom to copy and redistribute it, with or without modifying it, either commercially or noncommercially. Secondarily, this License preserves for the author and publisher a way to get credit for their work, while not being considered responsible for modifications made by others.

This License is a kind of "copyleft", which means that derivative works of the document must themselves be free in the same sense. It complements the GNU General Public License, which is a copyleft license designed for free software.

We have designed this License in order to use it for manuals for free software, because free software needs free documentation: a free program should come with manuals providing the same freedoms that the software does. But this License is not limited to software manuals; it can be used for any textual work, regardless of subject matter or whether it is published as a printed book. We recommend this License principally for works whose purpose is instruction or reference.

1. APPLICABILITY AND DEFINITIONS

This License applies to any manual or other work, in any medium, that contains a notice placed by the copyright holder saying it can be distributed under the terms of this License. Such a notice grants a world-wide, royalty-free license, unlimited in duration, to use that work under the conditions stated herein. The "Document", below, refers to any such manual or work. Any member of the public is a licensee, and is addressed as "you". You accept the license if you copy, modify or distribute the work in a way requiring permission under copyright law.

A "Modified Version" of the Document means any work containing the Document or a portion of it, either copied verbatim, or with modifications and/or translated into another language.

A "Secondary Section" is a named appendix or a front-matter section of the Document that deals exclusively with the relationship of the publishers or authors of the Document to the Document's overall subject (or to related matters) and contains nothing that could fall directly within that overall subject. (Thus, if the Document is in part a textbook of mathematics, a Secondary Section may not explain any mathematics.) The relationship could be a matter of historical connection with the subject or with related matters, or of legal, commercial, philosophical, ethical or political position regarding them.

The "Invariant Sections" are certain Secondary Sections whose titles are designated, as being those of Invariant Sections, in the notice that says that the Document is released under this License. If a section does not fit the above definition of Secondary then it is not allowed to be designated as Invariant. The Document may contain zero Invariant Sections. If the Document does not identify any Invariant Sections then there are none.

The "Cover Texts" are certain short passages of text that are listed, as Front-Cover Texts or Back-Cover Texts, in the notice that says that the Document is released under this License. A Front-Cover Text may be at most 5 words, and a Back-Cover Text may be at most 25 words.

A "Transparent" copy of the Document means a machine-readable copy, represented in a format whose specification is available to the general public, that is suitable for revising the document straightforwardly with generic text editors or (for images composed of pixels) generic paint programs or (for drawings) some widely available drawing editor, and that is suitable for input to text formatters or for automatic translation to a variety of formats suitable for input to text formatters. A copy made in an otherwise Transparent file format whose markup, or absence of markup, has been arranged to thwart or discourage subsequent modification by readers is not Transparent. An image format is not Transparent if used for any substantial amount of text. A copy that is not "Transparent" is called "Opaque".

Examples of suitable formats for Transparent copies include plain ASCII without markup, Texinfo input format, LaTeX input format, SGML or XML using a publicly available DTD, and standard-conforming simple HTML, PostScript or PDF designed for human modification. Examples of transparent image formats include PNG, XCF and JPG. Opaque formats include proprietary formats that can be read and edited only by proprietary word processors, SGML or XML for which the DTD and/or processing tools are not generally available, and the machine-generated HTML, PostScript or PDF produced by some word processors for output purposes only.

The "Title Page" means, for a printed book, the title page itself, plus such following pages as are needed to hold, legibly, the material this License requires to appear in the title page. For works in formats which do not have any title page as such, "Title Page" means the text near the most prominent appearance of the work's title, preceding the beginning of the body of the text.

The "publisher" means any person or entity that distributes copies of the Document to the public.

A section "Entitled XYZ" means a named subunit of the Document whose title either is precisely XYZ or contains XYZ in parentheses following text that translates XYZ in another language. (Here XYZ stands for a specific section name mentioned below, such as "Acknowledgements", "Dedications", "Endorsements", or "History".) To "Preserve the Title" of such a section when you modify the Document means that it remains a section "Entitled XYZ" according to this definition.

The Document may include Warranty Disclaimers next to the notice which states that this License applies to the Document. These Warranty Disclaimers are considered to be included by reference in this License, but only as regards disclaiming warranties: any other implication that these Warranty Disclaimers may have is void and has no effect on the meaning of this License.

2. VERBATIM COPYING

You may copy and distribute the Document in any medium, either commercially or noncommercially, provided that this License, the copyright notices, and the license notice saying this License applies to the Document are reproduced in all copies, and that you add no other conditions whatsoever to those of this License. You may not use technical measures to obstruct or control the reading or further copying of the copies you make or distribute. However, you may accept compensation in exchange for copies. If you distribute a large enough number of copies you must also follow the conditions in section 3.

You may also lend copies, under the same conditions stated above, and you may publicly display copies.

3. COPYING IN QUANTITY

If you publish printed copies (or copies in media that commonly have printed covers) of the Document, numbering more than 100, and the Document's license notice requires Cover Texts, you must enclose the copies in covers that carry, clearly and legibly, all these Cover Texts: Front-Cover Texts on the front cover, and Back-Cover Texts on the back cover. Both covers must also clearly and legibly identify you as the publisher of these copies. The front cover must present the full title with all words of the title equally prominent and visible. You may add other material on the covers in addition. Copying with changes limited to the covers, as long as they preserve the title of the Document and satisfy these conditions, can be treated as verbatim copying in other respects.

If the required texts for either cover are too voluminous to fit legibly, you should put the first ones listed (as many as fit reasonably) on the actual cover, and continue the rest onto adjacent pages.

If you publish or distribute Opaque copies of the Document numbering more than 100, you must either include a machine-readable Transparent copy along with each Opaque copy, or state in or with each Opaque copy a computer-network location from which the general network-using public has access to download using public-standard network protocols a complete Transparent copy of the Document, free of added material. If you use the latter option, you must take reasonably prudent steps, when you begin distribution of Opaque copies in quantity, to ensure that this Transparent copy will remain thus accessible at the stated location until at least one year after the last time you distribute an Opaque copy (directly or through your agents or retailers) of that edition to the public.

It is requested, but not required, that you contact the authors of the Document well before redistributing any large number of copies, to give them a chance to provide you with an updated version of the Document.

4. MODIFICATIONS

You may copy and distribute a Modified Version of the Document under the conditions of sections 2 and 3 above, provided that you release the Modified Version under precisely this License, with the Modified Version filling the role of the Document, thus licensing distribution and modification of the Modified Version to whoever possesses a copy of it. In addition, you must do these things in the Modified Version:

A. Use in the Title Page (and on the covers, if any) a title distinct from that of the Document, and from those of previous versions (which should, if there were any, be listed in the History section of the Document). You may use the same title as a previous version if the original publisher of that version gives permission.

B. List on the Title Page, as authors, one or more persons or entities responsible for authorship of the modifications in the Modified Version, together with at least five of the principal authors of the Document (all of its principal authors, if it has fewer than five), unless they release you from this requirement.

C. State on the Title page the name of the publisher of the Modified Version, as the publisher.

D. Preserve all the copyright notices of the Document.

E. Add an appropriate copyright notice for your modifications adjacent to the other copyright notices.

F. Include, immediately after the copyright notices, a license notice giving the public permission to use the Modified Version under the terms of this License, in the form shown in the Addendum below.

G. Preserve in that license notice the full lists of Invariant Sections and required Cover Texts given in the Document's license notice.

H. Include an unaltered copy of this License.

I. Preserve the section Entitled "History", Preserve its Title, and add to it an item stating at least the title, year, new authors, and publisher of the Modified Version as given on the Title Page. If there is no section Entitled "History" in the Document, create one stating the title, year, authors, and publisher of the Document as given on its Title Page, then add an item describing the Modified Version as stated in the previous sentence.

J. Preserve the network location, if any, given in the Document for public access to a Transparent copy of the Document, and likewise the network locations given in the Document for previous versions it was based on. These may be placed in the "History" section. You may omit a network location for a work that was published at least four years before the Document itself, or if the original publisher of the version it refers to gives permission.

K. For any section Entitled "Acknowledgements" or "Dedications", Preserve the Title of the section, and preserve in the section all the substance and tone of each of the contributor acknowledgements and/or dedications given therein.

L. Preserve all the Invariant Sections of the Document, unaltered in their text and in their titles. Section numbers or the equivalent are not considered part of the section titles.

M. Delete any section Entitled "Endorsements". Such a section may not be included in the Modified Version.

N. Do not retitle any existing section to be Entitled "Endorsements" or to conflict in title with any Invariant Section.

O. Preserve any Warranty Disclaimers.

If the Modified Version includes new front-matter sections or appendices that qualify as Secondary Sections and contain no material copied from the Document, you may at your option designate some or all of these sections as invariant. To do this, add their titles to the list of Invariant Sections in the Modified Version's license notice. These titles must be distinct from any other section titles.

You may add a section Entitled "Endorsements", provided it contains nothing but endorsements of your Modified Version by various parties— for example, statements of peer review or that the text has been approved by an organization as the authoritative definition of a standard.

You may add a passage of up to five words as a Front-Cover Text, and a passage of up to 25 words as a Back-Cover Text, to the end of the list of Cover Texts in the Modified Version. Only one passage of Front-Cover Text and one of Back-Cover Text may be added by (or through arrangements made by) any one entity. If the Document already includes a cover text for the same cover, previously added by you or by arrangement made by the same entity you are acting on behalf of, you may not add another; but you may replace the old one, on explicit permission from the previous publisher that added the old one.

The author(s) and publisher(s) of the Document do not by this License give permission to use their names for publicity for or to assert or imply endorsement of any Modified Version.

5. COMBINING DOCUMENTS

You may combine the Document with other documents released under this License, under the terms defined in section 4 above for modified versions, provided that you include in the combination all of the Invariant Sections of all of the original documents, unmodified, and list them all as Invariant Sections of your combined work in its license notice, and that you preserve all their Warranty Disclaimers.

The combined work need only contain one copy of this License, and multiple identical Invariant Sections may be replaced with a single copy. If there are multiple Invariant Sections with the same name but different contents, make the title of each such section unique by adding at the end of it, in parentheses, the name of the original author or publisher of that section if known, or else a unique number. Make the same adjustment to the section titles in the list of Invariant Sections in the license notice of the combined work.

In the combination, you must combine any sections Entitled "History" in the various original documents, forming one section Entitled "History"; likewise combine any sections Entitled "Acknowledgements", and any sections Entitled "Dedications". You must delete all sections Entitled "Endorsements."

6. COLLECTIONS OF DOCUMENTS

You may make a collection consisting of the Document and other documents released under this License, and replace the individual copies of this License in the various documents with a single copy that is included in the collection, provided that you follow the rules of this License for verbatim copying of each of the documents in all other respects.

You may extract a single document from such a collection, and distribute it individually under this License, provided you insert a copy of this License into the extracted document, and follow this License in all other respects regarding verbatim copying of that document.

7. AGGREGATION WITH INDEPENDENT WORKS

A compilation of the Document or its derivatives with other separate and independent documents or works, in or on a volume of a storage or distribution medium, is called an "aggregate" if the copyright resulting from the compilation is not used to limit the legal rights of the compilation's users beyond what the individual works permit. When the Document is included in an aggregate, this License does not apply to the other works in the aggregate which are not themselves derivative works of the Document.

If the Cover Text requirement of section 3 is applicable to these copies of the Document, then if the Document is less than one half of the entire aggregate, the Document's Cover Texts may be placed on covers that bracket the Document within the aggregate, or the electronic equivalent of covers if the Document is in electronic form. Otherwise they must appear on printed covers that bracket the whole aggregate.

8. TRANSLATION

Translation is considered a kind of modification, so you may distribute translations of the Document under the terms of section 4. Replacing Invariant Sections with translations requires special permission from their copyright holders, but you may include translations of some or all Invariant Sections in addition to the original versions of these Invariant Sections. You may include a translation of this License, and all the license notices in the Document, and any Warranty Disclaimers, provided that you also include the original English version of this License and the original versions of those notices and disclaimers. In case of a disagreement between the translation and the original version of this License or a notice or disclaimer, the original version will prevail.

If a section in the Document is Entitled "Acknowledgements", "Dedications", or "History", the requirement (section 4) to Preserve its Title (section 1) will typically require changing the actual title.

9. TERMINATION

You may not copy, modify, sublicense, or distribute the Document except as expressly provided under this License. Any attempt otherwise to copy, modify, sublicense, or distribute it is void, and will automatically terminate your rights under this License.

However, if you cease all violation of this License, then your license from a particular copyright holder is reinstated (a) provisionally, unless and until the copyright holder explicitly and finally terminates your license, and (b) permanently, if the copyright holder fails to notify you of the violation by some reasonable means prior to 60 days after the cessation.

Moreover, your license from a particular copyright holder is reinstated permanently if the copyright holder notifies you of the violation by some reasonable means, this is the first time you have received notice of violation of this License (for any work) from that copyright holder, and you cure the violation prior to 30 days after your receipt of the notice.

Termination of your rights under this section does not terminate the licenses of parties who have received copies or rights from you under this License. If your rights have been terminated and not permanently reinstated, receipt of a copy of some or all of the same material does not give you any rights to use it.

10. FUTURE REVISIONS OF THIS LICENSE

The Free Software Foundation may publish new, revised versions of the GNU Free Documentation License from time to time. Such

new versions will be similar in spirit to the present version, but
may differ in detail to address new problems or concerns. See
http://www.gnu.org/copyleft/.

Each version of the License is given a distinguishing version number.
If the Document specifies that a particular numbered version of this
License "or any later version" applies to it, you have the option of
following the terms and conditions either of that specified version or
of any later version that has been published (not as a draft) by the
Free Software Foundation. If the Document does not specify a version
number of this License, you may choose any version ever published (not
as a draft) by the Free Software Foundation. If the Document specifies
that a proxy can decide which future versions of this License can be used,
that proxy's public statement of acceptance of a version permanently
authorizes you to choose that version for the Document.

11. RELICENSING

"Massive Multiauthor Collaboration Site" (or "MMC Site") means any
World Wide Web server that publishes copyrightable works and also
provides prominent facilities for anybody to edit those works. A public
wiki that anybody can edit is an example of such a server. A "Massive
Multiauthor Collaboration" (or "MMC") contained in the site means
any set of copyrightable works thus published on the MMC site.

"CC-BY-SA" means the Creative Commons Attribution-Share Alike 3.0
license published by Creative Commons Corporation, a not-for-profit
corporation with a principal place of business in San Francisco, California, as well as future copyleft versions of that license published by that
same organization.

"Incorporate" means to publish or republish a Document, in whole or
in part, as part of another Document.

An MMC is "eligible for relicensing" if it is licensed under this License,
and if all works that were first published under this License somewhere
other than this MMC, and subsequently incorporated in whole or in
part into the MMC, (1) had no cover texts or invariant sections, and
(2) were thus incorporated prior to November 1, 2008.

The operator of an MMC Site may republish an MMC contained in the
site under CC-BY-SA on the same site at any time before August 1,
2009, provided the MMC is eligible for relicensing.

ADDENDUM: How to use this License for your documents

To use this License in a document you have written, include a copy of the License in the document and put the following copyright and license notices just after the title page:

```
Copyright (C)  year  your name.
Permission is granted to copy, distribute and/or modify this document
under the terms of the GNU Free Documentation License, Version 1.3
or any later version published by the Free Software Foundation;
with no Invariant Sections, no Front-Cover Texts, and no Back-Cover
Texts.  A copy of the license is included in the section entitled ''GNU
Free Documentation License''.
```

If you have Invariant Sections, Front-Cover Texts and Back-Cover Texts, replace the "with. . . Texts." line with this:

```
with the Invariant Sections being list their titles, with
the Front-Cover Texts being list, and with the Back-Cover Texts
being list.
```

If you have Invariant Sections without Cover Texts, or some other combination of the three, merge those two alternatives to suit the situation.

If your document contains nontrivial examples of program code, we recommend releasing these examples in parallel under your choice of free software license, such as the GNU General Public License, to permit their use in free software.

Appendix H Index of Command Line Options

This appendix contains an index of all GNU `tar` long command line options. The options are listed without the preceding double-dash. For a cross-reference of short command line options, see Section 3.4.3 [Short Option Summary], page 47.

-

--keep-directory-symlink, summary
.... 36

A

absolute-names 120
absolute-names, summary 29
add-file......................... 100
after-date 117
after-date, summary.............. 29
anchored......................... 108
anchored, summary................ 29
append 63, 64
append, summary.................. 28
atime-preserve 138
atime-preserve, summary 29
auto-compress 135
auto-compress, summary 30

B

backup........................... 81
backup, summary.................. 30
block-number 53
block-number, summary 30
blocking-factor 161
blocking-factor, summary 31
bzip2, summary 31

C

catenate......................... 67
catenate, summary................ 28
check-device, described 85
check-device, summary 31
check-links, described 141
check-links, summary............. 32
checkpoint 53
checkpoint, defined.............. 53
checkpoint, summary.............. 31

checkpoint-action 53
checkpoint-action, defined 53
checkpoint-action, summary 31
compare.......................... 69
compare, summary 28
compress......................... 134
compress, summary 32
concatenate 67
concatenate, summary............. 28
confirmation, summary 32
create, additional options 69
create, complementary notes 61
create, introduced............... 11
create, summary 28
create, using with '--verbose' .. 12
create, using with '--verify' ... 176

D

delay-directory-restore 76
delay-directory-restore, summary.. 32
delete........................... 68
delete, summary 28
delete, using before --append ... 64
dereference 141
dereference, summary............. 32
diff, summary 28
directory 119
directory, summary............... 32

E

exclude.......................... 101
exclude, potential problems with 105
exclude, summary 32
exclude-backups 104
exclude-backups, summary 32
exclude-caches 104
exclude-caches, summary 33
exclude-caches-all 104
exclude-caches-all, summary 33
exclude-caches-under 104

`exclude-caches-under`, summary 33
`exclude-from` 101, 102
`exclude-from`, summary 33
`exclude-ignore` 103
`exclude-ignore`, summary 33
`exclude-ignore-recursive` 103
`exclude-ignore-recursive`, summary
.... 33
`exclude-tag` 104
`exclude-tag`, summary 33
`exclude-tag-all` 105
`exclude-tag-all`, summary 33
`exclude-tag-under` 104
`exclude-tag-under`, summary 33
`exclude-vcs` 103
`exclude-vcs`, summary 33
`exclude-vcs-ignores` 102
`exclude-vcs-ignores`, summary 34
`extract` 17
`extract`, additional options 71
`extract`, complementary notes 62
`extract`, summary 28
`extract`, using with
`--listed-incremental` 86

F

`file` 97
`file`, short description 97
`file`, summary 34
`file`, tutorial 7
`files-from` 100
`files-from`, summary 34
`force-local`, short description 156
`force-local`, summary 34
`format`, summary 34
`full-time`, summary 34

G

`get`, summary 29
`group` 71
`group`, summary 35
`gunzip`, summary 35
`gzip` 134
`gzip`, summary 35

H

`hard-dereference`, described 142
`hard-dereference`, summary 35
`help` 10

`help`, introduction 49
`help`, summary 35

I

`ignore-case` 109
`ignore-case`, summary 35
`ignore-command-error` 79
`ignore-command-error`, summary 35
`ignore-failed-read` 71
`ignore-failed-read`, summary 35
`ignore-zeros` 72
`ignore-zeros`, short description 164
`ignore-zeros`, summary 35
`incremental`, summary 36
`incremental`, using with `--list` 86
`index-file`, summary 36
`info-script` 170
`info-script`, short description 157
`info-script`, summary 36
`interactive` 59
`interactive`, summary 36

K

`keep-newer-files` 74
`keep-newer-files`, summary 36
`keep-old-files` 74
`keep-old-files`, introduced 73
`keep-old-files`, summary 36

L

`label` 173, 174
`label`, summary 37
`level`, described 85
`level`, summary 37
`list` 15
`list`, summary 29
`list`, using with `--incremental` 86
`list`, using with `--listed-incremental`
.... 86
`list`, using with `--verbose` 15
`list`, using with file name arguments .. 16
`listed-incremental`, described 84
`listed-incremental`, summary 37
`listed-incremental`, using with
`--extract` 86
`listed-incremental`, using with `--list`
.... 86
`lzip` 134
`lzip`, summary 37

lzma................................. 134
lzma, summary 37
lzop................................. 134

M

mode 69
mode, summary 37
mtime................................ 70
mtime, summary 37
multi-volume 169
multi-volume, short description 157
multi-volume, summary 38

N

new-volume-script 170
new-volume-script, short description
    157
new-volume-script, summary..... 36, 38
newer.............................. 117
newer, summary 38
newer-mtime 117
newer-mtime, summary.............. 38
no-anchored 108
no-anchored, summary.............. 38
no-auto-compress, summary 38
no-check-device, described 85
no-check-device, summary 38
no-delay-directory-restore........ 76
no-delay-directory-restore, summary
    38
no-ignore-case 109
no-ignore-case, summary 39
no-ignore-command-error 79
no-ignore-command-error, summary .. 39
no-null, described 101
no-null, summary 39
no-overwrite-dir, summary 39
no-quote-chars, summary 39
no-recursion 118
no-recursion, summary 39
no-same-owner 139
no-same-owner, summary 39
no-same-permissions, summary 39
no-seek, summary 39
no-unquote 99
no-unquote, summary 39
no-wildcards 108
no-wildcards, summary 39
no-wildcards-match-slash 109

no-wildcards-match-slash, summary
    39
null, described 101
null, summary 40
numeric-owner 139
numeric-owner, summary 40

O

occurrence, described............... 64
occurrence, summary................. 40
old-archive, summary............... 40
one-file-system 119
one-file-system, summary 40
one-top-level, summary 40
overwrite........................... 73
overwrite, introduced 73
overwrite, summary................. 41
overwrite-dir 74
overwrite-dir, introduced 72
overwrite-dir, summary 41
owner............................... 70
owner, summary 41

P

pax-option 143
pax-option, summary............... 41
portability, summary.............. 41
posix, summary 41
preserve........................... 140
preserve, summary.................. 41
preserve-order 80
preserve-order, summary 41
preserve-permissions.............. 75
preserve-permissions, short description
    140
preserve-permissions, summary..... 41

Q

quote-chars, summary.............. 42
quoting-style 110
quoting-style, summary 42

R

read-full-records 71, 72
read-full-records, short description
    164
read-full-records, summary 42

record-size, summary.............. 42
recursion 118
recursion, summary................ 42
recursive-unlink.................. 75
recursive-unlink, summary 42
remove-files 79
remove-files, summary 42
restrict, summary................. 42
rmt-command, summary.............. 42
rsh-command 156
rsh-command, summary.............. 42

S

same-order 80
same-order, summary............... 43
same-owner 138
same-owner, summary............... 43
same-permissions.................. 75
same-permissions, short description
.... 140
same-permissions, summary...... 41, 43
seek, summary 43
show-defaults 50
show-defaults, summary 43
show-omitted-dirs................. 53
show-omitted-dirs, summary 43
show-snapshot-field-ranges 207
show-snapshot-field-ranges, summary
.... 43
show-stored-names 16
show-stored-names, summary 43
show-transformed-names 114
show-transformed-names, summary ... 43
skip-old-files, introduced 73
skip-old-files, summary 44
sort, summary 44
sparse............................ 137
sparse, summary 44
sparse-version 138
sparse-version, summary 44
starting-file 79
starting-file, summary 44
strip-components.................. 113
strip-components, summary 45
suffix............................ 81
suffix, summary 45

T

tape-length 169
tape-length, short description 157

tape-length, summary.............. 45
test-label 174
test-label, summary............... 45
to-command 77
to-command, summary............... 45
to-stdout......................... 77
to-stdout, summary 45
totals............................ 52
totals, summary 45
touch 75, 138
touch, summary 45
transform 114
transform, summary................ 45

U

uncompress 134
uncompress, summary 32, 46
ungzip............................ 134
ungzip, summary 35, 46
unlink-first 74
unlink-first, introduced 73
unlink-first, summary 46
unquote........................... 99
unquote, summary 46
update 66
update, summary 29
usage............................. 50
use-compress-program.............. 135
use-compress-program, summary 46
utc, summary 46

V

verbose........................... 51
verbose, introduced............... 8
verbose, summary 46
verbose, using with '--create' 12
verbose, using with '--list' 15
verify, short description......... 176
verify, summary 46
verify, using with '--create' 176
version........................... 49
version, summary 46
volno-file 170
volno-file, summary............... 47

W

warning, explained................ 57
warning, summary 47
wildcards 108

`wildcards`, summary................ 47

`wildcards-match-slash`............ 109

`wildcards-match-slash`, summary.... 47

X

`xform`............................. 114

`xform`, summary 45

`xz` 134

`xz`, summary 47

Appendix I Index

%

'%s: Directory has been renamed from %s', warning message 58

'%s: Directory has been renamed', warning message 58

'%s: Directory is new', warning message 58

'%s: directory is on a different device: not purging', warning message 58

-

–after-date and –update compared ... 117

–newer-mtime and –update compared 117

.

.bzrignore 102

.cvsignore 102

.gitignore 102

.hgignore 103

A

'A lone zero block at', warning message 57

abbreviations for months 125

absolute file names 120, 158

Adding archives to an archive........ 67

Adding files to an Archive 64

ADMINISTRATOR 88

Age, excluding files by 116

ago in date strings 127

all 57

alone-zero-block 57

alternative decompression programs .. 133

am in date strings 126

Appending files to an Archive........ 64

appending files to existing archive 63

Arch, excluding files 103

archive 1

Archive creation 97

archive member 2

Archive Name 97

Archive, creation of 10

Archives, Appending files to 64

archives, binary equivalent 146

Archiving Directories................. 14

ARGP_HELP_FMT, environment variable 187

arguments to long options 25

arguments to old options 26

arguments to short options 25

atrributes, files 138

'Attempting extraction of symbolic links as hard links', warning message 58

authors of parse_datetime 130

Avoiding recursion in directories 118

B

backup options 80

backup suffix 81

BACKUP_DIRS 88

BACKUP_FILES 89

BACKUP_HOUR 88

backups 81, 83

bad-dumpdir 58

basic operations 62

Bazaar, excluding files 103

Bazaar, ignore files................. 102

beginning of time, for POSIX 129

bell, checkpoint action 55

Bellovin, Steven M. 130

Berets, Jim.......................... 130

Berry, K............................. 130

binary equivalent archives, creating .. 146

block 159

Block number where error occurred ... 53

BLOCKING............................ 88

blocking factor 165

Blocking Factor..................... 161

Blocks per record 161

bug reports.......................... 4

Bytes per record 161

bzip2 132

C

cachedir............................ 57

calendar date item 124

case, ignored in dates 124

cat vs concatenate.................. 68

Changing directory mid-stream 119
Character class, excluding characters from
    107
checkpoints, defined 53
Choosing an archive file 97
combined date and time of day item .. 127
comments, in dates 124
compress 132
Compressed archives 132
concatenate vs cat 68
Concatenating Archives 67
'contains a cache directory tag',
    warning message 57
contiguous-cast 58
corrupted archives 83, 135
Creation of the archive 10
'Current %s is newer or same age',
    warning message 58
CVS, excluding files 103
CVS, ignore files 102

D

Darcs, excluding files 103
DAT blocking 165
Data Modification time, excluding files by
    116
Data modification times of extracted files
    75
date and time of day format, ISO 8601
    127
date format, ISO 8601 125
date input formats 123
day in date strings 127, 128
day of week item 127
decompress-program 58
Deleting files from an archive 68
Deleting from tape archives 68
dereferencing hard links 141
Descending directories, avoiding 118
Device numbers, changing 191
Device numbers, using in incremental
    backups 85
Directories, Archiving 14
Directories, avoiding recursion 118
Directory, changing mid-stream 119
DIRLIST 89
displacement of dates 127
doc-opt-col 188
'door ignored', warning message 57
dot, checkpoint action 55
Double-checking a write operation 176

DUMP_BEGIN 91
DUMP_END 91
DUMP_REMIND_SCRIPT 90
dumps, full 83
dup-args 187
dup-args-note 188

E

echo, checkpoint action 53
Eggert, Paul 130
End-of-archive blocks, ignoring 72
End-of-archive info script 170
entry 3
epoch, for POSIX 129
Error message, block number of 53
Exabyte blocking 165
exclude 102
exclude-caches 104
exclude-from 102
exclude-tag 104
Excluding characters from a character
    class 107
Excluding file by age 116
Excluding files by file system 101
Excluding files by name and pattern .. 101
Exec Mode, genfile 214
exec, checkpoint action 55
existing backup method 81
exit status 22
'Extracting contiguous files as
    regular files', warning message
    58
extracting nth copy of the file 64
extraction 2
Extraction 17

F

file attributes 138
'file changed as we read it', warning
    message 57
'file is on a different filesystem',
    warning message 57
'file is the archive; not dumped',
    warning message 57
'file is unchanged; not dumped',
    warning message 57
File lists separated by NUL characters
    211
file name 2
File Name arguments, alternatives 99

File name arguments, using '--list' with
.... 16
'file name read contains nul
    character', warning message 57
file names, absolute 120
File names, excluding files by 101
File names, terminated by NUL 101
File names, using hard links 141
File names, using symbolic links 141
'File removed before we read it',
    warning message................. 57
'File shrank by %s bytes', warning
    message......................... 57
File system boundaries, not crossing.. 119
file-changed 57
file-ignored 57
file-removed 57
file-shrank 57
file-unchanged 57
FILELIST.............................. 89
filename-with-nuls................... 57
find, using with tar............ 99, 118
first in date strings................ 123
format 0, snapshot file 206
format 1, snapshot file 206
format 2, snapshot file 206
Format Options 161
Format Parameters 161
Format, old style 142
fortnight in date strings 127
free documentation 217
full dumps 83
future time stamps................. 146

G

general date syntax 123
Generate Mode, genfile 211
genfile 211
genfile, create file 211
genfile, creating sparse files 212
genfile, generate mode 211
genfile, reading a list of file names .. 211
genfile, seeking to a given offset 211
Getting program version number 49
git, excluding files 103
Git, ignore files 102
GNU archive format 143
GNU.sparse.major, extended header
    variable 205
GNU.sparse.map, extended header
    variable 204

GNU.sparse.minor, extended header
    variable 205
GNU.sparse.name, extended header
    variable 204
GNU.sparse.name, extended header
    variable, in v.1.0 205
GNU.sparse.numblocks, extended header
    variable 203
GNU.sparse.numbytes, extended header
    variable 203
GNU.sparse.offset, extended header
    variable 203
GNU.sparse.realsize, extended header
    variable 205
GNU.sparse.size, extended header
    variable 203
gnupg, using with tar 136
gpg, using with tar................. 136
gzip 132

H

hard links, dereferencing............ 141
header-col 189
hook................................. 91
hour in date strings 127

I

ignore-archive 57
ignore-newer 58
Ignoring end-of-archive blocks........ 72
'Ignoring unknown extended header
    keyword '%s'', warning message .. 58
'implausibly old time stamp %s',
    warning message................ 58
Info script......................... 170
Interactive operation 59
ISO 8601 date and time of day format
    127
ISO 8601 date format 125
items in date strings 123

L

Labeling an archive 174
labeling archives 173
Labeling multi-volume archives 174
Labels on the archive media 174
language, in dates.................. 124
Large lists of file names on small machines
    80

large values 146
last day 127
last in date strings 123
Laszlo Ersek........................ 136
lbzip2............................. 136
leap seconds 124, 125, 129
Listing all tar options............... 49
listing member and file names......... 15
Listing volume label 174
Lists of file names................... 99
Local and remote archives 98
long options 24
long options with mandatory arguments
  25
long options with optional arguments.. 25
long-opt-col 188
lzip 132
lzma 132
lzop 132

M

MacKenzie, David 130
'Malformed dumpdir: 'X' never used',
   warning message................ 58
member 2
member name 2
members, multiple 65
Members, replacing with other members
   64
Mercurial, excluding files 103
Mercurial, ignore files 102
Meyering, Jim 130
Middle of the archive, starting in the .. 79
midnight in date strings............. 126
minute in date strings............... 127
minutes, time zone correction by 126
Modes of extracted files 75
Modification time, excluding files by.. 116
Modification times of extracted files ... 75
month in date strings............... 127
month names in date strings........ 125
months, written-out................ 124
MT 89
MT_BEGIN.......................... 90
MT_OFFLINE 90
MT_REWIND......................... 90
MT_STATUS......................... 91
Multi-volume archives.............. 169
multiple members................... 65
Mutli-volume archives in PAX format,
   extracting using non-GNU tars .. 147

Mutli-volume archives, extracting using
   non-GNU tars................. 147

N

Naming an archive 97
negative time stamps................ 146
new-directory 58
next day 127
next in date strings................. 123
none 57
noon in date strings 126
now in date strings 128
ntape device 166
NUL-terminated file names 101
Number of blocks per record........ 161
Number of bytes per record.......... 161
numbered backup method 81
numbers, written-out................ 123

O

Obtaining help 49
Obtaining total status information 52
Old GNU archive format 143
Old GNU sparse format 202
old option style..................... 26
old options with mandatory arguments
   26
Old style archives.................. 142
Old style format 142
opt-doc-col 189
option syntax, traditional............ 26
optional arguments to long options 25
optional arguments to short options ... 25
options for use with '--extract' 71
Options when reading archives........ 71
Options, archive format specifying ... 161
Options, format specifying........... 161
options, GNU style 24
options, long style 24
options, mixing different styles 27
options, mnemonic names 24
options, old style 26
options, short style................. 25
options, traditional................. 25
ordinal numbers 123
Overwriting old files, prevention 73

P

parse_datetime 123

pattern, `genfile`..................... 212
PAX archive format................. 143
Permissions of extracted files 75
Pinard, F.......................... 130
`pm` in date strings 126
POSIX archive format 143
Progress information 52
Protecting old files.................. 73
pure numbers in date strings........ 128

R

RCS, excluding files................ 103
Reading file names from a file......... 99
Reading incomplete records........... 71
record 159
Record Size 161
'`Record size = %lu blocks`', warning
      message........................ 58
`record-size` 58
Records, incomplete................. 71
Recursion in directories, avoiding 118
relative items in date strings........ 127
Remote devices...................... 98
remote tape drive.................. 157
Removing files from an archive........ 68
`rename-directory` 58
Replacing members with other members
      64
reporting bugs....................... 4
`RESTORE_BEGIN` 91
`RESTORE_END` 91
Resurrecting files from an archive 17
Retrieving files from an archive 17
return status 22
`rmargin`........................... 189
`rmt` 157
`RSH` 89
`RSH_COMMAND` 89
Running out of space................. 79

S

Salz, Rich 130
SCCS, excluding files............... 103
short options 25
short options with mandatory arguments
      25
short options with optional arguments
      25
`short-opt-col` 188
simple backup method 81

`SIMPLE_BACKUP_SUFFIX`............... 81
`sleep`, checkpoint action 55
`SLEEP_MESSAGE` 90
`SLEEP_TIME` 90
Small memory....................... 79
snapshot file field ranges 207
snapshot file, format 0 206
snapshot file, format 1 206
snapshot file, format 2 206
snapshot files, editing 191
snapshot files, fixing device numbers.. 191
'`socket ignored`', warning message.... 57
Sparse Files 137
sparse files v.0.0, extracting with
      non-GNU tars................... 150
sparse files v.0.1, extracting with
      non-GNU tars................... 150
sparse files v.1.0, extracting with
      non-GNU tars................... 149
Sparse files, creating using `genfile` .. 212
sparse files, extracting with non-GNU tars
      149
sparse formats...................... 202
sparse formats, defined 137
sparse formats, Old GNU............ 202
sparse formats, v.0.0 203
sparse formats, v.0.1 204
sparse formats, v.1.0 205
sparse versions...................... 202
Specifying archive members........... 98
Specifying files to act on.............. 98
Standard input and output 97
Standard output, writing extracted files to
      77
Storing archives in compressed format
      132
SVN, excluding files................ 103
Symbolic link as file name 141
`symlink-cast` 58

T

`TAPE`................................. 8
tape blocking....................... 165
tape marks 166
tape positioning 166
`TAPE_FILE`.......................... 88
Tapes, using '`--delete`' and 68
`tar`................................... 2
`TAR`............................... 90
tar archive 1
Tar archive formats 131

tar entry 3
tar file 3
tar to a remote device 98
tar to standard input and output 97
tar-snapshot-edit 191
TAR_ARCHIVE, checkpoint script
    environment 56
TAR_ARCHIVE, info script environment
    variable 171
TAR_ARCHIVE, to-command environment
    78
TAR_ATIME, to-command environment
    78
TAR_BLOCKING_FACTOR, checkpoint
    script environment 56
TAR_BLOCKING_FACTOR, info script
    environment variable 171
TAR_BLOCKING_FACTOR, to-command
    environment 78
TAR_CHECKPOINT, checkpoint script
    environment 56
TAR_CTIME, to-command environment
    78
TAR_FD, info script environment
    variable 171
TAR_FILENAME, to-command environment
    78
TAR_FILETYPE, to-command environment
    77
TAR_FORMAT, checkpoint script
    environment 56
TAR_FORMAT, info script environment
    variable 171
TAR_FORMAT, to-command environment
    78
TAR_GID, to-command environment 78
TAR_GNAME, to-command environment
    78
TAR_MODE, to-command environment .. 78
TAR_MTIME, to-command environment
    78
TAR_OPTIONS, environment variable
    23
TAR_REALNAME, to-command environment
    78
TAR_SIZE, to-command environment .. 78
TAR_SUBCOMMAND, checkpoint script
    environment 56
TAR_SUBCOMMAND, info script
    environment variable 171
TAR_UID, to-command environment 78

TAR_UNAME, to-command environment
    78
TAR_VERSION, checkpoint script
    environment 56
TAR_VERSION, info script environment
    variable 171
TAR_VERSION, to-command environment
    78
TAR_VOLUME, info script environment
    variable 171
TAR_VOLUME, to-command environment
    78
tarcat 173
this in date strings 128
time of day item 125
'time stamp %s is %s s in the future',
    warning message 58
time zone correction 126
time zone item 124, 126
timestamp 58
today in date strings 128
tomorrow in date strings 128
totals, checkpoint action 55
ttyout, checkpoint action 55
TZ 129

U

Ultrix 3.1 and write failure 158
'Unknown file type '%c', extracted as
    normal file', warning message ... 58
'Unknown file type; file ignored',
    warning message 57
unknown-cast 58
unknown-keyword 58
unpacking 2
Updating an archive 66
usage-indent 189
Using encrypted archives 136
ustar archive format 143
uuencode 81

V

v7 archive format 142
VCS, excluding files 103
VCS, excluding patterns from ignore files
    102
VCS, ignore files 102
Verbose operation 51
Verifying a write operation 176
Verifying the currency of an archive ... 69

version control system, excluding files
.... 103
Version of the `tar` program 49
`version-control` Emacs variable 81
`VERSION_CONTROL` 81
volno file 170
`VOLNO_FILE` 89
Volume label, listing 174
Volume number file 170

W

`week` in date strings 127
Where is the archive? 97
Working directory, specifying 119

Writing extracted files to standard output
.... 77
Writing new archives 97

X

`xdev` 57, 58
`XLIST` 89
`xsparse` 149

Y

`year` in date strings 127
`yesterday` in date strings 128

Short Contents

1   Introduction 1

2   Tutorial Introduction to `tar` 5

3   Invoking GNU `tar` 21

4   GNU `tar` Operations 61

5   Performing Backups and Restoring Files 83

6   Choosing Files and Names for `tar` 97

7   Date input formats 123

8   Controlling the Archive Format 131

9   Tapes and Other Archive Media 155

10   Reliability and Security 179

A   Changes 185

B   Configuring Help Summary 187

C   Fixing Snapshot Files 191

D   Tar Internals 193

E   Genfile 211

F   Free Software Needs Free Documentation 217

G   GNU Free Documentation License 219

H   Index of Command Line Options 229

I   Index 235

Table of Contents

1 Introduction 1
- 1.1 What this Book Contains 1
- 1.2 Some Definitions 1
- 1.3 What `tar` Does 2
- 1.4 How `tar` Archives are Named 3
- 1.5 GNU `tar` Authors 3
- 1.6 Reporting bugs or suggestions 4

2 Tutorial Introduction to `tar` 5
- 2.1 Assumptions this Tutorial Makes 5
- 2.2 Stylistic Conventions 5
- 2.3 Basic `tar` Operations and Options 6
- 2.4 The Three Most Frequently Used Operations 7
- 2.5 Two Frequently Used Options 7
  - The '`--file`' Option 7
  - The '`--verbose`' Option 8
  - Getting Help: Using the '`--help`' Option 10
- 2.6 How to Create Archives 10
  - 2.6.1 Preparing a Practice Directory for Examples ... 11
  - 2.6.2 Creating the Archive 11
  - 2.6.3 Running '`--create`' with '`--verbose`' 12
  - 2.6.4 Short Forms with '`create`' 13
  - 2.6.5 Archiving Directories 14
- 2.7 How to List Archives 15
  - Listing the Contents of a Stored Directory 16
- 2.8 How to Extract Members from an Archive 17
  - 2.8.1 Extracting an Entire Archive 17
  - 2.8.2 Extracting Specific Files 17
  - 2.8.3 Extracting Files that are Directories 18
  - 2.8.4 Extracting Archives from Untrusted Sources ... 19
  - 2.8.5 Commands That Will Fail 19
- 2.9 Going Further Ahead in this Manual 20

3 Invoking GNU `tar` 21
- 3.1 General Synopsis of `tar` 21
- 3.2 Using `tar` Options 23
- 3.3 The Three Option Styles 24
  - 3.3.1 Long Option Style 24
  - 3.3.2 Short Option Style 25
  - 3.3.3 Old Option Style 26
  - 3.3.4 Mixing Option Styles 26

3.4   All `tar` Options 28
   3.4.1   Operations 28
   3.4.2   `tar` Options 29
   3.4.3   Short Options Cross Reference 47
3.5   GNU `tar` documentation 49
3.6   Obtaining GNU `tar` default values 50
3.7   Checking `tar` progress 51
3.8   Checkpoints 53
3.9   Controlling Warning Messages 56
3.10   Asking for Confirmation During Operations 59
3.11   Running External Commands 59

4   GNU `tar` Operations 61

4.1   Basic GNU `tar` Operations 61
4.2   Advanced GNU `tar` Operations 62
   4.2.1   The Five Advanced `tar` Operations 62
   4.2.2   How to Add Files to Existing Archives: '`--append`' 63
      4.2.2.1   Appending Files to an Archive 64
      4.2.2.2   Multiple Members with the Same Name 65
   4.2.3   Updating an Archive 66
      4.2.3.1   How to Update an Archive Using '`--update`' 66
   4.2.4   Combining Archives with '`--concatenate`' 67
   4.2.5   Removing Archive Members Using '`--delete`' 68
   4.2.6   Comparing Archive Members with the File System 69
4.3   Options Used by '`--create`' 69
   4.3.1   Overriding File Metadata 69
   4.3.2   Ignore Fail Read 71
4.4   Options Used by '`--extract`' 71
   4.4.1   Options to Help Read Archives 71
   Reading Full Records 72
   Ignoring Blocks of Zeros 72
   4.4.2   Changing How `tar` Writes Files 72
   Options Controlling the Overwriting of Existing Files 72
   Overwrite Old Files 73
   Keep Old Files 74
   Keep Newer Files... 74
   Unlink First 74
   Recursive Unlink 75
   Setting Data Modification Times 75
   Setting Access Permissions 75
   Directory Modification Times and Permissions................ 75
   Writing to Standard Output 77
   Writing to an External Program 77
   Removing Files... 79
   4.4.3   Coping with Scarce Resources 79
   Starting File 79

         Same Order 80
4.5 Backup options 80
4.6 Notable `tar` Usages 81
4.7 Looking Ahead: The Rest of this Manual 82

5   Performing Backups and Restoring Files . . . 83

5.1 Using `tar` to Perform Full Dumps 83
5.2 Using `tar` to Perform Incremental Dumps 84
5.3 Levels of Backups 87
5.4 Setting Parameters for Backups and Restoration 88
    5.4.1 General-Purpose Variables 88
    5.4.2 Magnetic Tape Control 90
    5.4.3 User Hooks 91
    5.4.4 An Example Text of '`Backup-specs`' 92
5.5 Using the Backup Scripts 92
5.6 Using the Restore Script 94

6   Choosing Files and Names for `tar` 97

6.1 Choosing and Naming Archive Files 97
6.2 Selecting Archive Members 98
6.3 Reading Names from a File 99
    6.3.1 `NUL`-Terminated File Names 101
6.4 Excluding Some Files 101
    Problems with Using the `exclude` Options 105
6.5 Wildcards Patterns and Matching 106
    Controlling Pattern-Matching 107
6.6 Quoting Member Names 109
6.7 Modifying File and Member Names 113
6.8 Operating Only on New Files 116
6.9 Descending into Directories 118
6.10 Crossing File System Boundaries 119
    6.10.1 Changing the Working Directory 119
    6.10.2 Absolute File Names 120

7   Date input formats 123

7.1 General date syntax 123
7.2 Calendar date items 124
7.3 Time of day items 125
7.4 Time zone items 126
7.5 Combined date and time of day items 126
7.6 Day of week items 127
7.7 Relative items in date strings 127
7.8 Pure numbers in date strings 128
7.9 Seconds since the Epoch 129
7.10 Specifying time zone rules 129

7.11 Authors of `parse_datetime` 130

8 Controlling the Archive Format 131

8.1 Using Less Space through Compression 132
    8.1.1 Creating and Reading Compressed Archives 132
        8.1.1.1 Using lbzip2 with GNU `tar`....................... 136
    8.1.2 Archiving Sparse Files 137
8.2 Handling File Attributes.................................... 138
8.3 Making `tar` Archives More Portable 140
    8.3.1 Portable Names 140
    8.3.2 Symbolic Links...................................... 141
    8.3.3 Hard Links.. 141
    8.3.4 Old V7 Archives..................................... 142
    8.3.5 Ustar Archive Format 143
    8.3.6 GNU and old GNU `tar` format 143
    8.3.7 GNU `tar` and POSIX `tar`........................... 143
        8.3.7.1 Controlling Extended Header Keywords........... 143
    8.3.8 Checksumming Problems.............................. 146
    8.3.9 Large or Negative Values............................. 146
    8.3.10 How to Extract GNU-Specific Data Using Other `tar`
        Implementations...................................... 147
        8.3.10.1 Extracting Members Split Between Volumes....... 147
        8.3.10.2 Extracting Sparse Members 149
8.4 Comparison of `tar` and `cpio`............................... 151

9 Tapes and Other Archive Media.......... 155

9.1 Device Selection and Switching............................. 155
9.2 Remote Tape Server....................................... 157
9.3 Some Common Problems and their Solutions................ 159
9.4 Blocking.. 159
    9.4.1 Format Variations 161
    9.4.2 The Blocking Factor of an Archive 161
9.5 Many Archives on One Tape 166
    9.5.1 Tape Positions and Tape Marks....................... 167
    9.5.2 The `mt` Utility..................................... 168
9.6 Using Multiple Tapes...................................... 168
    9.6.1 Archives Longer than One Tape or Disk 169
    9.6.2 Tape Files 173
    9.6.3 Concatenate Volumes into a Single Archive 173
9.7 Including a Label in the Archive............................ 173
9.8 Verifying Data as It is Stored 176
9.9 Write Protection 177

10   Reliability and Security 179
   10.1   Reliability 179
      10.1.1   Permissions Problems 179
      10.1.2   Data Corruption and Repair 179
      10.1.3   Race conditions 179
   10.2   Security 180
      10.2.1   Privacy 180
      10.2.2   Integrity 180
      10.2.3   Dealing with Live Untrusted Data 181
      10.2.4   Security Rules of Thumb 182

Appendix A   Changes 185

Appendix B   Configuring Help Summary . . . 187

Appendix C   Fixing Snapshot Files 191

Appendix D   Tar Internals 193
   Basic Tar Format 193
   GNU Extensions to the Archive Format 201
   Storing Sparse Files 202
      Old GNU Format 202
      PAX Format, Versions 0.0 and 0.1 203
      PAX Format, Version 1.0 204
   Format of the Incremental Snapshot Files 205
   Dumpdir 207

Appendix E   Genfile 211
   E.1   Generate Mode 211
   E.2   Status Mode 213
   E.3   Exec Mode 214

Appendix F   Free Software Needs Free
Documentation 217

Appendix G   GNU Free Documentation License
. . . . 219

Appendix H   Index of Command Line Options
. . . . 229

Appendix I   Index 235

www.ingramcontent.com/pod-product-compliance
Lightning Source LLC
LaVergne TN
LVHW060138070326
832902LV00018B/2847